GIVE US THIS DAY

*A Daily Bible Study, Devotion, Meditation,
and Prayer for the Whole
New Testament*

Volume 1—The Gospel of Matthew

FR. CHARLES ERLANDSON

St. Bede Press
Tyler, TX

Cover art: *Bread of Heaven, No. 1* by Paul Erlandson
Cover design: Bethany Hoyt

ISBN—978-0-9828198-0-7

Published by St. Bede Press
Tyler, TX

Printed in the United States of America

Testimonials for Give Us This Day

"*Give Us This Day* is lively, provocative, and engaging. With it, Charles Erlandson has given us all good inducement to dig deep into the Word of Life. Highly recommended."

GEORGE GRANT—Author of more than 50 books and pastor of Parish Presbyterian Church in Franklin, Tennessee

"I and my wife have been using Fr. Charles Erlandson's *Give Us This Day* meditations on the readings from the lectionary in the Prayer Book for several years, and we do so with great delight and benefit. I especially look forward to the applications he always has because they are always so helpful in thinking about how to put God's Word into practice every day."

BISHOP DANIEL MORSE—Missionary Diocese of the Central States, the Reformed Episcopal Church

"Many daily devotional books seem to have the goal of offering the reader a small slice of comfort to help him through the day. This one is different. Fr. Charles Erlandson sets forth a daily sermon accompanied by prayers and reflections. The zeal, the intensity of faith, and the intelligence of these messages are contagious. Praying these prayers and reflecting deeply on God's Word in this way will give you more than a pious gush. They will equip you to go into the world as a soldier of Christ's Church."

THE REV. PAUL S. HOWDEN—Rector of Grace Reformed Episcopal Church, Scranton, Pennsylvania

"I use *Give Us This Day* as a daily meditation in conjunction with my prayer discipline using the 1928 *Book of Common Prayer* Order for Morning Prayer. I have found it to consistently glorify God, and spiritually substantive and edifying as part of my discipline. May God bless these meditations further for His glory and the good of His people."

FATHER DEWAYNE ADAMS—Ascension & St. Mark's Episcopal Church, Bridgeport, Texas

"Father Charles writes with the grace and wisdom that all seekers of God's kingdom can faithfully identify with. *Give Us This Day* has been pivotal in my daily discipline of shaping my heart and mind in His image."

DARBY LOGAN—Long-time *Give Us This Day* reader

Table of Contents

Introduction to GIVE US THIS DAY

Welcome to *Give Us This Day*, the daily Bible devotional I've written for every passage in the New Testament. I began to write *Give Us This Day* in the summer of 2006, in response to the promptings of the Holy Spirit for me to write a daily Bible devotional based on the ancient way of reading the Scriptures known as the *lectio divina*. Originally called *Daily Bread* for the first five years of its existence, my daily devotionals began as a daily e-mail I sent out to a growing readership. However, for some time it has been my goal to publish the entire series of devotionals so that there would be a daily Bible devotional for every passage of the New Testament. Some of you have been reading *Give Us This Day* from the beginning, and I thank all of you who have been its faithful readers over the years.

While I originally wrote *Give Us This Day* primarily for the Reformed Episcopal Church in Hot Springs, Arkansas at which I was serving as rector (St. Chrysostom's then, but now called Christ Anglican), I became aware that many others might profit by these devotionals. When I first began writing, I surveyed the other daily devotionals that were out there and immediately noticed some differences between what I was writing and what others had written. I was concerned that most of the other devotionals only dealt with a verse of the Bible for each day, and I could find none that provided a devotional for every passage of the New Testament. I also noticed that what I had written was usually longer than the uniformly bite-sized devotionals that seemed to be the publishing norm. In addition, most other devotionals did not include suggestions for further meditations and virtually none offered suggested resolutions to help put into effect what God had revealed through a given passage. At the end of each *Give Us This Day* meditation, I therefore offer not only a Prayer but also some Points for Further Reflection and a Daily Resolution.

This particular volume covers St. Matthew's Gospel and is the first in what will be an eight-volume series which covers the entire New Testament. *Give Us This Day* will be made available as a printed book, an e-book, and also, hopefully, available as a daily devotional that is sent each day to those on my list.

"Give us this day our daily bread" is the most fundamental prayer we can ask on behalf of ourselves. Knowing this, our Lord not only commanded us to pray for this every day but also offers Himself to us *as* our daily bread.

As the Bread of Life that offers Himself to us each day as true spiritual food,

Jesus comes to us in many ways. The feedings of the 4000 and 5000 (especially in the Gospel of St. John) remind us that it is through faithful participation in the covenantal meal of the Holy Communion that Jesus feeds us. Through the creatures of bread and wine, Jesus gives His Body and Blood to us and feeds us at His heavenly banquet.

But He feeds us in other ways. In one of his sermons, St. Augustine expressed his belief that the feeding of the 4000 isn't just about filling the bellies of men with bread and fish, nor is it solely about the Holy Communion. For St. Augustine and others, the Bread of Life is also the Holy Scriptures, upon which we are to feed every day, for they are the words of life. That the Word of God is also the Bread of God is satisfyingly illustrated by the Collect for the Second Sunday in Advent in the *Book of Common Prayer*, in which we ask God to "Grant that we may in such wise hear them [the Scriptures], read, mark, learn, and inwardly digest them."

However, Christians in the twenty-first century often do not properly eat or digest the Word of God. I've noticed some of you snacking in a sort of hit and run fashion, as you rush to lead your "real life." "I'll squeeze in a chapter of Bible reading today," you think. Some of you are to be commended for devoting yourself to studying the Scriptures, but unfortunately it is in such a way that only the mind is fed. Meanwhile, the soul gets spiritual kwashiorkor, which may easily be identified by your distended spiritual belly.

Scripture must therefore be eaten with prayer, which may be likened to the spiritual blood into which the bread of life must be digested and ingested. Through a life of prayer, the Word of God is carried into every part of your life and becomes your life, just as a piece of digested food is broken down, enters the blood, and is carried to every part of your body. Only through a life of prayer, which is a third means by which Jesus becomes our daily bread, will the Word of God become spiritual food for us. After all, haven't many of us had teachers of the Bible in college who have read and studied the Word but who, apart from a life of prayer and obedience, use their studies to starve themselves and others?

The most fruitful way I know of to receive my daily bread of Scripture is through the ancient practice of the *lectio divina*, or divine reading, with which I hope many of you are familiar. The essence of the *lectio divina* is not just another Bible study to inform our minds. Instead, the *lectio divina* is *formative* reading, in which we allow the Holy Scriptures, under the inspiration of the Holy Spirit, to form our very being. There are four basic steps in this divine reading:

1. *lectio*—reading/ listening
   a. Cultivate the ability to listen deeply.
   b. Your reading is slow, formative reading.
   c. Your reading is based on previous reading and study.

2. *meditatio*—meditation
   a. Gently stop reading when you have found a word, phrase, or passage through which God is speaking to you personally.
   b. Ruminate over this passage, as a cow ruminates or chews its cud.
   c. Say the passage over and over, noticing different aspects—"taste" it!
   d. Allow God's Word to become His word for you at every level of your being and to interact with your inner world of concerns, memories, and ideas.

3. *oratio*—prayer
   a. Pray—or dialogue with God—over the passage.
   b. Interact with God as one who loves you and is present with you.
   c. Allow God to transform your thoughts, memories, agendas, tendencies, and habits.
   d. Re-affirm and repeat what God has just told you.

4. *contemplatio*—contemplation
   a. Rest in the presence of the One who has come to transform and bless you.
   b. Rest quietly, experiencing the presence of God.
   c. Leave with a renewed energy and commitment to what God has just told you.

Daily reading of the Holy Scriptures through the *lectio divina* is just the food we need to nourish and correct our impoverished spiritual lives, our over-emphasis on the intellect, and our random foragings into the Bible that leave us unsatisfied.

A Few Words of Advice:

1. Use what is profitable, and don't worry about the rest.

2. Don't feel the need to meditate on every part of every *Give Us This Day*. It's not good to exhaust yourself spiritually. Also, don't feel it necessary keep up with a different Resolution every day: you'll drive yourself crazy in the process and unnecessarily feel like a failure! Work on what God is calling you to work on. Use the *Give Us This Day* as it is most profitable *for you*.

3. If God stops you and tells you to do something different—for example to

meditate on one small part of the lesson and apply it to your life today—drop everything else and listen to Him!

4. Most importantly: once you've developed the godly habit of meditating on the Bible every day—don't ever let go of it!

Ways to Profitably Eat Give Us This Day

1. Find and use some system for reading Scripture on a daily basis. I've organized *Give Us This Day* in the canonical order of the New Testament: from Matthew to Revelation. But many church traditions use a lectionary system of reading the New Testament. With your favorite lectionary in hand, you can read *Give Us This Day* according the daily New Testament assigned by that lectionary. The Roman Catholic Church uses a form of the Revised Common Lectionary (RCL), which is also used by the American Baptist Churches, the Disciples of Christ, The Episcopal Church, the Evangelical Lutheran Church in America, the Missouri Synod Lutheran Church, the Presbyterian Church in the U.S.A., the Reformed Church in America, the United Church of Christ, and the United Methodist Church. Other churches, such as my own Reformed Episcopal Church, use a different lectionary system.

2. *Give Us This Day* was written with the conscious aim of encouraging the reader to think more actively about the act of interpretation. While the literal meaning of the text is always the beginning point, the Bible can legitimately be applied in other ways. I've especially tried to suggest that the Bible is best read with the interpretation of the entire Church in mind.

3. I've also written *Give Us This Day* so that it could serve as a reference point for Bible study: in other words, as a kind of commentary to be consulted and not only a daily devotional to be used only once.

4. The Resolutions found in each *Give Us This Day* are another resource that should not be neglected. It may be neither desirable nor possible to follow the prescribed Resolution for each day. But these Resolutions can be returned to for further reference and used even apart from the devotional for the day.

5. The Prayers of *Give Us This Day*, many of which have been taken from a variety of historical sources, are also a rich resource that bears repeated use. Together, the prayers form a kind of treasury of prayer that can be used in any of a variety of ways. They especially include a number of different ways to think about how to pray the Lord's Prayer.

6. Finally, in the future I hope to add even greater resources to *Give Us This Day*, such as an index of keywords and topics and possibly artwork and interactivity.

A Note on Interpretation

Most of us who believe the Bible is the Word of God naturally assume that God intends it all for *me*, but even if this is true, the question remains as to *how* it applies to me. This is *the* task of all interpretation, including teaching and preaching. Historically, the Church has read the Bible in four senses or kinds of interpretations: the *literal, allegorical, moral* (or *tropological*), and *anagogical*. The *allegorical* meaning, of which so many Bible-believing Christians are afraid, is simply applying a given passage to Jesus Christ or the Church Militant (the Church still here on earth). We interpret the Bible *allegorically* all the time whenever we read the Old Testament and find Jesus Christ in it, for the literal meaning may be about the entrance into the Promised Land or about kings or about the delicate art of sacrificing animals. Yet we know that such passages also teach us about Christ. The *moral* sense is also one we use all the time, even if we claim we are only being literal. A *moral* interpretation of a passage involves applying it to yourself or other Christians. The *anagogical* interpretation means applying the passage to the heavenly realities and is thus (here goes another big word) *eschatological* in nature, applying the Word of God to the end things, or the world to come, on which we think too infrequently.

Give Us This Day is designed to be primarily *moral* in its interpretation because I want each of you to apply the Word of God to your life. But your life is not merely your own: it belongs to Christ, and so we seek Jesus Christ in His Church (*allegorical* interpretation). And all who are truly Christians are part of the Body of Christ and hopefully part of a local body, and therefore much of what the Bible says must be *allegorical* in this sense.

May God bless you through *Give Us This Day*, however you choose to use it, however you allow God to use it in your life. It is, in essence, but one way to make sure God's people are meditating on His Word even as they pray. Feel free to share it with friends and pass along those parts that may be profitable to your brothers and sisters in Christ.

Father Charles Erlandson

Matthew 1:1-17

Host:	Hello, I'm your host, Guy Smiley. And now it's time to play *Fun with Genealogies*, that wacky Bible trivia game in which our contestants try to see who can come up with the most creative way to stay awake while reading biblical genealogies. Last week we had a woman who stapled her eyelids open and a man who installed an IV drip of Starbucks into his body.
	Our contestant this week is Father Charles Erlandson who has a unique method for staying awake while reading a biblical genealogy. Father Charles, some have called you a fanatic or a space cadet. Would you tell us about your novel approach?
Fr. Charles:	Sure, Guy. I'm going to attempt to read the first genealogy in the New Testament, from Matthew chapter 1. I plan to actually read every word and study the names, looking for special significance.
Host:	Father Charles, if I may. Hasn't that method been tried before and been shown to induce extreme states of somnolence?
Fr. Charles:	That depends.
Host:	Depends on what?
Fr. Charles:	On what somnolence means. Actually, most people just skip over the genealogy of Jesus Christ. But I'm going in. Here I go!

. . .

It's strange, isn't it, that the first words of the New Testament would be some of the least read of the words of the New Testament? Doesn't it seem *unseemly* for God to have begun things like this? Now if He had started with John 1, I could understand. The majesty of John 1 matches the majesty of Genesis 1: "In the beginning was the Word, and the Word was with God, and the Word was God."

But to start with this: "The book of the genealogy of Jesus Christ, the Son of David, the Son of Abraham, yada, yada, yada..."

Actually, there are a lot of stimulating things I find in Matthew's genealogy of

Christ. It's different from Luke's and appears to give Jesus' genealogy through Joseph's line, while Luke gives it through Mary's. Then there's the fact that Matthew divides up Jesus' ancestors into three groups of 14 names. I could speak about why genealogies were important to the Jews and how important it is.

But I want to focus instead on four simple names: Tamar, Rahab, Ruth, and Uriah's wife. There's something unusual about these four people in the genealogy of Jesus Christ. In the first place, in case you hadn't noticed, they're all *women*! Look up any of the Old Testament genealogies, and what do you see? The names of a bunch of men. Since men are biblically the head of the family covenant and tribes of Israel, it makes sense for the genealogies to be traced through the father. When Paul traces our genealogy in Romans and Corinthians, he traces our sin back not to Eve but to Adam.

The fact that Matthew chooses to put four women in his genealogy is already significant and is in keeping with what we will soon learn about this Jesus who is to be born. If you remember Jesus as we see Him in the Gospels, you'll remember that He went to the outcasts and those of low degree: tax collectors, prostitutes, Samaritans, and *women*. You'll remember the sudden prominence that women have in the Gospel story, after the Crucifixion, when all the men have left, from fatigue or fear or confusion. Isn't it just like God to color outside the lines and reach down and put women into the genealogy of the Son as a permanent part of His inspired Word?

But there's more. These aren't just any women that God has chosen to record as part of the genealogy of His Son. It's important that Matthew chose to include these *particular* women, while he has clearly left out other names.

First, we find Tamar. Who's she? Her life is a sordid, sensational tale that I don't have time to tell. Moses tells it better in Genesis 38 anyway. Suffice it say that Judah, the patriarch from whom the Christ would come, was a fool. He was a man who didn't keep his vow to his daughter-in-law Tamar and ended up sleeping with her. It's O.K., though. He didn't know that she was his daughter-in-law: he thought she was a prostitute! Tamar took such desperate measures because Judah had treated her evilly, and even he acknowledged she was more righteous than he was. Still, she's not exactly the kind of person you would put into the genealogy of Christ, unless you had a very important point to make. And unless you had the authority and audacity of God!

Second, there's Rahab. You know Rahab—Rahab, the *prostitute*. What is it with Jesus and prostitutes? He not only talked to them, in violation of the social customs of his day, but also dared to have two as his ancestresses. There's no getting around the fact that Rahab was a prostitute, and not just a woman driven to pretend to be one. Worse yet, she was a *Canaanite*, that accursed race that God was determined to destroy and drive out of the Promised Land. But you'll remember that she acted favorably toward the people of God and hid the spies. Further, she is put into the famous Hebrews 11 "Hall of Faith" because of her faithful actions. Still, she's a pretty shady character to put into the genealogy of the Son of God.

Third, we have Ruth. Another non-Israelite. Ruth was a Moabitess, but one who left her home and her people to follow the true God. She sounds a lot like the first disciples Jesus called, who left families and jobs to follow Him. For her faithfulness, she was not only rewarded by getting to marry Mr. Right, Boaz, but was also privileged to become David's great-grandmother, and therefore an ancestor of Jesus.

And then there is the wife of Uriah. Who was this mysterious wife of Uriah? Matthew's modesty conceals the fact that she was none other than Bathsheba. Yes, Bathsheba, another woman in another sex scandal—this time for adultery, not prostitution. We know the consequences for her and David because of their sin: Uriah was murdered and David and Bathsheba's firstborn son together died. But out of that union came Solomon, the wisest of men.

Why are these women in the genealogy of Jesus Christ? If the Bible were heavily edited by those who wanted to tidy things up and make the story look better, don't you think they'd have thought to get rid of these scandalous women? Just what did Matthew think he was gaining for his Master's cause by including them?

In these women, I see the good news of Jesus Christ. I see a God who reaches down to the poor, the humble, the fallen, and the sinful, and out of love chooses them to be a part of His people. I see a holy God who, out of love, dares to associate with those who would defile Him and who have blatantly chosen to disobey Him.

In the blood of Jesus Christ was the blood of these sinful, scandalous women, taken from among the people who were not God's people. In Jesus' DNA were remnants of the DNA of Tamar and Rahab, Ruth and Bathsheba.

How scandalous! How shocking! Most shocking of all: I see myself in these women. For *I* am the outcast, the poor, and the sinful one. I am the one who rightfully stands outside of God and His people. But I am also the one who God adopted and made a part of His family.

You and I have also now been grafted into the genealogy of Jesus Christ, not as ancestors and not as descendants, but as His *brothers and sisters*. Like Tamar, Rahab, Ruth, and Bathsheba, we have found favor with God, in spite of ourselves.

In the story of these four women, incarnated in the "boring" genealogy of Matthew 1 (the very first thing we read in the New Testament), I find the gospel of Jesus Christ. In their stories, I find His story, which is now also my story.

Prayer:
Abba, Father! Thank You for adopting me as Your child and making me Your heir. Thank You for accepting me, in spite of my sinfulness, because of the perfect righteousness of Your Son, Jesus Christ. Help me to walk today as a child of light that I may give You all glory and honor and praise. Amen.

Points for Meditation:
1. How does it make you feel to know that, though sinful, you have been made a child of God?
2. How does it illuminate your life to remember that you are a brother or sister of Jesus Christ?

Resolution:
I resolve to meditate on the mystery of being reclaimed as a child of God and to offer God appropriate thanks, praise, and obedience.

Matthew 1:18-25

Emmanuel—"God with us." That is the great theme of Christmas.

When God became man, even His infant presence brought blessing to all who beheld Him. We think of faithful Anna, ministering at the temple, and of Simeon. John the Baptist kicked in the womb when he felt the presence of Mary and of the blessed Jesus still inside her. And, of course, Mary was the most highly favored one of all.

The characters and plots of the Christmas story are familiar to all of us. But there is one person who is often neglected in the Christmas story, someone who has much to teach us. He is the focus of much of the first two chapters of the Gospel of Matthew. He is who I call "The Forgotten Man of Christmas," and his name is Joseph.

Where is Joseph in the whirlwind of activity of the birth of the Savior of the world?

As I meditated on the life of Joseph, I took an informal survey of the portrayal of the Christmas story in art through the centuries. I looked at approximately 100 paintings depicting scenes such as the birth in the stable, the visits of the shepherds and the magi, and the flight into Egypt. I was amused at what I found. In some paintings I found just what I expected: a Joseph in the thick of things, looking adoringly at his son who was also the Son of God. But in a large percentage of the paintings I found Joseph portrayed in the following ways:

Absent; to the side; way in the back; way in the back to the side; way in the back beating chestnuts (in one painting); with his back to us; with his back to us carrying a saw; and asleep (sometimes with his head in his hands). The consensus opinion of tradition seemed to portray Joseph as "bewildered and inadequate," "tired and burdened."

But when I read the Gospel according to St. Matthew, that isn't the portrait I see. Instead, I marvel at how much attention Matthew gives to this Joseph. I find a Joseph who is a godly father and a Joseph who is an example to us of faith, as well as an example of God's grace in our lives.

If you try to imagine Christmas without Joseph, if you imagine for a moment the Holy Family, there is a gaping hole without the silent but strong presence of Joseph. Without a Joseph, Jesus would grow up the son of an unwed mother.

It would be hard to imagine the Jews seriously considering His claims had he grown up in such a fashion. It's probable that Joseph already had to contend with jeers and sneers on account of the fact that Mary was pregnant before she married him. But in time these would have been forgotten because the fact was that Jesus did have a human father.

Joseph was a true father to Jesus. And *I* think *I've* got a lot of pressure on me as a father! Can you imagine what a burden it would have been to have to raise a son who was the Son of God? When do you assert your fatherly prerogatives, and when do you hold back for fear that you might be in the wrong? What do you do when your little son begins correcting *you*?

And how must Joseph have worried at times, knowing he was the human protector of and provider for God's Son on earth! In spite of the angelic words of comfort, wouldn't he have been a little afraid when he heard Herod wanted to kill this special son of his, whom he was to protect?

But Joseph was truly the father of Jesus.

Joseph was there to give Jesus advice as He grew in grace and stature. He was there to teach Jesus about God from the time He was born. Children form a great deal of their conception of God from their fathers. Even the mere presence of Joseph, who is all too often absent in art, would have been important to Jesus. And Jesus had to grow in His knowledge of God just like the rest of us. It must have been the wisdom, righteousness, and faithfulness of Jesus' earthly father that provided him with much of his ever-growing knowledge of His heavenly Father.

Joseph gave Jesus his trade. In time, the Son of God became a carpenter, just like his earthly father. Joseph must have spent many hours with his son Jesus teaching him the tools and techniques of his trade. And although Jesus was without sin, that doesn't mean that he could drive a nail straight the first time he held a hammer or that he never hit Joseph's thumb when learning to hammer. After all, Jesus would still have been a little human boy holding sharp objects in his hands!

Joseph gave Jesus his name, lineage, and inheritance. He gave Jesus his good name, even though Jesus wouldn't be his natural son. He unhesitatingly adopted Jesus as his own son and treated him just as a natural born son, giving him the place as his firstborn, with all of the attendant rights and privileges. Joseph agreed to make Jesus a part of his family and to give his name to one who wasn't of his flesh and blood.

We know that Mary pondered or treasured all of the events surrounding Jesus in her heart. But what must have Joseph felt, knowing that it was his name that was to be given to Jesus: Jesus bar Joseph of Nazareth? In fact, it was Joseph who was given the privilege of naming the child, in obedience to the angel's word. Unlike his relative Zacharias, Joseph believed and obeyed: Joseph called his son's name Jesus, "He saves."

Joseph was also a righteous man of God whose example of faith we would do well to follow, for wherever we find Joseph in the Gospels we find him doing what is right.

Even before Joseph hears the good news of his son, Matthew makes a point of telling us that Joseph was a just man. Though his wife-to-be, Mary, had apparently gotten herself pregnant out of wedlock by a man other than him, we see no signs of jealousy or hatred or revenge on the part of Joseph. Instead, we find in Matthew 1:19 that he, "*being a just man, and not willing to make her a public example, was minded to put her away secretly.*" Even though he had apparently been wronged, he would not do wrong back. He had no desire to "teach Mary a lesson" or publicly humiliate her.

Next, we find Joseph being visited by the angel for the first time. The angel tells Joseph to not be afraid to take Mary as his wife, for that which is conceived in her is of the Holy Ghost. Now I'm sure Joseph had many questions about what the angel said. There was so much he must not have understood, for who could comprehend such marvelous and mysterious words?! But we see no sign of hesitation in Joseph, only a simple comment in verse 24: "*Then Joseph, being raised from sleep, did as the angel of the Lord had bidden him...*"

How different from the response of Abraham and Sarah, or of Zacharias when he was told the news of John the Baptist, also by an angel! They laughed or questioned: Joseph quietly believed and obeyed.

Joseph responded just as faithfully when the angel told him to flee to Egypt from Herod's slaughter of the innocents. When it was time to return back to Israel, we find that Joseph was afraid to go back, for the son of Herod was now ruling. Amazingly, we read in Matthew 2:22, "*But when he heard that Archelaus did reign in the room of his father Herod, he was afraid to go there. Notwithstanding, being warned of God in a dream, he turned aside into the parts of Galilee.*"

Isn't Joseph, in this passage, the very essence of faith? Isn't faith obeying the Word of God, regardless of what personal consequences are which that obedience may bring? In this forgotten man of Christmas, we find the kind of faith we all wish we had.

There is one final reason we should remember Joseph this Christmas, and that is because he is a symbol of the grace which we all receive from Jesus Christ.

"Hail, Mary full of grace!!" the angel sang. But he could just have easily sung "Hail, Joseph, full of grace!" It's true that Mary carried the Son of God in her womb, but Jesus was no less a son of Joseph, whose name and inheritance, and blessing and trade he took.

Joseph, of all the men who ever lived, was chosen to be the father of our Lord Jesus Christ. As we have already seen, this was no easy task, and perhaps the old masters were right in painting Joseph as burdened and tired, bewildered and inadequate. But he was faithful in all that God had given him to do while here on earth. The fact that he obeyed, even while burdened and tired and bewildered and inadequate, is even more wonderful.

If Mary, the recipient of an angelic visit, was full of grace, then Joseph, the recipient of *three* angelic visits, was certainly also full of grace. God's unmerited favor, His grace, came down upon Joseph.

We have already seen that Jesus was adopted into the family of Joseph and given his name. But in a more important sense Joseph was adopted into the family of Jesus: the family of God. Joseph, being a just man who feared God, had to be brought to a knowledge of Jesus, his son, as Jesus the Son of God.

This, above all other things in the life of Joseph, demonstrated the grace of God.

In a way, many of us may feel like forgotten men, women, and children. Forgotten, neglected—even rejected. Maybe someone on your Christmas card list forgot to send you a card or maybe some of you kids didn't get for Christmas all that you expected. Maybe for some of us the gifts we could afford weren't quite as nice this year. Or perhaps more seriously for some reason we can't seem to find it within ourselves to rejoice in this season of Christmas or at whatever time of the year it is that you are reading this. Maybe there are trials on the job or at home, within our own families.

At times, we all feel forgotten.

But Christmas (and every day is Christmas for the Christian!) is a time for all to remember, to remember that God is indeed with us. If you believe that Jesus, the son of Joseph, is the Lord who was born to die for our sins, then you will be adopted as a child of God. God has adopted us, and like Joseph He has made us all a part of His Holy Family—the Church.

There are no forgotten Christians at Christmas time, or at any other time, for God has remembered His people. God came to earth to be with us, and when He came, He came bearing gifts for all who love Him.

Prayer:

Almighty God, who hast given us thy only-begotten Son to take our nature upon him, and as at this time to be born of a pure virgin; Grant that we being regenerate, and made thy children by adoption and grace, may daily be renewed by thy Holy Spirit; through the same our Lord Jesus Christ, who liveth and reigneth thee and the same Spirit ever, one God, world without end.

(The Collect for Christmas from *The Book of Common Prayer*)

Points for Meditation:

1. How can I be more faithful in my calling, as Joseph was in his calling as a father?
2. How can I demonstrate more faith, as Joseph did in accepting Mary and Jesus and protecting them in the face of fear?
3. How can I accept more freely and joyfully the grace of Jesus Christ in my life today?

Resolution:

I resolve to practice today seeing my lot and calling in life as being from the Lord and then treating them accordingly.

Matthew 2:1–12

I want to talk this morning about zombies...

Yes, zombies—you know, the living dead that you see in horror movies.

I don't watch a lot of movies, but in my time I've watched a number of strange movies. One of them was *The Night of the Living Dead*, which is basically about an attack by zombies. (For the connoisseur, check out *Dawn of the Dead,* which takes place in a shopping mall!) Zombies, the living dead, seek out the living that they might turn them into the living dead. They find a living human, focus on them, follow them, and then feed on them.

All of us in many ways are like these zombies: we find something significant, we focus on it, we follow or pursue it, and then finally we feed on or consume in some way what we have found so that we may find life.

Like zombies, we also often walk around spiritually half-dead. And like zombies, we seek one who is living.

But unlike zombies, who turn the living into the living dead, we find, focus on, follow, and feed on Jesus Christ, who is the Living One. And He turns us, the living-dead, into ones who truly live.

First, we need to find Jesus Christ. The magi or wise men found Jesus Christ. How did this happen? They spent time seeking Him. They studied the sky, and they spent time pondering Him and how to find Him. They not only had to find the star but also had to know what it meant. And so they found His star because they were "star struck." Of course they were looking for the greater Star that the star of Bethlehem could lead them to, for Jesus Christ is the true Star of Bethlehem.

We, too, need to be star struck by Christ Himself. But God uses many kinds of stars, each with its own glory, to lead us to His Son. This is why I subscribe to the sacramental worldview (it comes to my front door every morning) in which every part of the creation is a way to come to the Creator. God uses different means to entice and capture each of us. There are many parts of His creation that are flashy and glorious. But what should really catch our attention and hold it, as with all wise men, is Jesus Christ Himself.

It's not enough just to find or hear about this most stellar of people. We must focus on Him in order to finally feed on Him. And so the Magi *focused* on the Star of Bethlehem. Presumably, they came from Arabia or Persia which were 1000 to 1200 miles away. To come to the One who was the Star would take 3–12 months—by camel! To make the journey would take weeks of preparation. They probably arrived to see Jesus months after He had been born. During that whole time they never lost their focus on the star and the One to whom it would lead them. They spared no expense to come to Him.

Like the Magi, we must not lose focus. How long can you stare at a single object without looking away or being distracted? How long can you look at something without moving your eyes or blinking? My son Charlie says he can do it for 92 seconds, although this has yet to be replicated in lab tests.

It is so easy to get distracted in this life. One of the greatest blessings of having gone to Belize for a mission trip for a week was the blessing of leaving my distractions (which are often my blessings) back home. No TV, no Internet, no e-mail. No "To Do List." Just a simple rediscovery of John Milton's, "They also serve who only stand to wait."

We may have the best of intentions to find and follow Jesus at the beginning of the day. And then when we finally wake and the day comes, it has a way of just happening. Our lives are swept away by a tidal wave of activity, a sky filled with threatening clouds of To Do Lists that destroy our real purpose in life. For one of the things that almost never makes it onto these lists is to seek, find, and follow Jesus Christ. How often do we safely reach the end of the day by the grace of God and say or feel, "I wish I had stayed more focused on Jesus Christ"?

Once you have found Jesus Christ, so much of the rest of the Christian life is simply not to lose focus.

Once we have found Jesus Christ and focused on Him, we must choose to follow Him. After the Magi had seen the star in the East, they followed it all the way to Bethlehem and where the Christ child lay.

Wherever the star went, the wise men followed, for they sought Christ. Having found Him, to be truly wise, we must follow Him. Wherever Jesus Christ goes before us, we must follow. The people of God have seen a great light, and we must follow it until we join with it.

This might—it *will*—involve changing our plans. It must involve changing our direction, and actually it does, every day. We have Stars of Bethlehem to lead us to Christ: they are the Word of God and His Church, and we must align our lives with God, not the other way around.

After we have found, focused on, and followed Jesus Christ, what do we do, as holy zombies? We get to feed on Him. The wise men fed by rejoicing in the presence of God and worshiping Him: "When they saw the star, they rejoiced with exceedingly great joy. And when they had come into the house, they saw the young Child with Mary His mother, and fell down and worshiped Him."

Having come to Bethlehem, the House of Bread, to Jesus, we must then feed on Him. He is a feast for our souls! We feast on His presence and light, and we participate in His glorious, loving presence. In His light, we become light.

"Arise, shine, for your light has come! And the glory of the Lord is risen upon you. Then you shall see and become radiant, and your heart shall swell with joy" (Isaiah 60:1, 5).

We eat the Bread of Life until we find life and become part of the Life that is the light of the world.

This is wisdom, this is faith. *Faith = Find + Focus + Follow + Feed.*

Prayer:
O God, who by the leading of a star didst manifest thy only-begotten Son to the Gentiles; Mercifully grant that we, who know thee now by faith, may after this life have the fruition of thy glorious Godhead; through the same thy Son Jesus Christ our Lord. Amen.

(The Collect for Epiphany from *The Book of Common Prayer*)

Points for Meditation:
1. Meditate upon each aspect of wisdom and faith: finding, focusing, following, and feeding. Which of these is something to which God is calling you in particular?
2. Jesus is the Bread of Life: how can you feast on Him today with joy and satisfaction?

Resolution:
I resolve to find Jesus today and focus on Him throughout the day. In particular, I resolve to follow Him wherever I hear Him calling me, feeding on Him along the way.

Matthew 2:13-23

I am amazed and humbled again at the obedience of Joseph. Now it's true that Joseph was especially privileged to have heard angels speak to him in dreams, upon several occasions. Yet he still had to obey. And especially if it's true that Mary was perpetually virgin (considering the implications for Joseph's sex life), then Joseph is nothing short of heroic!

Joseph, not yet understanding that Jesus was conceived by the Holy Spirit, wanted to do the right thing and privately put away his pregnant, betrothed wife. When told by an angel that he should still marry Mary because what was conceived in her was from the Holy Spirit, Joseph "did as the angel of the Lord commanded him and took to him his wife, and did not know her till she had brought forth her firstborn Son."

The angel comes again to Joseph and tells him to take the child and mother and flee to Egypt, for Herod was seeking his son's life. And when Joseph arose, he did just as the angel had commanded. When Herod was dead, the angel comes and tells Joseph to go back to Israel because the one seeking the child was dead. But Joseph also hears that Archelaus, Herod's son, is ruling in his place, and he is afraid. But the angel warns him to go to Galilee, and so Joseph goes to dwell in Nazareth.

If I were Joseph, I know I certainly would feel like I was being jerked around. All I did was betroth myself to a young woman I loved. And then she gets pregnant without me. And then, I'm told to marry her anyway because somehow this is from God. And then, just as I'm getting used to the idea that my son is special, what with the angels and shepherds, and magi and so on, I'm told to flee with my wife and child to Egypt. Egypt, of all places! Couldn't it be Samaria or Syria or someplace like that? And, just as I'm settling down there, I'm told again to move, right into the heart of the enemy who wants to destroy my son and probably me and my entire family. I'm told again that I should go to Galilee, Nazareth. Finally, back home!

What a lesson for me! If only I would listen to God, He would safely lead me home, back to hick Galilee. There will be dangers on the way, but God will lead me safely through them. But these dangers will be proportional to the greatness of the ministry God has given me. Joseph was given the ministry of raising and protecting God's own Son, and so life suddenly became wonderful and difficult for Joseph. And yet, Joseph got jerked around, humanly speaking.

But God also blessed him immeasurably. Even though he may even have been frustrated sexually, God blessed Joseph immeasurably—because of the greatness of the ministry and because of Joseph's faithfulness.

To what ministry is God calling me? What dangers and obstacles will I face? But what blessing does God have in store for me, if only I would learn not to fear those who can kill the body but to fear the One who has power over both my body and my eternal soul?

Lord, give me ears to hear!

So what is it that I hear God saying to me? I hear several things distinctly. I am so glad I taught my kids the other night to begin listening to God and knowing that He speaks to them throughout the day, especially through their consciences. Here's a short list of things that I already hear God calling me to do. And yes, they will probably involve Him "jerking me around"!

1. I must surrender every labor of work, home, family, and self to God as a way of knowing and seeking Him, and not treat it as something distinct from my life with Him.

2. I must renew my labors on the most important things God is calling me to, in spite of the persistent obstacles He's put in my life.

3. I must continue writing (and reading!) *Give Us This Day*, no matter how tired I am or how difficult it is at times. For it is bearing fruit in my life and the lives of others, and I believe it will lead me to more.

4. I must not fritter away any more time.

5. I must remain open to the thrilling and dangerous and exhilarating call God has upon my life, no matter where it leads.

6. I must speak passionately and fearlessly about Jesus Christ to anyone who is willing to listen to me.

As I closely observe Joseph, the father of my Lord, he's taught me. I, too, want to listen intently to the Lord, no matter how He speaks. I, too, want to follow wherever He leads me. I used to think that maybe God was eventually calling me to Africa, to Kigali or Nairobi or Nigeria. Maybe He was calling me to be daring in encountering another form of Anglicanism. And so He led me to places like wild St. Andrew's in exotic Fort Worth, Texas; humble St. Chrysostom's in Hot Springs, Arkansas; and back to good old Good Shepherd in Tyler, Texas!

The point is: I want to vow to keep listening and obeying, as Joseph did.

What if...? What if all of us vowed to be like Joseph: to seek the Lord, to listen for Him, and to do whatever He told us to do, even if He sent us a virgin birth or to Egypt or to a place where we might be killed?

I think maybe we'd turn the world upside down all over again!

Prayer:

Lord, I ask that You would reveal Yourself to me today. Although You may not come to me through angels or dreams but through the small still voice, I ask that You would increase my spiritual ears and my ability to hear You when You speak. Strengthen my spiritual muscles so that when I hear You I will have the strength to obey, in the Name of Your Son and through the power of Your Spirit. Amen.

Points for Meditation:

1. What has the Lord been telling you recently? If you don't know, then spend some time today becoming very quiet and still, and then listen for what He's saying.
2. What distracts you from listening better to the Lord? How can you over-come this?

Resolution:

I resolve to listen for the Lord today until I hear Him speak.

Matthew 3:1–12

"Repent! For the Kingdom of Heaven is at hand!"

There, that's what you came to hear me say, wasn't it. It's what I'm most famous for.

Some called me Elijah. But they were wrong. Others called me The Prophet. They, too, were wrong. Some actually thought I was the Messiah, if you can believe that—me, John. You may call me the John the Baptist, as most do, or John son of Zechariah, or just John.

All my life I knew I was special. My father always reminded me of the angelic visitation and promises, and my mother too was always telling me of God's purposes for my life. I grew up differently from other kids. I wasn't allowed to drink wine or to cut my hair, because I had taken a Nazarite vow. I also had what you today might call an overdeveloped conscience, if such a thing exists. I saw sin everywhere and lamented it. Even as a kid I remember my anger whenever I saw the other kids lying and stealing and often getting away with it. Of course I was labeled, and other kids didn't want to have anything to do with me. I knew that obeying my parents and the will of God was a good thing, but I almost— almost—resented it being so difficult. Sometimes I wished I weren't so special.

In my twenties I gravitated toward the wilderness, full of wildness myself and ready to conquer the wilderness. It conquered me. I was wild at first. I mean I was wild with energy and ideas like a young man ought to be. But I matured in my solitariness, and my head cleared. Sometimes, it almost seemed as if God and I were the only beings in existence, and I basked in His fellowship.

In the wilderness I loved God, and my constant prayers were for God to show me His work. All I ever wanted was a chance to serve Him, and yet even this holy desire seemed thwarted. I prayed without ceasing for the coming of the Messiah, for God had shown me what my work was to be: I was to be the forerunner of the Messiah, the long-awaited King of Israel. God had elected me for this most exalted human role. My parents had reminded me of this my whole life, and in the wilderness sun it was burned into my soul indelibly.

It was so burning that it dried up my eyes: my vision began to fail. I thought maybe God had forgotten or more likely that my parents were deceived or mistaken in what they'd told me. I thirsted to drink of the mission God had given me. I wanted to *charge* into the cities of Israel, *grab* the first person I saw, and *shake* him, shouting my sermons until he repented. I wanted to carve out the Kingdom of Heaven from the wilderness and seize it and carry it away with the force and violence of my own energy.

You can forgive me. Maybe some of you are like I was: tired of waiting for God to come and to move in your life. Maybe you've given up on Him. Maybe you've said to yourself that God doesn't care or that He isn't really there. Maybe you've fooled yourself into being mad at God for the way your life is, without considering how much God loves you and is preparing you for maturity.

But God IS there, and He does care.

One day, without warning, without my planning it, and just as I'd learned to be patient, God told me it was time. The day had come when I was to go into the cities and preach repentance, for the *Kingdom of Heaven was at hand*! God's long-awaited Messiah was coming, the light of the world, and my moment of service was imminent.

I trembled within myself; my knees knocked; a storm swept through my gut. I was finding out I was not as impregnable as I'd imagined myself to be. The wilderness seemed tame compared to the wild herds of society I must face and to whom I was now a stranger.

I'm sure I created quite an impression. I'd forgotten what a wild-looking specimen I'd become. I'd grown used to my coat of camel's hair and leather belt, and I liked my locusts and wild honey, even as those in the cities liked their bread and wine. To me, I was just a man like any other, and I was just as shocked at their appearance as they were at mine.

But *you should have seen them!* You would have thought they'd seen the face of the Almighty Himself! How *terrible* my words must have sounded to them! "*Repent, for the kingdom of God is at hand.*" (v. 2), or to the Pharisees: "*O generation of vipers, who warned you to flee from the coming wrath?!*" (v. 7) Again, I was alone, even though surrounded by many. Not everyone wanted to hear what I had to say. But I was never lonely because I was filled with the Spirit and at that very moment fulfilling my eternal destiny.

Many responded in faith. It was very gratifying, yet I purposed in my heart to never let my "success" go to my head, because it was all the work of God. There is nothing a man has received that does not come from God. Even when they asked me if I were the Messiah, I did not give in to temptation but faithfully proclaimed that I was not He but only his humble messenger. Sometimes, when I saw the lostness of their souls and the hunger in their faces, I wanted to be that One. Everyone's looking for a leader, someone worth following, and many of us are tempted to think we are Him.

"*No!* I am not He," I said. "I am not worthy even to undo the latch on his sandals," I told them. If you want to know the stark truth, I wasn't worthy of anything: I wasn't worthy to be his prophet; I wasn't worthy to be his cousin; I wasn't worthy to be mentioned in the same breath with Him. God had taught me that He must be greater than I am: He alone is God. I must be second, for this is the lot of mankind.

In the wilderness I'd had a lot of time to think about this, and I'd made my peace with God about always being second best. There's a part of each of us that wants to be #1, that wants to say "I am worthy: I should have my desires met first." Some of you may be second best. Maybe there's someone in your life who is always a little faster, a little stronger, a little smarter, a little richer. I was special beyond my peers, and yet I was nothing compared to He who was truly #1. Considering who God is, being second best isn't so bad after all.

One of the hardest things wasn't just being second best or my self-doubts, or even my reluctance that it was Jesus, my own cousin Jesus, who was the Promised One. Think about it: if one of your cousins was, well, *God*, it'd make you think, too. What was even more difficult was that I hadn't exactly counted on being thrown in prison, and so I began to doubt again. I, who of all people should know—I who had seen the Spirit descend on Him in the body of a dove—doubted. I even sent some of my disciples from prison to make sure of who He was.

But even this wasn't the most difficult thing.

The hardest thing of all was accepting that my role was now over: as quickly as it had come, like a flower in the wilderness, it was gone. One day I was released from years in the wilderness and into the city, preaching, baptizing, and the center of the attention of all of God's Chosen People. The next day, I withered. I was done. I was in prison, watching everything God had created me to prepare and usher in.

All of these things were hard.

And yet it was the easiest thing in the world to do because it was right. It was the very thing for which I was created. In the end, I played my part well. I did all that God had commanded me to do.

If you will permit a man dead for nearly two millennia to speak to you today for but a few more minutes, to proclaim my one last sermon, I will continue.

Jesus the Messiah said of me that I was the greatest man of those born to a woman. But He also said that even the least of you who are in the Kingdom of Heaven is greater than me. And indeed you are. I bore witness to the first coming of Christ, but you have already seen Him and must bear witness to His Second Coming. This requires patience like mine, but even greater. Each of you must live your life as if He's coming back today, with all His cloud of angels and glorious, blinding light.

You are greater than I. I saw Him baptized with water, but you have seen Him crucified, resurrected, ascended, and seated at the right hand of the Father. You have a great responsibility for this great knowledge, a greater responsibility than mine for you have been given a greater light. For when God shows you His truth, like He did to me, He gives you the awesome responsibility to be righteous and speak the truth. These things aren't just good ideas: they're the Law.

I had the Scriptures of the Old Testament, but you all have the entire Scriptures, the complete revelation of Jesus Christ. Go home and read them every day. God has given you His revelation that you might read it for yourselves and proclaim it to all.

Finally, I had the Holy Spirit for a season, but you have the Spirit within you forever and are His temple. The same Spirit who made me kick in my mother's womb is in each of you, and each of you should be kicking and leaping for joy because you have seen Jesus Christ and you know Him. Pray, and the Spirit will guide you into all truth and will give you strength to profess, if you do not quench Him.

I beseech you, then, my greater brethren, do as I did. Faithfully confess Christ to all men, preach righteousness, do what is right, and do not be afraid of being second to God.

You, my greater brethren, who are greater than me because you come after me, must surpass my works. It is you who are now living who must prepare the way of the Lord. Behold! our Lord comes to you. Prepare ye the way for Him, for unto you is given the commandment to be greater than me, John the Baptist, by serving the One who is the greatest One of all.

Prayer:

Almighty God, by whose providence thy servant John the Baptist was wonderfully born, and sent to prepare the way of thy Son our Savior by preaching repentance: Make us so to follow his doctrine and holy life, that we may truly repent according to his preaching; and after his example constantly speak the truth, boldly rebuke vice, and patiently suffer for the truth's sake; through the same thy Son Jesus Christ our Lord, who liveth and reigneth with thee and the Holy Spirit, one God, for ever and ever.

(The Collect for the Nativity of John the Baptist from *The Book of Common Prayer*, 1979)

Points for Meditation:

1. How willing are you to serve Jesus Christ, becoming less that He might become greater?
2. In what ways is God asking you to be a prophet, making Him and His ways known to others? What fears do you have of being a prophet like John?

Resolution:

I resolve to find one way today that I can actively and humbly submit myself to my Lord.

Matthew 3:13–17

Have any of you ever been a marked man—or woman?

I mean, have you ever had the feeling that someone is just out to get you?

Maybe you had an enemy who was hell-bent on tracking you down and seeing you brought down at whatever cost, or maybe you feel as if you have a big X marked all over you.

Though you wouldn't guess it to look at me, *I* am a marked man. Not *was* a marked man—*am*. I *am* a marked man. Now you might be thinking: "Just who is this guy who I thought was a godly priest." But let me explain.

You see, I've been a marked man all my adult life, and I remember the day and hour I became a marked man. It's really my own fault. It's something I volunteered to do—well, sort of. It was towards the end of my freshman year in high school, in the spring. I remember my twin brother, Danny, was with me: we had been singled out from a group of teenagers I think maybe there was one other guy as well.

They made us come forward in front of everyone and face a large crowd of adults. And that's when they marked me.

That's when the minister took his hand, placed it in water, and marked my forehead with the sign of the cross.

The day I was baptized was the day I became a marked man. And the day you were baptized was the day you became a marked man as well.

You and I—all of us who are Christians—are marked men. You see, God puts the sign of His name upon us at baptism and claims us publicly for His own.

At that moment, even if we don't realize it, there are a lot of amazing things that begin to happen to us. Suddenly, the stakes for our life become a lot higher. God declares Himself for us, but Satan is out to get us: he is the hunter. With every decision you make from that moment you will either be confirming the mark that is on you, or you will be denying the One who put it there.

When you are baptized, you become a part of the Church. And when you become a part of the Church, you are united with Jesus Christ in all of His life.

. . .

I want us to try to understand what Jesus' baptism has to do with us. When Jesus was baptized, it was easy for everyone present to see the earthly and physical aspects of His baptism—how the water was placed on Him by John the Baptist. But there was a heavenly aspect as well: God is always working behind the scenes in baptism.

Three heavenly things happened to Jesus when He was baptized: the heavens were opened; the Holy Spirit descended; and the Father was well-pleased. But here, if you're like me, you might have a question about baptism. If baptism for the Christian is being made a part of the body of Christ, as well as a dedicating of one's life to God, then why was it necessary for Jesus Christ to be baptized? What did it signify for Him, and why did God act so dramatically?

In baptism, Jesus was anointed to three offices. He was anointed ("Messiah" or "Christ" means "Anointed One") to be a prophet, one who proclaims the Word of the Lord, the Good News of salvation. He was anointed to be a priest, our High Priest who offers up the perfect sacrifice that truly took away the sins of the world. And He was anointed as a king, in fact, the King of Kings.

Immediately after, and only after, His baptism, Jesus began the work for which He was born. We rightly celebrate the birth of Jesus Christ at Christmas, God made man. But God was made man in the person of Jesus for a purpose. This is the connection between the baptism of Jesus Christ and your baptism: when you are baptized God is equipping you for ministry, to serve *as* Jesus Christ served, for it is His ministry and life into which you are baptized.

There's another reason Jesus was baptized: Jesus was baptized so that He might baptize us. Jesus was baptized that He might serve us and baptize us with His Spirit, that we might be united to Him in all things.

In the Church year, we celebrate and rehearse the life of Christ: God became man that man might come to God or become like God. In baptism, we put on Christ, and we are united with Him and are made a part of His body. We think, act, and speak as Jesus thought, acted, and spoke.

In fact, in baptism, we are given our eternal *identity*: baptism makes us *Christians* and identifies us to the world, both visible and invisible, as Christians. Everyone today is looking for an identity: we've all heard of people having identity crises. You can see it in the way people change their hair or cars or even their lifestyles, searching for their "true" identity, when all along the identity of each human is to be one created in the image of God

When you are baptized, three heavenly things happened that marked your new identity, as they did with Jesus. First, the heavens were opened: you now have access to God. Second, you were given the Holy Spirit who equips you for spiritual battle and life in Christ. Third, God is well pleased with you as His adopted child.

In baptism, God makes you one of His sheep. He puts His mark on you and claims you as one of His own: He *brands* you! Then He cares for you like a shepherd cares for His sheep. He feeds you and clothes you; He protects you and blesses you in every way. Praise God from whom all blessings flow!

But when you accept the mark of God upon you, you have taken a *vow*: when you were baptized, you signed your life away. You signed up for God's army, the Church, and agreed to submit to the rules and discipline, as well as the rewards, of life in Christ and in His Body.

Like Jesus, in your baptism you were anointed to three offices. You were anointed to be a prophet who speaks the word of God. You were anointed as a priest who is to make spiritual sacrifices with your lips and life to God, a sacrifice of thanksgiving and praise. You are to worship Him! And you were anointed as a king who is to rule over your body and whatever else God has given you.

Once baptized, you are marked men and women. You have entered a spiritual war, and baptism makes clear to the enemy which side of the battle you are on. Just as Jesus was immediately led into the wilderness to be tempted after He was baptized, you will be tempted as a Christian. You have a glowing cross on your uniform which Satan and his minions see as a big, fat target.

You will be tempted to do things your way, which is too often Satan's way. You will be tempted to forget that you are a Christian, signed with the name of the Holy Trinity. You will suffer in this life, and God's enemy will seek to use this to make you question God and your identity as one of His children.

But the God who has marked you as His child and made you a member of the body of His Son will protect you from all evil if you are faithful to Him.

In the midst of a pagan nation to whom he had come in order to make them Christians, St. Patrick knew who he was. He could have been discouraged by how hard his life was and how often he must have been rejected and dejected. But everywhere around him he saw a world that reminded him of the presence of Jesus Christ.

He saw clearly that he was in Christ and that Christ was his life. He knew that being baptized into Christ was what made Him a Christian, marked before God and man as being the property of Jesus Christ.

When St. Patrick rose in the morning, he awoke with a sense of his Christian identity: he arose by invoking the strong name of the Trinity, into whose name he was baptized. When he rose each morning, he put on Jesus Christ and used all of creation to remind him that he was a Christian. He arose each day with a sense that he was identified with Jesus Christ through baptism

Just as the life of Christ guides us through the Christian year, it guides us through each day:

> "I bind this day to me forever,
>   by power of faith, Christ's Incarnation; (Christmas)
>   his baptism in the Jordan river (Epiphany)
>   his death on the cross for my salvation (Good Friday)
>   his bursting from the spicèd tomb (Easter)
>   his riding up the heavenly way; (Ascension)
>   his coming at the day of doom: (Second Coming)
>   I bind unto myself today."

St. Patrick's identity in Jesus Christ is what gave him strength, which is why the hymn from which these words are taken is called "St. Patrick's Breastplate".

When Jesus Christ was baptized, He was anointed to begin His ministry of salvation for you and for me. When you were baptized, you were anointed to a life in union with Jesus Christ and His ministry. When you were baptized you became marked men and women, marked by God as one of His.

May we choose to live our lives as St. Patrick lived his, with a sense of his Christian identity and with a sense of Jesus Christ in every part of his life.

Prayer:

Christ be with me,
Christ within me,
Christ behind me,
Christ before me,
Christ beside me,
Christ to win me,
Christ to comfort
and restore me.
Christ beneath me,
Christ above me,
Christ in quiet,
Christ in danger,
Christ in hearts of
all that love me,
Christ in mouth of
friend and stranger. Amen.

(From "St. Patrick's Breastplate" as translated by Cecil F. Alexander)

Points for Meditation:

1. Sing St. Patrick's Breastplate today (hymn #268 in the 1940 Episcopal Hymnal).
2. In which of the three anointed offices is God calling you to work more faithfully?
3. How can you practice binding yourself to Christ today so that He is your breastplate and your identity?

Resolution:

I resolve to find one specific way to put Jesus Christ on today.

Matthew 4:1-11

Baptism—Fasting—Feasting. This is the pattern of the life of Christ in Matthew 4, and it is the pattern of our lives as well. You can even see this pattern in the Church Year that the Church has created and preserved. Advent and Christmas are kinds of baptisms or new beginnings: Advent is the initiation of the church year in which we prepare for Christ, and Christmas is the initiation of the life of Christ, to whose life we join ourselves. Epiphany is an extension of the life of Christ and Incarnation, and then come the weeks before Lent and Lent itself, which is the period of fasting. This fasting leads to the climax and crisis of Good Friday, and then comes the glorious feast of Easter in which we leave the fast behind and celebrate the new life that God has given. Trinity, the green season of growth, is a season of lesser feasting, as we continue to celebrate this new life.

But here, in Matthew 4, the pattern is laid down in the life of Jesus. In verse 1 we read that *"Jesus was led up by the Spirit into the wilderness."* Jesus didn't rush out into the wilderness to be tempted by the devil of his own accord: He was led there by the Spirit. And where is it that we find Christ first filled with the Spirit? It is after his baptism. This may seem puzzling at first, since I've said that the pattern of the life of Christ is Baptism, Fasting, and Feasting, and in Matthew 4 there appears to be a fast without a baptism before it. If we read the Gospel of Matthew as an entirety, and not as a collection of verses and chapters (which were added later) we wouldn't miss such patterns.

In the book of Exodus, we find that this pattern of fasting and temptation applies not only to Christ but also to Moses, as the mediator of the Old Covenant. In Exodus 14 Moses leads the Israelites through the Red Sea, which represented their baptism. Not only do we have the obvious water symbolism represented here to confirm that this is a baptism, but we also have the testimony of Paul in 1 Corinthians 10:2 that *"all were baptized unto Moses in the cloud and in the sea."* Immediately following the baptism of the Israelites, they fasted, or were tempted for forty days. There are two aspects of this fasting.

First, Moses himself fasted for forty days and nights on the mountain of God, as Exodus 34 tells us. As the mediator of the Old Covenant, it is not surprising that Moses should undergo the same kind of fasting and temptation which His Master was to undergo. (It's interesting that Christ, Moses, and Elijah, all of whom appeared on the mount of transfiguration, had all first undergone 40 day periods of fasting.)

The second fasting that takes place involved the Israelites. Even as Moses was fasting and receiving the Law for 40 days, the people faced a different kind of fasting and temptation. They were without their godly representative for forty days and nights. How would they handle this time without their leader upon whom they depended for everything? The answer is all too clear. They broke the fast and set up a golden calf to be their leader and god in Moses' absence. This failure on the part of the Israelites led to another testing period of 40, this time the 40 years of wandering in the wilderness.

But Jesus succeeded where the Israelites, and even Moses, could not, for even Moses was tempted in the wilderness to smite the rock of water twice, and thus was disabled from leading the children into the Promised Land. It was Joshua, which is only another form of the name "Jesus," who was to lead them into the Promised Land.

Now it's interesting to me that the same Spirit with which Jesus has been baptized is the one who immediately leads him into the *wilderness – to be tempted.* Maybe that isn't as startling to us as it ought to be. The Spirit of God which baptizes us also leads us into the wilderness after baptism to be tempted and tested. We don't usually hear much about this aspect of the Spirit's ministry. In fact, sometimes when we face trials and temptations it's assumed that they occurred because of a *lack* of the Spirit in the life of a believer. But God's Holy Spirit has a purpose in leading His people into the wilderness.

Let's look more closely at how Christ was tempted after His baptism and how He endured it.

Verse 2 says, *"And when He had fasted forty days and forty nights* (and here comes an understatement so extraordinary it seems almost comical), *afterward, he was hungry"*!! So Jesus was already engaged in one kind of temptation even before Satan showed up. In denying Himself food for 40 days Jesus was at the same time subjecting himself to the temptation to break the fast He was to endure.

Satan's first temptation was only an intensification of a temptation Christ was already enduring. It was an appeal to the desires of the flesh which Satan brought to Christ's mind in a new way. But Christ rebuked Satan with Scripture. And Jesus had bread that Satan did not know about. He had the Word of God, and He had the food of doing the will of the Father (John 4:34), which sustained Him, in spite of temptation. Romans 10:8 states that, *"The word is near you, even in your mouth."* Indeed, the Word of God was so near to Jesus and His mouth that it was what sustained Him during His fasting. Man shall not live by bread alone but by every word of God. Jesus was not alone in His fasting; instead, He was accompanied by the Word of God, and the Father and His will, and we can be sure that He occupied His time in prayer as well, inhabited by the same Spirit who had led Him to the wilderness. With these weapons did Jesus subdue the Tempter.

Satan's second attempt to seduce Jesus was the temptation to doubt. This was, perhaps, the most subtle of Satan's temptations. After all, what could possibly be wrong with Jesus fulfilling Scripture and casting himself down? Surely the angels of God would save Him. But this is the same temptation which Satan planted in the mind of Eve and to which she succumbed. "Hath God said?" was Satan's question to her. "Did God really say that you couldn't eat from the Tree of the Knowledge of Good and Evil?"

Satan's third and final attempt was an appeal to riches and power, the temptation of the world. Satan wanted Jesus to accept an easy glory that came from his hand, instead of the difficult and costly glory which must come from the Father. Jesus' response is the same which he offered to Peter, when Peter attempted to seduce Him from walking the path to the Cross: *"Get behind me Satan." "For thou shalt worship the Lord thy God, and him only shalt thou serve."* It is the spirit of Satan that attempts to have us serve anything but God.

Once again, Jesus dispatches Satan through His use of Scripture.

And so the story ends. The good guy wins again. End of story.

Or is it?

So far we have seen that after Baptism will come Fasting. But Fasting itself gives way to Feasting. The period of Fasting which Christ endured, which we must endure and which we celebrate particularly in Lent but also throughout all of our lives, will end.

In verses 17 and following, the verses immediately after today's lesson, we read that Jesus began to preach, saying, *"Repent, for the kingdom of heaven is at hand!"* He then calls the disciples who were fishermen to become fishers of men, and, beginning in verse 23, He goes about Galilee teaching, preaching, and healing. Christ's period of Fasting prepared Him for His public ministry here on earth, in which He was greatly glorified. And during this time, as the disciples of John the Baptist discovered, there was Feasting as well.

Likewise, the period of feasting for the Israelites began when they entered the Promised Land after being tested in the wilderness for 40 years. Their 40 year fast, like the 40 days of Christ and the 40 days of Lent, was not in vain. It was during this time that God was preparing them for holy warfare against the Canaanites. They entered the Promised Land, the land flowing with milk and honey and enormous pomegranates and figs (as well as giant men), ready to do God's will on the earth.

Well what about us? Does this pattern of Baptism—Fasting—and Feasting apply to us? We've seen how it's found in the life of Moses and Israel, the life of Jesus, and in the Church year, which rehearses the life of Christ for us. But it's also found in the life of the Church, even if there were no Church calendar. For the Church, both individually and corporately, is baptized into the name of Christ. Once we are baptized, we immediately enter into a period of fasting, which is to last the remainder of our earthly lives.

The early church recognized the connection between baptism, fasting, and temptation in its baptismal services, into which was incorporated an exorcism or a putting off of the devil. This is reflected in *The Book of Common Prayer* in the service of baptism. Here the minister asks those to be baptized, "Dost thou renounce the devil, and all his works, the vain pomp and glory of the world, with all covetous desires of the same, and the sinful desires of the flesh, so that thou wilt not follow, nor be led by them?" And again, "We receive this person into the congregation of Christ's flock; and do sign him with the sign of the Cross, in token that hereafter he shall not be ashamed to confess the faith of Christ crucified, and manfully fight under his banner, against sin, the world, and the devil."

In a way, then, all of our life is a season of fasting, for as Mark 2:20 reminds us, a day will come when the bridegroom will be absent and the bride will fast. While the Lord is absent, we must fast and put off the deeds of the flesh. There is, for the life of the believer, as long as he shall live here on earth, a perpetual Lent, a perpetual fasting.

Mardi Gras is a traditional celebration that developed along with the tradition of Lent, but its roots are also in pagan festivals such as the Saturnalia, bacchanalia, and carnival. Mardi Gras, which means "Fat Tuesday" and whose slogan is "Let the good times roll," is the day before Ash Wednesday. Since Ash Wednesday, as the first day of Lent, meant a temporary end to the pleasures of this world, "Fat Tuesday" became a day when all of those pleasures, sometimes including illicit ones, were fulfilled.

But this is exactly backwards. We fast first, and then we feast. Lent, and then Easter. Some contemporary sermons and even entire worship services make a similar mistake. They begin with feasting and end with feasting. They have no desire to fast or to observe Lent. They won't say a confession of sin or even sing songs in a minor key! Life is good. Let's eat, drink, and be merry. Let the good times roll because health and wealth are just around the corner! Woo-hoo!

The Israelites, when Moses was receiving the very oracles of God, did not keep the fast either, but chose to enjoy the pleasures of sin and make a false idol. As Paul quotes in 1 Corinthians 10:7, *"The people sat down to eat and drink, and rose up to play."*

Just as the church must proceed from baptism to fasting, it must also anticipate going from fasting to feasting. When Christ the Bridegroom returns, then the church, His Bride, will feast. You all, if you truly believe on the name of Christ, are invited to the Marriage Feast of the Lamb. As we proceed from fasting to feasting, let us keep in mind that after we have endured the years of the wilderness we shall enter the Promised Land.

 This is not just the pattern of our lives on the grand scale but on a daily basis. Every time we begin to draw closer to Christ and initiate a new life in Him, we are often tempted, and often a time of fasting comes. But if we persevere and eat the Bread of Heaven, the Word of God, and the bread of obedience, we will be sustained and our lives will turn into a feast.

Yes, even in this life, there is, ultimately, feasting because He who is the Bread of Life offers Himself to us every day. Although in this life it is mixed with the fast, the feast which is Christ is also always offered to us.

Baptism—Fasting—and Feasting. It was God's pattern for Christ's life, and it is His pattern for our lives.

Prayer:

Father, I praise You for baptizing me into Your Son and the Name of the Holy
Trinity; I thank You for sharing Your life with me. When I am in fasting, remind
me that to do Your will is my food, according to Your Word. When I am feasting, remind me that You are the giver of every good gift. In all things, unite me
with Yourself, through Your Son, Jesus Christ my Lord. Amen.

Point for Meditation:

Where are you in the cycle of Baptism—Fasting—Feasting? What is it that the
Lord would have you do in this place? If you have initiated a renewed life in
Christ, meditate on what He is asking of you. If you are in a period of fasting,
meditate on how you should be sustained during this time. If you are in a period
of feasting, then rejoice and give thanks!

Resolution:

I resolve to meditate on where my life in Christ is at this moment and, having
meditated, to respond appropriately, recognizing that He is with me in all times
and circumstances.

Matthew 4:12-25

"And Jesus, walking by the Sea of Galilee, saw two brothers, Simon called Peter, and Andrew his brother, casting a net into the sea; for they were fishermen. Then He said to them, 'Follow me, and I will make you fishers of men.' They immediately left their nets and followed Him."

I want to try one of my favorite tricks when reading the Bible. It's a technique I pioneered when I was in 2nd and 3rd grade. Ever since 2nd grade, I've always wanted to be a writer, by which I mean writing stories and novels. I remember when I was in college, I still wanted to believe that when I finished my first novel I would get rich and famous and not have to lead a real life. The grand irony, of course, was that back then I had nothing to write about but had the desire and time. Now I have something more to write about but much, much less time.

But I digress. In 2nd and 3rd grade, I liked to write funny stories, especially if I could get my classmates to laugh along with me. So I wrote a story once with an entire page of "very"s. You know, something like, "It was a very very very very very very very very very very very very very very very very very very very very very very very very very very very very very very very very very very very very very very very very very very very very very very very very very very very very very very very very hot day."

My teacher wrote at the top of the page something like, "Don't ever do this again."

I wrote slapstick stories about people falling into pools and having tree branches thwack them so that they fell down, etc., it seemed particularly funny to the 3rd grade boy mind if I had these things happen to a girl.

One of my favorite techniques was to allow for audience participation. I would write a story, complete except for several adjectives that I left blank. The class would then get to vote from a multiple choice list of adjectives that they could fill in. They were nearly always negative adjectives, and the sentences would go something like, "The girl was: a) smelly, b) dirty, c) ugly, d) all of the above."

One time I had the idea for leaving blanks and allowing for one of my classmates to have his name be put into the story.

And that's what I'd like to do this morning in Matthew chapter 4. Only you're the lucky classmate whose name I'd like to put into the story. Here goes!

"And Jesus, walking by _____ (name of your city,) saw _____ (your name) as (s)he was _____ (typical activity you do on a daily basis), for (s)he was a(n) _____ (your occupation). Then He said to him (her), "Follow me, and I will make you _____ (what you think Jesus may be calling you to be)."

After you've had a while to fill in the blanks for yourself, the story continues, and this is where I need even more audience participation. The rest of the story for the disciples went like this: "They immediately left their nets and followed Him."

 The other ending, for the other brothers who were fisherman, reads like this in verse 22: "And immediately they left the boat and their father, and followed Him." But now, after you've filled in all the blanks above, I need you to write a sentence that describes your response to what Jesus told you to do and called you to be when He passed by and called to you.

There are several things, then, that you should get out of this passage. I'll summarize them for those of you who like bullet points.

1. Put yourself in the story. Imagine that Jesus is coming to see you today. (He *is*, you know!) *Your job is to look and listen for Him today as He comes to you.*

2. He sees who you are and calls you to follow Him. *Your job is to follow Him and come closer to Him, ready to do what He asks.*

3. He calls you to become something more than you are, as you follow and serve Him. *Your job is to immediately follow Him when He tells you what your next assignment is.*

That's pretty much it for today, from me. The rest is up to you. I can give you a few hints from Matthew 4, but your circumstances will be different and Jesus' call to you will be different. We know that Jesus called the disciples to do two things: one was simply to follow Him, without knowing the wheres and the whys. The other was that He was calling them to be fisher of men.

Your call, then, is definitely to follow Him wherever He asks you to go, even if you don't understand it all. And He is probably calling to you help make fishers of men, that is, to be a disciple who makes disciples.

We know as well what Jesus then began to do, with His disciples observing and learning all that He did: He taught, preached, and healed the sick. Again, these are the broad categories of what He is likely asking you to do. Again, it will look different on you than it did on Peter and Andrew and James and John.

What would each of these look like in your life? I've got some ideas, but I, and others, would like to hear your ideas!

Prayer:

Almighty God, who didst give such grace unto thy holy Apostle Saint Andrew, that he readily obeyed the calling of thy Son Jesus Christ, and followed him without delay; Grant unto us all, that we, being called by thy holy Word, may forthwith give up ourselves obediently to fulfill thy holy commandments; through the same Jesus Christ our Lord. Amen.

(The Collect for St. Andrew's Day from *The Book of Common Prayer*)

Point for Meditation:

See the meditation above and finish it!

Resolution:

I resolve to follow Jesus in the way He has told me to follow Him today, even when I don't understand the whys and wheres.

Matthew 5:1–16

The Sermon on the Mount in general and the Beatitudes in particular are as dense as a black hole! It's a little intimidating trying to say something meaningful about the Beatitudes in such a small space, but here goes.

The first thing that strikes me is the very name Beatitudes. This name, of course, isn't found in the original manuscripts but comes from the Latin word "*beatus*" for "blessing" or "blessed." As opposed to the rest of the Sermon on the Mount, which seems to amount to a list of things to do and not to do (it's much more than this!), the Beatitudes only imply what we should do. They say, indirectly, "If you are poor in spirit or meek or hunger and thirst for righteousness, etc., then you will be blessed."

More accurately, they begin with God and His blessing, and not what we must do. And this is why reading the Beatitudes is refreshing and invigorating—because they begin with God and not me, and therefore they begin with blessing and grace, and not my works.

To back up a little bit, the Sermon on the Mount comes immediately after Jesus has begun his public ministry, which we have seen involved teaching, preaching, and healing. It begins with Jesus going up to a mountain to proclaim the Word of the Lord. Some have likened the Sermon on the Mount to a new giving of the Law, and I think that makes sense. But there are some interesting similarities and differences.

Like Moses, Jesus goes up to a mountain. Of course, the interesting part, behind the scenes, is that God the Son first had to descend to earth before He ascended. Like Moses, Jesus gives the commandments and revelation of the Lord. But unlike Moses, He does it on His own authority. While Moses clearly lays out both blessing and cursing, Jesus begins with blessing—the Beatitudes. As we read through the Sermon on the Mount together, you'll notice that Jesus begins with the Law of Moses but goes far beyond it in a radical, delightful, and challenging way.

The promises of God given through Moses were future-oriented, for those blessings had not yet come to pass. But the promises Jesus gives are not only for the life to come but also for the present, the here and now. For Moses was the mediator of the Old Covenant, but Jesus Christ *is* the New Covenant.

This is why the Beatitudes, quiet though they are, stir up such passion in me. This is why, meek and lowly as they appear, they are revolutionary!

The word "blessed" is used to begin eight sentences in a row. Repetition in the Bible always means something: it's a way of shouting or using a larger font. Here's the way I see it:

One use of the word "blessed" is a fact. It says "blessing."

Two uses of the word "blessed" is emphatic. It says, "blessing."

But *eight* uses of the word "blessed" is to take the Giant Hammer and bop us over the head! It says, "blessed!"

Now that God has your attention, what could He possibly mean? It surely means something that the first word Jesus teaches with in Matthew's Gospel (with the exception of 4:17) is "Blessed." Why? This is God's desire for humanity: that He might bless them. It was for this reason that Jesus came into the world.

I write a lot in *Give Us This Day* about what God desires for us to do. You may have guessed that I think being a Christian is very demanding and requires a life of sacrificing oneself to God. But I hope you haven't missed the reason for all of these things: to come to God and be blessed. This is how I see the Beatitudes: as a proclamation of God's blessings upon His people, with some instructions for how to receive this blessing.

The next thing I notice about the Beatitudes is that they are meant not only for heaven but also for the present. "Blessed *are*" is what Jesus says. Not "Blessed you will be," but "blessed *are*." The blessing of God, the state of beatification, is possible—*here and now!*

This is the best news of the day, of the week—of my life! I can receive God's blessing upon my life—*now!*

Isn't that the deepest, secret desire of everyone with any interest in God—to be blessed by Him? Immediately, I want to know how.

What does Jesus say? He gives me eight ways I can choose to live that I might receive His blessing. In fact, the eight ways of living that will receive His blessing aren't even things I have to go out and seek: the circumstances necessary to achieve them already exist in my life, and all I have to do is see them in such a way that they will lead to God's blessing.

They all involve the same basic thing: seeking God and His Kingdom. What Jesus is proclaiming so loudly that we still hear it 2000 years later is that if we seek

God and His Kingdom, we will find Him and live in His Kingdom, starting right *n-n-n-n-n-n-ow*! You have the ability to choose to live in God's kingdom now, for the kingdom of heaven has been opened to all believers! The Kingdom of Heaven comes to earth whenever we do the will of the Lord. And God's deepest desire and will for us is only that we come to Him!

Look at each of the eight blessings: see how each involves us coming to God to find Him and submit ourselves to Him. *"Blessed are the poor in spirit, for theirs is the kingdom of heaven"* (v. 3). Who are the poor in spirit? Those who don't think too highly of themselves but have the same mind which was also in Christ Jesus, who humble themselves before God, and who are ready to do His will. If you live this way today, then yours *is* the kingdom of heaven.

I won't go through each Beatitude and apply it: that's your job today. Here's what you need to know: that God desires to bless you. In fact, that's His deepest desire. To that end, He sent His Son, who is His blessing in your life. God desires to bless you *today*. More than this, He *promises* to bless you today, if you will only come to Him, seeking Him with your whole heart.

Are you broken or crushed or down today? That's terrible—unless you allow God to use it as a way to humble yourself before Him. The moment you do that, you place yourself in God's Kingdom and are in a condition where God may bless you.

Do you mourn because of the evil in the world and in your life? Are you burdened by your sins and the sins of the world? That can be a heavy, heavy weight. Or it can be the one thing that drives you into the arms of the Lord, where He may bless you.

The Beatitudes are God's public proclamation that He desires to bless *you*, right now, right here, in whatever circumstances you find yourself today.

Don't think you have to be perfect before you come to Him (which may be a form of pride). Don't think you must be persecuted or be completely pure or mournful. The one thing that is necessary is that you are meek and lowly before Him—and that you come.

If you do this one necessary thing today, then the blessing of God will rest upon you!

Prayer:

Father, I submit myself before your merciful Hand. You are the One who hates a proud look and casts down those who exalt themselves. You resist the proud, but give grace to the humble. Forgive me for exalting myself and thinking and acting as if I were You and don't need You. Here I willingly submit myself to You in all things, for You are my deepest desire in this life. Make me poor in spirit that I may dwell in Your blessed kingdom, and grant me a pure heart that I may see You. In all things give me the mind of Your Son, Jesus Christ, in whose Name I pray. Amen.

Points for Meditation:

1. Pick one of the Beatitudes that God is directing you to today. How might it apply in your life, and how might you seek the Lord's blessing today?
2. How can you receive all that God has given you today in a spirit that will lead to blessing?
3. What form might God's blessing take in your life?

Resolution:

I resolve to put aside all distractions today and humbly come before the Lord today that He may bless me!

Matthew 5:17–26

The Sermon on the Mount, as I alluded to in my commentary on Matthew 5:1–16, is Jesus' perfect exposition of the Law. He who gave the Law and perfectly kept it is also its most perfect interpreter. After establishing that God's Law will not pass away, Jesus begins to apply it in a most perfect and, therefore, most exacting way.

We would do well not to explain away or diminish the radical, revolutionary, and perfect nature of what our Lord commands.

Jesus immediately raises the bar high—way high! "*Unless your righteousness exceeds the righteousness of the scribes and Pharisees, you will by no means enter the kingdom of heaven*" (v. 20). One common way on interpreting this verse and similar ones is to pick on our favorite target: the Pharisees. You see, they were really hypocrites and very unrighteous. They didn't truly love God but were merely religious to make themselves feel good.

Or so goes the common myth of the Pharisees. In this scenario, then, we're being called to a higher standard: to more perfectly love God and not be hypocrites.

But I find that a little too reassuring, a little too easy. It seems to diminish the force of the other things Jesus says. What if Jesus is really saying something more radical and discomforting?

Since we are still in the beginning of Matthew 5, and Jesus hasn't had any run-ins with the Pharisees in Matthew's account, what are we to think of the Pharisees and scribes? The natural view of them would be a very favorable one—the Pharisees and scribes would have been considered the most righteous of the Jews, who were the most righteous people. We should be careful to read what Jesus says about the Pharisees in context, and not what we know will be revealed about them later.

What if Jesus is saying that to enter the kingdom of heaven we have to be more righteous than the most righteous people known to the world at that time? If this is true, then think of the implications in the mind of the first century Jewish audience of Jews. Wouldn't they be amazed, mystified, and eager to hear the resolution to this terrifying puzzle?

Jesus intensifies the Law, sets the bar higher, immediately when He begins to talk about murder. He teaches that the Law was never just about murder but also about anger. *"Whoever is angry with his brother without a cause shall be in danger of the judgment...But whoever says, 'You fool!' shall be in danger of hell fire"* (v. 22).

Have you ever been angry without a just cause? Then, Jesus says, you are in danger of hell fire. Who, then, can be saved?

I think Jesus' point may be that our righteousness *does* not surpass that of the Pharisees. In fact, it's probably a little pharisaical to think that we are more righteous than the Pharisees. Wasn't that *their* schtick? I think Jesus may be teaching us that we, too, are far from perfect, as *even* the Pharisees and scribes were not perfect enough.

It's not about comparing ourselves to the Pharisees and keeping score so that we might be accounted more righteous. How would you even begin to keep score at home? Is there some calculus by which we can compute the severity of our sins? Murder is worth so much, and anger so much less. And then you have to make sure you multiply by the hypocrisy factor. Don't forget to factor in the natural abilities and environment of the sinner in question. There's probably a degree of difficulty multiplier, just as in Olympic diving competitions.

Ultimately, Jesus reveals that only He can keep the Law. Only He is righteous and perfectly kept the Law. I think the ultimate teaching about the Law and righteousness is that Jesus *is* our righteousness and that without Him we are all lost in our sins.

There are two implications of this teaching.

First, in order to deal with our sins, we must first turn to the Righteous One of Israel. We are unable to be more righteous than the Pharisees and scribes. We must, by faith, unite ourselves to Him who is the Law-giver and the Law-keeper.

Second, God really does care about our sins, enough to send His Son to the Cross. We, too, are supposed to care about our sins, and in Christ, we have the ability to deal with them. In this case, God not only cares about murder, the unlawful taking of the life of one made in His image, but also its much more common cause: anger. Anger does not work the righteousness of God but only seeks the good of the one who is angered. To think or act in anger (with rare exceptions) is to think or act in selfishness and pride.

God cares about anger because He cares about the roots of the great tree of sin that we have allowed to grow in His garden, which is us. He cares, primarily, to restore our relationship with Him, which is why He sent His Son and why we must unite ourselves to Him in order to be restored to a right relationship with

God. In fact, the word *righteousness* has everything to do with a *right* covenantal relationship with God.

But God also cares about our human relationships. They are reflections of our relationship with Him and because He cares about them in their own right. So important are our relationships that Jesus even teaches that they are, in certain cases, more important than our worship! If you are about to bring your gift to the altar of the Temple and remember that you are angry at your brother or not in peace with Him, then first be reconciled with your brother, *even before* you offer your gift.

In fact, to restore a relationship for the love of Christ *is* to offer your gift. To humble yourself before your brother is to humble yourself before the Lord and to offer yourself as a living sacrifice before Him. It is, thus, the most profound act of worship! It is an act of righteousness.

And, therefore, when we obey the Lord's command we also unite ourselves to Him. To obey *is* to worship and without obedience our worship becomes vain ritual and ceremony. So much is our obedience valued by the Lord that He says that whoever *does* His commandments and teaches them shall be called great in the Kingdom of Heaven!

And that, in the end, is exactly what I want. I've always wanted to be great. I think that's what I was after when I wanted to be the world's record holder in the mile and what I wanted when I wrote my first novel and imagined myself being interviewed by David Letterman. I wanted to be great: I just had the wrong measure.

All I really had to do to be great was to follow my Master and, by His grace, obey Him!

Prayer:

Father, I earnestly repent of my sins and desire to be in love and charity with my neighbors. I intend to lead a new life, following Your commandments and walking from now on in Your holy ways. Strengthen me by Your Son so that I may draw near to You with faith and find Your blessing. Amen.

(Paraphrased from *The Book of Common Prayer*, Exhortation, p. 75)

Points for Meditation:

1.   Do you have a problem with anger? Confess your anger and angry thoughts and actions to God and ask for His help. If you have wronged your brother, go and make peace today.
2.   Practice seeking Jesus Christ and His righteousness today, instead of relying on your own strength to keep His commandments.

Resolution:

I resolve to seek Jesus today in the way He has been telling me to seek Him, that I might receive His blessing and righteousness.

Matthew 5:27–37

In the previous passage in the Sermon on the Mount we talked about how Jesus' teaching is an intensification of the Law: to not get angry is much more difficult than to not murder. Likewise, today, to not lust is much, much more difficult than to not commit adultery. It's not so much that Jesus is trying to make the Law harder: He's simply explaining what the Law meant all along.

Sometimes we have a tendency to think of God's Law as arbitrary. God gave the Law and made up a bunch of laws because He could, and by these arbitrary laws He tests our morality. These laws are arbitrary shows of force, and there isn't necessarily any connection between them and our lives, except that He says there is.

The truth is that God's Law is a natural emanation from Who He Is. The Law is an outward manifestation of God and His loving, holy character, and therefore, the Law, and each Law in particular, is really about love and right relationships. This love is either love of God or love of neighbor (or both).

We also talked yesterday of how far we are from being able to keep God's true standard. We are not only to avoid outright murder and adultery but also their inner manifestations and motivations: anger and lust. The Law, therefore, is the pillar of cloud of the Israelites: it is a cloud and darkness over our lives in that it hovers over and points to our dark sins. But it is also a light by night in that it also hovers over and points to Jesus Christ, the Just One of Israel who not only kept the Law but keeps it for us. He is the end or goal of the Law.

With these things in mind, let's consider Jesus' teaching on marriage and adultery. In Moses' Law we have heard the familiar commandment: "*Thou shalt not commit adultery.*" (Exodus 20:14) If we rightly understood what adultery actually constituted, we would see it for the horror that it is. But to properly understand adultery, we have to understand not only the sacramental character of marriage but also the nature of God's relationship with us.

What is adultery, at its heart, once you get past the sex part? It's fundamentally the human will to eat the forbidden fruit, to choose what one wants instead of what God wants and to tear apart what God has joined together. There's a reason that adultery was a capital offense in the Old Testament: God hates it.

Humanly speaking, you might say that adultery is just about sex. What could possibly be so harmful about sex with someone else on the side, since sex is just about pleasure, and sex with someone else might be more pleasurable? That seems to be the message our culture sends. Though we generally still believe adultery is wrong, we don't think of it in particularly dire or severe terms.

But God does. Typically, women understand the true consequences more than men because they seem to believe more completely that sex is never just about sex but is a sacramental joining together into one flesh. Adultery is not just about sex and not even just about a man or woman choosing to be faithful to each other: it's also about our faithfulness or unfaithfulness to God. Our relationship with God is pictured in marriage, and so adultery is a terrible picture of what we do when we're not faithful to God.

Adultery, as we know, wrecks marriages. It doesn't just wreck them once the innocent party finds out, it begins to wreck them from the moment the act of adultery is committed because adultery is an act of betrayal toward the two people in life you've vowed to be faithful to—your spouse and God.

As an aside, I don't even think on a human level we realize how devastating divorce is. I can't tell you how many sullen, depressed, black, Goth, vacant, zombie-like, angry, confused kids I've seen come out of divorced households. We blithely go into marriage based on infatuation and even lust, and then wonder why predictably a year or 18 months afterward we're no longer in love and the marriage is on the rocks. As Christians, we don't take seriously what Jesus says about divorce and assume that if we don't like the relationship we can always get out of it again.

It would take a book to chronicle the devastating consequences of divorce, and, personally, I believe a lot of our social ills are directly due to divorce and the culture that permits it. These consequences are often lifelong and therefore perpetuated multi-generationally: as one study found, concerning the consequences of divorce: "Little children often have difficulty falling asleep at bedtime or sleeping through the night. Older children may have trouble concentrating at school. Adolescents often act out and get into trouble. Men and women may become depressed or frenetic. Some throw themselves into sexual affairs or immerse themselves in work."

What's worse is that in this passage Jesus speaks not only of adultery but also of lust. So terrible is lust that Jesus says, "If your right hand causes you to sin, cut it of and cast it from you; for it is more profitable for you that one of your members perish than for your whole body to be cast into hell." I'd like to see a show of hands of those who think they should take every part of the Bible completely literally. Eh? What's that? Oh, you can't because all the literalists are already handless!

The point isn't that we should mutilate ourselves. If we really did this, we'd soon be a race of eyeless, handless freaks! The point is that we should go to any lengths imaginable to make sure we don't lust. Why? Because God takes it that seriously.

But here we run into a problem. We can tolerate the strict commandment against adultery because there's a good chance we'll be able to keep this law. But when Jesus tells me it's also about lust, suddenly my chances of keeping this law are vastly diminished!

Now all of this would be devastating—and should be—if we take the burden of our sins upon ourselves. But Jesus' teaching isn't meant to crush but to refresh those of us who are weary and heavy laden. If you insist on ignoring your sins or trying to deal with them yourself—you *will* be crushed! This is true, of course, for all of your sins, and not just ones involving lust or adultery.

But if you confess your sins to the Just One, He will forgive you your sins. He offers today to take your burden upon Him. He offers true freedom and life, but you've got to come to Him and desire Him. In a delightful irony, even our sins, black and deadly as they are, can become the very means by which we are driven to God! My misery in my sins and my own weakness in overcoming them are wonderful means for remembering to come back to Jesus every day.

And so, for the Christian, even our sins should not defeat us, for we are united to the One who has taken them on Himself and defeated them!

This is the meaning of the Law, once again: *Jesus Christ*, and that we might remember to come to Him today!

Prayer:

Almighty God, Father of our Lord Jesus Christ, maker of all things, judge of all men: I acknowledge and bewail my manifold sins and wickedness, which I from time to time most grievously have committed, by thought, word, and deed, against thy divine Majesty, provoking most justly thy wrath and indignation against me. I do earnestly repent, and am heartily sorry for these my misdoings; the remembrance of them is grievous unto me, the burden of them is intolerable. Have mercy upon me, have mercy upon me, most merciful Father; for thy Son my Lord Jesus Christ's sake, forgive me all that is past; and grant that I may ever hereafter serve and please thee in newness of life. Amen.

(Revised from the General Confession from *The Book of Common Prayer*)

Almighty God, my heavenly Father, who of his great mercy hath promised forgiveness of sins to all those who with hearty repentance and true faith turn unto him, have mercy upon me, pardon and deliver me from all my sins, confirm and strengthen me in all goodness, and bring me to everlasting life; through Jesus Christ my Lord. Amen.

(Revised from the Absolution from *The Book of Common Prayer*)

Points for Meditation:

1. Meditate on the love of God, that He would take away all of your sins, and then give thanks!
2. Do you have a daily time when you confess your sins before God, that you might be brought closer to Him? Is God calling you to establish one?

Resolution:

I resolve to practice confessing my sins before the Lord today that I might receive forgiveness and be brought closer to Him.

Matthew 5:38–48

Love is the strongest thing known to man. This only makes sense when you remember that we were wrought in love and formed from the substance of God's love. How could we not be made for love?

However, I find that there are a lot of counterfeits out there to the *agape* kind of love to which God is calling us (and He's calling us to Himself, who *is* love). It reminds me of an ad that appeared in the very first issue of *Mad* magazine, titled "Beware of Imitations!" In it, there's a newsstand with 30 different magazines, all with titles that are variations of *Mad*—*Mid, Mod, Med, Mod, Mord, Mard, Madd, Maddd, Shmad, Admay,* etc. The proprietor of the store is trying to palm a copy of *Mud* off on the kid who is standing there.

Sometimes, of course, we confuse *eros* love for *agape* love, or worse yet, we confuse lust or infatuation with love. Relationships built on lust or infatuation have a very short half-life. Sometimes in romantic relationships, what we're really in love with is the idea of being in love and of having somebody to call or own. This is simply a variation on the most common theme of confusing love with pride. In many ways, what we often say is being done out of love is, in reality, quite self-serving.

We also accept lesser forms of love. It feels good to be liked and loved, and so it's natural that we would show more love to those who love us. This is where love shows itself to be the strongest and toughest, for true love expresses itself not only towards those who reciprocate but even towards those who not only don't reciprocate but who, in fact, mistreat us or hate us.

Here's how Jesus expresses it: "You have heard it said, '*You shall love your neighbor and hate your enemy.*' But I say to you, *love your enemies, bless those who curse you, do good to those who hate you, and pray for those who spitefully use you and persecute you, that you may be sons of your Father in heaven*" (verses 43–45).

We all know how not only Jesus but also the first Christian martyr, St. Stephen, lived out this commandment. But did you know that Hegesippus records a similar kind of love in the life of St. James, the brother of the Lord? The Pharisees and scribes set James on the summit of the Temple so that all the Jews gathered for the Passover in A.D. 62 could hear how James would "set them straight" about who Jesus was.

Here's how Hegesippus records the story:

"They cried aloud to him, and said: 'O just one, whom we are all bound to obey, forasmuch as the people is in error, and follows Jesus the crucified, do thou tell us what is the door of Jesus, the crucified.' And he answered with a loud voice: 'Why ask ye me concerning Jesus the Son of man? He Himself sitteth in heaven, at the right hand of the Great Power, and shall come on the clouds of heaven.'

And, when many were fully convinced *by these words*, and offered praise for the testimony of James, and said, 'Hosanna to the son of David,' then again the Pharisees and scribes said to one another, 'We have not done well in procuring this testimony to Jesus. But let us go up and throw him down, that they may be afraid, and not believe him.' And they cried aloud, and said: 'Oh! oh! the just man himself is in error.' So they went up and threw down the just man, and said to one another: 'Let us stone James the Just.' And they began to stone him: for he was not killed by the fall; but he turned, and kneeled down, and said: 'I beseech Thee, Lord God our Father, forgive them; for they know not what they do.'

And, while they were thus stoning him to death, one of the priests, the son of Rechab, the son of Rechabim, to whom testimony is borne by Jeremiah the prophet, began to cry aloud, saying: 'Cease, what do ye? The just man is praying for us.' But one among them, one of the fullers, took the staff with which he was accustomed to wring out the garments *he dyed*, and hurled it at the head of the just man. And so he suffered martyrdom; and they buried him on the spot, and the pillar erected to his memory still remains, close by the temple." [1]

· · ·

Richard Wurmbrand tells this story:

"We were in a prison cell; some 30 or 40 prisoners. The door was unlocked and the guards pushed in a new prisoner. He was dirty like we were. We had not washed ourselves in 3 years. So he was dirty, and we were dirty. He was shorn and had the striped uniform of a prisoner. In the half darkness of the cell we did not recognize him, but at a certain moment, one of us exclaimed, 'This is Captain Popescu, I recognize him!'

Captain Popescu had been one of the worst torturers of Christians. He had beaten and tortured even some of us who were now in the same cell with him. We wondered how he had become a prisoner of the communists and how

---

1   Peter Kirby. "Fragments of Hegesippus," *Early Christian Writings*, 2 Feb. 2006. http://www. earlychristianwritings.com/hegesippus.html.

he had been put in a prison cell reserved for Christians. So we surrounded him and asked him his story.

With tears in his eyes, he told us that a few months ago he sat in his office. The soldier on duty knocked at the door and said, 'Outside is a boy of 12 or 13 who has a flower for your wife.' The captain scratched his head. He did not remember that it was his wife's birthday, but in any case, he allowed the boy to enter.

The boy entered with the flower in his hand, very shy, but very decided, and said, 'Comrade Captain, you are the one who has put my father and mother in prison. Today is my mother's birthday. I have the habit every year on this day, out of my little pocket money, to buy a flower for her. Because of you, I have no mother to gladden today. But my mother is a Christian and she taught me since I was a little child to love my enemies and to reward evil with good. Because of you, I have no mother to gladden today, I thought to give joy to the mother of your children. Please take this flower to your wife and tell her about my love and about the love of Christ.'

It was too much even for a communist torturer. He was also a creature of God. He also has been enlightened with the light which enlightens every man who comes into this world. He embraced this child. He could not beat any more. He could not torture anymore. He was no longer useful as an officer of the communist secret police. He came to suffer together with the children of God and was happy for this new state." [2]

I often wonder how Jesus, Stephen, James, and this boy could have so much love for those who hated them. And then I remember, "Oh yeah, that's what God did for me." Don't you see, that this kind of love comes from the Father Himself, the Father who so loved the world that He sent His only begotten Son into it? Don't you see that it comes from the Son Himself who taught us what love was: the just dying for the unjust? And don't you see that this love must be the work of the Spirit in our lives?

Do you want to be a son or daughter of your heavenly Father? Then (verse 45) learn to love your enemies the way He loves you.

There is a principle in anthropology and sociology that seems to be universal: it's called *reciprocity*. Reciprocity means that if I give you something, you feel obligated to give me something back. It was an integral part of the Greek world.

---

2   Excerpt from Wurmbrand, Richard. *If Prison Walls Could Speak,* Voice of the Martyrs Australia, April 1997 Edition. http://members.cox.net/wurmbrand/doubledose.html.

Go re-read *The Odyssey* by Homer, and you'll see what I mean! So fundamental is this to our existence that salesmen have found many ways to exploit it. You know those "free" gifts you receive in the mail? They are only one means of making you feel compelled to give something back.

It's our nature to want to give back what we have received. If I have received the love of God, then my impulse ought to be to return that love to God. In fact, I think the law of reciprocity is God-ordained as a part of the creation order, and I'm only beginning to understand it. Love begets love.

But if what I have received is hatred and persecution, then my Old Man immediately wants to give back hatred and persecution. And here is where *agape* love triumphs over human nature. Whereas the natural human instinct is to return hatred for hatred, the Christian instinct of love is to return love for hatred. In this way, hatred begets love so that for the Christian love and hate and everything in between all lead to the same response—love!

Even the tax collectors and sinners and the ungodly know how to love those who love them: but it takes the love of Christ to love those who hate you.

If you think about it, there are probably not that many people in your life who actively and personally hate you. There are a lot who hate Christians, but most of them don't know me. And yet I'm sure there are many people in your life who mistreat you and aren't nice to you. If you should love even those who hate you, what should be your response to those who mistreat or simply aren't nice to you?

Today's commandment: *"Love your enemies, bless those who curse you, do good to those who hate you, and pray for those who spitefully use you and persecute you, that you may be sons of your Father in heaven"* (vv. 44–45).

Prayer:

Love divine, all loves excelling,
Joy of heaven to earth come down;
Fix in us thy humble dwelling;
All thy faithful mercies crown!
Jesus, Thou art all compassion,
Pure unbounded love Thou art;
Visit us with Thy salvation;
Enter every trembling heart. Amen.

(From a hymn by Charles Wesley)

Points for Meditation:

1. Who are the people in your life who hate, mistreat, or are mean to you? How might you show them love?
2. Meditate on the love of God. Remember who you would be without the love of God; remember how God loved you before you loved Him; and then apply this principle of love to your life.

Resolution:

I resolve to find one way today to show love to someone who isn't loving to me.

Matthew 6:1–18

Jesus spoke at length about three spiritual disciplines that He assumes His disciples are practicing. These three disciplines Jesus are three that have for centuries been a part of Lent, as well as a fundamental part of the Christian life as a whole, until the time of the Reformation.

Can you name them?

They are:

1. almsgiving

2. prayer

3. fasting

Most of us know about prayer. But almsgiving is a neglected virtue, and fasting has all but vanished, except among Roman Catholics, Orthodox Christians, and some Anglicans. As comfortable as this is, I can't let myself off so easily. Why do we so easily accept the red-letter words of Jesus (you know: words spoken by Jesus Himself and which are often printed in red in Bibles) when we like them but so easily reject His other red-letter words? It would take a library of books to unpack the religious, cultural, and personal assumptions that allow us to so easily pick and choose (as consumers of Jesus' words) which we will obey and which we won't.

In Matthew 6, Jesus speaks about each of these, and the first assumption He makes is that His disciples are actually doing all three of these things. We know we're supposed to pray and need no convincing about the commandment to pray and the necessity of it for our souls. But what does Jesus say about almsgiving and fasting?

In verse 2 of Matthew 6, He says, *"When you give alms do not sound a trumpet before you,"* while in verse 3 He commands, *"When you give alms, do not let your left hand know what your right hand is doing."* Jesus' instruction on prayer takes the same form: *"When you pray, do not pray as the hypocrites"* (v. 5). On fasting, Jesus similarly teaches, *"When you fast, do not fast as the hypocrites"* (v. 16).

There are a few things that each of these three spiritual disciplines has in common.

The first is we should not express our *private* spirituality in an ostentatious way

(Jesus certainly isn't prohibiting the prayers of the people in the Temple and synagogue or the collecting of alms that the Jews and the early church practiced).

Secondly, each of these three spiritual disciplines is a crucifying of the flesh so that Christ might live in us. This is the real point of the spiritual disciplines and of the spiritual life: to deny self that we might come to Jesus. For this reason, these spiritual disciplines are *Spiritual* disciplines, with a capital "S," because they involve the work of the Spirit in our lives, which is to bring us to Christ.

Christian spirituality involves "giving up something" (*ourselves*) for the sake of the Lord. For this reason, it's appropriate that the three disciplines of almsgiving, praying, and fasting are seen particularly as Lenten disciplines. Of course, they're also meant for our entire lives.

We should keep in mind as well that we don't do any of these things for their own sakes.

But if we give alms, pray, and fast with Jesus Christ and through Him, we find that not only do we "give up something" but also that we get something much better in return, for Christ Himself, as we shall see, promises the reward of God.

When we give alms, we give up what we have worked for, the money, the fruit of our labor that is, humanly speaking, ours. It is hard to give alms because our money is a symbol of ourselves and of our power to get things for ourselves. But giving alms reminds us of 1 Corinthians 4:7, where Paul says, "*What do you have that you did not receive?*" Giving what God has first given us reminds us of the words of our Lord Jesus Christ: how He said it is more blessed to give than to receive.

Almsgiving is, therefore, a Christian duty, because God first gave to us. He is the giver of every good and perfect gift, and all that we have has come from His loving hand.

It wasn't something that Jesus said glibly, expecting His disciples to do as He said and not as He did: Jesus Himself went around doing good, healing, and spending time with the poor of this world. Much better than money, He gave Himself to the poor of this world.

What does this mean practically for us? Simply, we are to give to the poor. The Greek word for almsgiving generally means doing works of mercy and compassion. Although it is usually used to mean giving to the poor, I believe there are many ways to show mercy and compassion, especially when we remember that the poor are primarily the poor in spirit. This means we have an obligation to look for the poor around us, who may be closer than you think. They may be relatives, neighbors, or strangers—or the poor might even be someone half way around the world.

Almsgiving has declined in recent decades, at least partially because we have delegated this personal obligation to the government. In doing so, we are robbed of truly giving because the process is invisible and impersonal. The personal choice that one has to *make* to give is taken away if the government compels us to give alms by taking and redistributing wealth. In Jesus' time, the giver of alms would also know the beggar to whom he gave money. They knew his family and that he was really blind or lame and wasn't going to spend the money getting drunk.

How might you give alms in your life?

The second spiritual discipline is prayer. I won't spend much time on it because it's dealt with in other places in the New Testament. We might begin by observing that the spiritual disciplines are meant to work together in synergistic fashion. Some demons, after all, only come out by prayer *and fasting*.

Prayer is at the center of Christ's teaching on Christian disciplines, and rightly so. It is to be the most frequent and most important of all disciplines. What is given up is the biggest thing of all: your pride. In prayer, you must humble yourself before God and acknowledge that He is your God and you need Him. Prayer is a very humbling thing, which is why we know to kneel to pray. Perhaps the reason we sometimes avoid it is because it is so humbling.

But it was through a constant life of prayer that Jesus was able to have a constant life in the Father, whose will He perfectly obeyed. Amazing! that He who was also God found it necessary to pray so constantly to His Father! Throughout the Gospels, Jesus found places to pray. "*He went up on the mountain by Himself to pray*" (Matthew 14:23); *He "withdrew to the wilderness to pray*" (Luke 15:16); He prayed when His soul was troubled (Matthew 26:42 and the Garden of Gethsemane); and "*He rose up early in the morning to pray*" (Mark 1:35). He prayed constantly for His disciples (John 17) and intercedes for us even now at the right hand of the Father!

In fasting, we give up for a time the food that sustains us to remind ourselves of our dependence upon God for all things. Fasting is meant to teach us to let go of the things of this earth and to teach us to let go of ourselves. It is to remind us of our sin and mortality that we might turn all the more to God. Every time you have a hunger pang from something you have given up, it should remind you of God and all that Christ gave up for you.

Prayer and fasting should often go together. Consider not only Matthew 17:21

and the casting out of demons but also Nehemiah 1:4, as Nehemiah sought what the Lord would have him do in a ruined Israel, and Acts 13:3, when Paul and Barnabas were chosen by the Church.

There are other kinds of fasts, other than from food, but the essential thing is that we should periodically give up our daily physical food, or some other earthly good, to remind us to fill our greater hunger for the Bread of Life.

Jesus gave up not only food but also sleep, as He stayed up all night praying. At other times He was too busy or too crowded to eat, because his bread was to do the will of the Father.

When my twin brother Danny was in junior high and high school, he would play war-game solitaire for hours on end. I remember several occasions where he would park himself in the den beside *Panzer Blitz* or *Third Reich* and play against himself for an entire day. The good news is that he won. The bad news... Sometimes, he would not eat or drink (which meant he also probably didn't have to hit the bathroom) for the entire day.

That's the kind of intensity and desire (although not in every detail!) I want to have in my serving the Lord!

Jesus Christ loved each of us so much that He gave up His life for those around Him, especially at the Cross. This Cross was the ultimate fast: to give up not only one thing that He loved in this life but to give up life itself for love of another.

It is more blessed to give than to receive, and so in each of these three spiritual disciplines—almsgiving, prayer, and fasting—the ultimate blessing of which Jesus is speaking is the spiritual treasure we obtain, which is Jesus Christ Himself. They are not magical ceremonies, nor should they be onerous. For, in fact, they are the Cross of Jesus itself, by which we are united with Him.

Prayer:

Our Father, who art in heaven, hallowed be Thy name. Thy kingdom come. Thy will be done, on earth as it is in heaven. Give us this day our daily bread. And forgive us our trespasses, as we forgive those who trespass against us. And lead us not into temptation, but deliver us from evil. For Thine is the kingdom, and the power, and the glory, for ever and ever. Amen.

Point for Meditation:

To which of these three spiritual disciplines is the Lord calling you? How might you begin this discipline, if it is not already a discipline you practice?

Resolution:

I resolve to begin or renew one of these spiritual disciplines, if I hear the Lord calling me to do it. (Remember: Don't try and begin too many spiritual practices at once. If there is something else the Lord is calling you to do first, then do it!)

BONUS MEDITATION!
Matthew 6:5–15 (The Lord's Prayer)

I love antiques and artifacts. I love going to museums and experiencing their artifacts. I feel tangibly closer to dinosaurs or mummies, to van Gogh or van Eyck, when in a museum. I love old books and how they smell and their sturdy yellow pages and the fact that they connect me with the truth and lives of the past that are still meaningful today.

And so I read with fascination the archeological discoveries of the Holy Land. Recently, an archeologist thought he and his team may have discovered Herod's Temple. Several years ago, someone believed they discovered one small object from Solomon's Temple, and not too long ago the ossuary (box to hold bones) of St. James was found (although many are suspicious of this claim).

But look what *I* discovered today! It's an artifact that's been lying around for you and me to discover every day, and it's one of the most priceless artifacts of all: the Lord's Prayer. Forget about the Ark of the Covenant or the Holy Grail, which we'd probably make into an idol anyway: they're both dead objects. But in the Lord's Prayer, we have something very living and active and powerful, full of more power and glory than streamed from the Ark of the Covenant in the Indiana Jones movie.

When you pray *this*, the prayer of the Lord, you are standing on hallowed ground. You have come to the Prayer that the saints have prayed for 2000 years and which saints across the earth are all busy praying this very day. The Lord's Prayer is holy, not just because the Lord gave it to us, saying "Take, do this" but also because it is the prayer that He Himself first prayed and hallowed before He gave it to us. More than just praying it, He *lived* it. In the Lord's Prayer we should therefore see Jesus Christ Himself.

Do you realize that if you pray the Lord's Prayer once a day for 50 years, you'll have prayed it 18,262 times? How can you make the most of a prayer that you pray that often? How can you keep it from becoming old? One way is to pray it in depth so you'll have something to remember next time and so you can spend a life growing in the Lord with His prayer. Let's look at how we might pray the Prayer of the Lord *with* the Lord that we might receive His blessing.

. . .

"Our Father, who art in heaven, hallowed be Thy Name" (v. 9b).

In praying to our Father, we come remembering Who it is we are coming before. In praying "Our Father," we claim our right to come before Almighty God as we come before a father. And yet it is only because of Jesus Christ, the true Son, that we have this incalculable right. The Son makes us sons, too. He calls us His brother and has turned us from slaves and sinners into sons who are now heirs of God's riches. Because of the Son we can now come to our loving Father, who is the One who created us and cares for and blesses us. We are to come like little children before Him, like the Son Himself came, full of faith and humility.

But we have a problem in coming before the Father: He is in heaven, and we are on earth. He is as far above us as the heavens are above the earth. But Jesus came from heaven to earth as one of us; and He ascended from earth to heaven, for us. And now as the writer of Hebrews made clear, Jesus is in heaven *for us.* In praying "who art in heaven," we are asking to be brought into heaven, the throne of grace, through Jesus Christ. We must come in utter humility, not demanding, but begging, like the Prodigal Son, for what we have no right to.

When we pray "hallowed be thy name," we have another problem: this Father of ours is holy, and we are unholy sinners. God is a holy, consuming fire, so much so that when Uzzah reached out to try and steady the Ark of the Covenant which was being carried on a cart and was about to fall, God killed him because He dared to touch something holy that God said no man could not touch. But Jesus Christ kept the name of the Father holy by perfectly obeying Him. By His obedience and His holiness we can come into the presence of the Father. And like Jesus, every time we obey the Father, we hallow His name; but every time we disobey Him, we desecrate His Name.

. . .

"Thy Kingdom come, Thy will be done, on earth as it is in heaven" (v. 10)

Now that we are allowed to enter into God's presence, because of Jesus Christ, the heavenly and holy Son, we ask for the things that Jesus Christ the Son asked for while on earth and the things He now asks for in heaven, at the right hand of God. What a privilege to say and to pray the same things that our holy Lord did—and does!

He prays, and we pray with Him, that His kingdom would come. We know, from both His testimony and John the Baptist's, that the Kingdom of Heaven is already here. We know it's here because the King is here and is, in fact, ruling from heaven. And yet because we are sorrowfully aware that it is not here fully, and we groan as a result, we pray for the King and His Kingdom to come fully to all.

How does God's kingdom come? A king's domain is as large an area as he is able to maintain control over. God's Kingdom, His rule, is therefore present whenever He is obeyed and whenever His will is done. Obedience to the will of the Father is the essence of prayer and our lives in His kingdom. By obedience, the Kingdom of heaven is manifested. By the Son's perfect obedience, in becoming man, in suffering for us and by dying as our sacrifice, He made it possible for us to also do the will of the Father. Every time you obey, God's kingdom advances a little; but every time you disobey, His Kingdom retreats a little.

How did Jesus obey the will of the Father when He was on earth, and how does He obey the will of the Father, now that He is in heaven? Perfectly, that is: immediately, completely, and joyfully. And so we pray, with the Son and through the Son, that we might do the will of the Father just as perfectly here on earth.

. . .

"Give us this day our daily bread;" (v. 11)

But where shall we ever find the strength to obey, to show God's kingdom and hallow God's name? By asking for and receiving our daily bread. How did Jesus Christ find strength to do the will of the Father? By praying to the Father. The One who said, "My food is to do the will of the Father" becomes our daily bread. So when we pray for our daily bread, we're not just praying for our physical food (which we should) but are also praying for Jesus Christ Himself, the bread that comes down from heaven. He is your strength to obey the will of the Father. He is your food, and your food is to obey the Father with and through Him. He is with you in every part of your life: in joys and in sufferings. Every part of the day is your daily bread—if you receive it with thanksgiving and with Jesus Christ. Your daily bread, then, is your life: breakfast, the morning paper, work, chores, errands, recreation, and relationships. It's all your daily bread if you live it with Jesus Christ and see it as an occasion to turn to Jesus and feed off Him.

. . .

"And forgive us our trespasses, as we forgive those who trespass against us;" (v. 12)

But we have a hard time eating our daily bread and obeying the will of the Father; we don't truly want to come to Him but want to do our will—which is known as sin. But Jesus obeyed the Father for us, and now we *can* come to God.

Through Him, we have the right to confess our sins and ask forgiveness. Jesus died to forgive us all, even though He had never sinned, and the Father forgives us only because of His obedience and sacrifice.

Therefore, after feeding off Jesus and receiving His forgiveness, we are to be like God, forgiving those who sin against us. To truly receive God's gift of forgiveness, you must give it, becoming like Him. This is one way of eating your daily bread.

. . .

"And lead us not into temptation, but deliver us from evil" (v. 13).

A second way of eating your daily bread is to turn to Jesus in times of trouble. When we pray "and lead us not into temptation," we are praying not so much that God won't tempt us but that He will keep us safe from *tribulation*, which is probably a better translation of the Greek word in this context. Regardless of the kind of tribulation we face, even temptation, we are to turn to Jesus Christ to deliver us. He is the one who lead us out of the wilderness of Sin and into the Promised Land, for He is the true Joshua, leading His people in the true Exodus.

We ask as well that we would be delivered from evil, knowing that Jesus defeated every kind of evil: temptation, sin, the world, the flesh, and the devil. One way of translating this prayer is "deliver us from the Evil One," and Jesus knows how to do that, too, having defeated Satan not only in the wilderness of temptation but also at the Cross.

. . .

"For thine is the kingdom and the power and the glory."

In following Jesus in all things, in praying His prayer with Him (which also means *living* it), we proclaim the kingdom, the power, the glory of the Father. But something even more miraculous happens if we faithfully pray and live with Jesus: He allows us to share in His kingdom and power and glory. Every time you obey, you are showing that you live under the rule of the King, and you manifest His kingdom. By receiving the same Holy Spirit that came upon Jesus at His baptism and seeking His grace in all the ways He offers it, you receive His power to obey the Father and the power to make God known to others. And as you are made partakers of Jesus Christ through prayer and faith and obedience, He shares the riches of His glory with you!

To pray the Lord's Prayer, therefore, is to be drawn into the life and kingdom of Jesus Christ Himself. It is to follow Him in all things. It is not only to pray the prayer that He gave us but also to live the prayer that He lived. I think it's even possible that this prayer, the Prayer of the Lord's, was the very prayer He made holy by praying it in the wilderness when tempted by Satan and in the Garden of Gethsemane when tempted to avoid the Cross.

So, pray it faithfully with Him every day, and it will lead you to Him so you can more faithfully follow Him. And where He leads you is to the Cross: to self-denial, to the forsaking of your sins, and to perfect obedience to the will of the Father. But where He leads you is also to the Resurrection and to the Father, where you will find the kingdom, the power, and the glory.

Prayer:
(Hmmmm, I wonder what we should pray today?!)

Points for Meditation:
1. Pray with the Lord's Supper in mind: it will revolutionize the way you pray it!
2. Pray the Lord's Prayer in the garden of Gethsemane with Him, and see it come to life. Apply it to your own temptations and tribulations.
3. Meditate on a different phrase from the Lord's Prayer each day of this week.

Resolution:
I resolve to pray the Lord's Prayer slowly and meditatively throughout the day today.

Matthew 6:19-34

"You cannot serve two masters" (v. 24).

You can't serve both God and wealth, and you can't serve both God and self.

You've heard the saying, from old Westerns, "This town ain't big enough for the both of us." Well, your life ain't big enough for two opposing masters.

So who's your master? Who are you really serving?

There are, basically, 3 choices. Behind door #1 you get Pride: serving self and putting faith in self. Behind door #2 you get Idolatry: serving wealth and putting trust in your possessions (which is only another form of Pride). But don't answer yet! Behind door #3 lies faith: serving God and putting your trust in Him.

Pride is serving and trusting in self. The real starting point for reality and our lives is not ourselves or the world but God, who is the Giver of every good gift. God has created, sustained, and redeemed every part of your life. What do you have that you have not received as a gift? The invisible reality is that you own nothing outright, not even your own body: it is God's Temple. Any thought or action that denies God and that everything good is His gift is a sin. For this reason, pride is the center of sin and the mother of sins, and all other sins are relatives of it.

Idolatry, with which Jesus is concerned this morning, begins with pride. Without meaning to, we often end up in idolatry, serving another god instead of the true God: *but it starts with Pride—with trusting in one's self.*

The following pattern is what happens so often:

1. You receive God's good gifts

2. You are blessed by God and His gifts

3. You relax and get comfortable and come to believe that the good things you receive in this life are things you have gotten for yourself, apart from God

4. You believe that everything you have is not a gift but a reward and that God owes it to you because of your own merits, apart from Him

5. You begin to trust in yourself, instead of God

6.   Congratulations! You are now serving yourself instead of serving God! You have officially become proud (and idolatrous, too!)

As bad as trusting in ourselves is, it never stops there. It's all too natural to transfer the goodness and providence of God to His creation, to say, not that "God has given me this or will give me this" but that some material thing will give me this. At some point we find ourselves believing that the source of our strength and security and life is something other than God: money, a house, a job, another person, ourselves.

Here are some frank questions we all need to ask ourselves regularly, as a diagnostic for the sickness of our souls:

1.   Do I trust in money or my house or any possession to provide for my physical needs?

2.   Do I believe that my bank account or house or any possession will give me security?

3.   Do I trust in money or movies or cars or books or any physical possession to make me happy?

4.   Have I begun to believe that I am blessed because I have certain things that are good, rather than believing I am blessed because God has given me good things?

5.   Do I value myself or my sense of worth based on the things I have?

6.   Are possessions my goal? Have they become my treasure?

7.   Do I trust in my possessions or my gifts and talents to make me happy or joyful?

If you have answered "Yes" to any of these questions, then you have begun to make an idol out of our possessions. If you answered "Yes" to any of these questions, then there's a good chance you have begun to serve Mammon instead of God

What may be just as challenging is that worry is also related to pride. Why? Because worry puts you back in charge. Worry is not the same as concern or godly action. Proper concern, godly action, and worry all begin with a problem that provokes a reaction, often an emotional one. But worry departs from godly concern or action because it doesn't trust that God, working through you or others, will be able to accomplish His will. It may very well be that *you* are not able to do what needs to get done. But either God will provide a way for it to get done, or else God didn't demand that it gets done (even if you do). It may be that you are not strong enough or smart enough to accomplish your will in a situation. But this is only a source of worry when you forget about God.

Worry is therefore ultimately about who is in control, and it puts you, and not God, in charge.

This is why Jesus says, "Do not worry," or similar words, *five* times in this passage. It's not just that Jesus wants us to be peaceful and calm (He does): He also wants us to come to Him and trust Him, and not ourselves.

Worry is also related to idolatry and should make you ask the question, "Do my possessions possess me?" Like any disease, there are symptoms and warning signs of the idolatry of trusting in Mammon, and some of them have to do with worry. The same questions I asked you to ask yourself above apply to worry, as well as idolatry.

Jesus says that worry is the most important symptom of serving Mammon and not God. Worry is not just being anxious to have something but is also being overly concerned to keep what you have, to have more, and to have more than what is necessary.

Why do we worry? We fear that something bad will happen, because we're uncertain, because we're afraid that we won't get what we feel we are owed, and because we're afraid that the good things we have will be taken away from us. Worry means trusting in a false god that cannot help you. You have reason to worry if you make your sense of worth, your happiness, or your well-being based on material things. Worry means *not* trusting in the only one who can help you: God.

To all who are anxious or trust too much in money or possessions, Jesus says: "Do not worry about how much I have or have not given you. *I* am your treasure, and *I* am your security.

The birds are beautiful and elegant and do not have bank accounts to trust in. Yet I give them all that they need.

Do not worry or be anxious, for *I* am your true possession, and I am where true riches are to be found."

This morning, to all who are anxious and worried about anything and to all who are tempted to turn to self instead of God for what you need, Jesus says to you: "Do not worry about your life. You cannot add a day to your life, and you can't provide for yourself without Me. But come to Me with humility, and I will provide for you everything you truly need. Let me worry about what you need to wear, what you need to eat, and where you need to live. If I know how to take care of the grass and the lilies and the birds, don't you think I know how to give you all you truly need? Stop playing God, and I will truly be your God and provide all you need."

. . .

Pride, Idolatry, Mammon, Covetousness, and Worry are deadly diseases. But thank God, there is a cure! Here it is: seek Jesus Christ.

If you seek Jesus Christ, you will not seek yourself. If you serve Him, you will not serve Mammon. If you're satisfied with Him, you won't covet. And if you trust Him, you won't worry.

The point isn't to dwell on sin and think of ourselves as worms (though a little of that goes a long way!) The point is to be motivated to seek Him!

Whatever your worries, on the one hand; however secure you may seem to be on the other hand; wherever you are this morning: seek first the Kingdom of God and His righteousness, and all these things shall be added unto you. Whatever gets in the way of you seeking and seeing Him—pride, idolatry, possessions, covetousness, ingratitude, or worry—get rid of it, for He is what you really want!

Prayer:

Father, I pray that You would make Yourself to be my treasure and where my heart is today. Give me a heart that desires You above all else so that I may serve You only. Cast down all pretenders to Your throne in my life: pride, possessions, and worry, that I might be free to be your slave and find all that I most truly desire in You. Amen.

Points for Meditation:

1. Examine yourself. Have you put possessions before God? Do you worry? Is there any way in which you have allowed Pride to reign in your life?
2. In what ways could you seek Jesus more faithfully, so that He will reign in your life?

Resolution:

I resolve to practice putting my trust in the Lord today, that He might dethrone pride, idolatry, Mammon, and worry in my life.

Matthew 7:1-14

"God."

What does this word mean to you? When you think of God, what are the first images, thoughts, and feelings you experience? What stands out as His most important characteristic?

I'll give you some of my answers, since I'm into cooperative learning. When I think of "God," sometimes He is a concept I've been taught and believe. I may experience Him as an aloof power. I think of Him as the Almighty Creator who is omnipotent, omniscient, and omnipresent. And yet often I don't experience Him as any of these things, even though I believe them with my whole heart and head.

I want today to think of God in one of Jesus' favorite ways of portraying the Father—as your *loving heavenly Father*.

An interesting thing happens when you look up the word "father" in an exhaustive concordance (I'm using Young's): "Father" (as in *the* Father) is used 43 times in Matthew, 8 times in Mark, 19 times in Luke, and 114 times in John. "Father" is used 3 times in Acts (2 of which are by Jesus), 4 times in Romans, 8 times Corinthians, 12 times in Galatians and Ephesians, 8 times in Philippians and Colossians, 8 times in the letters to the Thessalonians, 4 times in the letters to Timothy, once in Titus, once in Philemon, twice in the letter to the Hebrews, 4 times, by James, 4 times by Peter, once by Jude, 12 times in 1 John, 4 times in 2 John, and 5 times in the Revelation.

What's the point of my little survey? It's Jesus who invokes the name of "Father" more than anyone else. "Of course He did," you might say. "He *is* the Son." Well said, my little theological friend. But what's really interesting is that Jesus turns "My Father" into *"Our* Father" in the Lord's Prayer. The Father who is eternally the Father of the Son is now also *our* Father! This is, of course, because we have been made sons by the Son, and we are now heirs of the blessing of this same Father. When He speaks of the Father, it's not just for His sake but for ours.

The second point one could draw from my survey is that it is St. John who especially loves to use the name "Father." Perhaps this is because he seems to have understood the love of the Father better than anyone else.

This is a gift from the Son: that we too may call His Father *our Father* and may cry out to Him and expect to receive His blessing. This is what the work of the Son most truly and wonderfully is: to make His Father *our Father*.

This truth has staggering implications for how we pray. It means, first of all, that we can come into the presence of the God who is a Living Fire not only with fear and trembling but also as beloved sons and daughters. When we come into the presence of this Holy Living Fire, the first thing we'll probably notice is how sinful and unworthy we are. Good! I'm glad you noticed! But there's an easy way to deal with this: confess your sins, seek His forgiveness, and vow to truly turn from them. This is an integral part of prayer.

When we come into the presence of the Almighty Creator, we will probably also notice how glorious and powerful and majestic He is. Hopefully, we won't be able to contain our impulse to worship, adore, and praise such a God. And this is also a part of what our prayer should be.

How can we come into His Presence and not also immediately be flooded with memories of all of the good things He has given to us? Giving Him thanks is, therefore, an essential part of prayer, and I hope you practice it every day.

At some point it should dawn on you that it's not right to always be the one talking when in the company of the Lord. For this reason, a silent listening is also a part of prayer, which is our conversation with God.

But the part of prayer that seems to be everyone's favorite is the part that Jesus especially deals with today, and that's asking God for things. The amazing truth is that when we come before the Holy Living Fire and Creator of Heaven and Earth, we are granted permission to ask for the things we need, as a child would ask his father!

As parents, Jackie and I haven't always been able to afford to give our kids much, and so when I took my kids to Six Flags one day, they were so appreciative. If even a stooge like me knows how to give good gifts to my kids, don't you think our heavenly Father will give good things to those who ask Him?

Do we accept and believe the words of Jesus? He says, "Ask, and it will be given to you; seek, and you will find; knock, and it will be opened to you." The bottom line is that Jesus teaches us to turn to the Father in prayer, believing that we will receive what we ask for.

If you're like me, you have a siren that's going off—you know, the one that detects an offer that just doesn't add up. Jesus couldn't possibly really mean this. O.K. So here goes the obligatory disclaimer:

"No, God isn't compelled to give you everything you ask for. You have to ask with faith, and you have to ask according to His will. But how do I know it's His will? Aye, there's the rub. Also, what if I ask for things that are selfish? (Janis Joplin sang about asking God to buy her a Mercedes Benz to be like her friends.) But sometimes God is trying to give you even more valuable things by making you wait because the best prayer and best answer to prayer is to be brought closer to God. This is so that what you desire and ask for is precisely what His desire is, which, by the way, is the answer to the dilemma above about having to ask according to God's will."

With this disclaimer in mind, we're back at the fundamental fact that God, your loving heavenly Father, desires for you to come to Him and ask Him for what you need. Just think of what you could ask for and might receive: love, joy, peace, long-suffering, gentleness, goodness, faith, meekness, self-control, holiness, righteousness, zeal, closeness to God, forgiveness of your sins, health, good relationships with others, clarity, wisdom, confidence, spiritual gifts and blessings and fruits for those you love, your work situation, family stability, family finances, the big decision you are facing, reconciliation, healing for that long and deep wound, spiritual revival, peace and justice in the world, your church, your city, your nation, etc., etc., etc.

Given the commandment of Jesus, the love of our Father, and our desperate need, why don't we pray? Here are just a few of the many reasons why we are weak in prayer: we're weak in faith; we're far from God because we don't pray or hear His Word; we don't live in the Body of His Son which is His ordained means of helping us; laziness; false humility (pride); pride; thinking we've got it made on our own; distraction; thinking God is too remote; thinking God's too busy; believing He doesn't really care; believing that what we need isn't important enough to ask for; believing prayer's too difficult; and refusing to schedule in time for God.

For each of these excuses there is an answer. But I'm not going to give it to you. Instead, I'm giving each of you a homework assignment: whatever reason you have for not coming to God to pray today (from the above list or for some other reason), I want you to write down what the excuse is, why that's not a good excuse, and what God would say to that excuse. Seriously. I want you to write these things down.

And then, having no excuse, get on your knees and pray!

Prayer:

Our Father, who art in heaven, hallowed be Thy name. Thy kingdom come. Thy will be done, on earth as it is in heaven. Give us this day our daily bread. And forgive us our trespasses, as we forgive those who trespass against us. And lead us not into temptation, but deliver us from evil. For thine is the kingdom, and the power, and the glory, for ever and ever. Amen.

Points for Meditation:

1. Keep a prayer list.
2. Keep a prayer journal of how God has answered your prayers and worked through prayer in your life.

Resolution:

I resolve to examine why I don't pray as I ought to and to write down my excuse(s) and reasons why they aren't valid. I further resolve to spend time in prayer today.

Matthew 7:13-29

When I lived in England with my family for 10 months several years ago (to begin my Ph.D. work at Lancaster University), we lived in student housing. We had a family flat which wasn't too bad—except that it was on the fourth floor. One of the most memorable experiences, and not a pleasant one, was being woken from a deep sleep at 2 or 4 a.m. by the most piercing, high-volume fire alarm imaginable. On several occasions the alarm sounded in winter at night, shocking us out of sleep. We threw on some warmer clothes and our shoes without socks, reassured our little children, and then bustled them down three flights of stairs to safety.

Little did I know that two years later, after I had returned to the U.S. that an alarm, even louder, even more piercing, even more disturbing than the one in England, would go off on the week of August 3rd, 2003.

But an ear-splitting, *church*-splitting alarm has gone off. Some were in a deep sleep and have only by such a loud and fearsome noise been wakened. Others have seen the building burning for some time and escaped before such a loud alarm had to go off. Sadly, many seem content to sleep through it and allow themselves and the building to burn all the way down.

I'm speaking about the Episcopal Church's decision to elect an openly homosexual man to be the bishop of New Hampshire.

Do you remember the first king of Israel? Saul was at first a righteous man, a man God hand-picked to lead Israel. Though he stood a head taller than those around him, he was so humble that he hid among the luggage when people came looking to crown him.

But his heart slowly turned from God. He began to do his own will, and not the will of His father in heaven. He offered up unholy sacrifices, consulted a witch, and became jealous over one more righteous than he. Ultimately, he died on the battlefield, along with his more noble son.

When David heard the news, rather than rejoicing, he lamented over Saul and Jonathan and taught his lament to Israel. He said: *"The beauty of Israel is slain on your high places. **How are the mighty fallen!**"* (2 Samuel 1:19)

And so we, too, might lament over the fall of our sister, the church formerly known as the Episcopal Church USA (now, simply The Episcopal Church).

So, how did we get here? How could it come to this? There are Anglicans in The Episcopal Church (TEC) who serve communion to the unbaptized, bless same-sex marriages, ordain and consecrate those who are openly homosexual, conduct Wiccan masses, deny the Bible is the Word of God, are Moslems and yet a Christian priest, etc. How could a once godly church now suffer through such shame and ungodliness?

The answer is that for years and years The Episcopal Church has failed to heed the warning of Jesus Christ found in Matthew 7:15–16: *"Beware of false prophets, who come to you in sheep's clothing, but inwardly they are ravenous wolves. You will know them by their fruits."*

As with all sin, it happened in stages. And it has all happened not in spite of the shepherds *but often because of them.* Go read about Bishops Pike, Robinson, Righter, Schori, Spong, and others if you want to learn about wolves in sheep's clothing.

As has often been said: "All that is necessary for the triumph of evil is for good men to do nothing."

"Beware of false prophets, who come to you in sheep's clothing, but inwardly they are ravenous wolves. You will know them by their fruits."

"But Father Charles," you might say, "how can we know false prophets when they come around? Sometimes it's confusing, and sometimes, even though I know they are wrong, they sound so intelligent."

Let me be very clear here: this battle we have just witnessed isn't really about homosexuality. Yes, that is the particular issue that has been raised, but there are even deeper issues at stake. Again, *the real issue is obedience to God and His Word*

At stake is not just this one sinful behavior: it is our entire relationship to God and His Word. This raises the issue of standards: how shall we know if we love God? How shall we know if someone who claims to love God truly does?

Fortunately, God has given us a standard by which to judge the fruits of men: and that is His holy Word. You shall know them by their fruits, and you shall know their fruits by comparing them with what God says in His Word.

Many today call themselves Christians and claim to love God. But God says in 1 John 5: 3, "For this is the love of God, that we keep His commandments."

If you love God, you will obey God. You shall know them by their fruits.

God is clear in His Word about what He believes about homosexuality—and about many other things. Go and find the passages on homosexuality yourself, and remember that fornication (which Jesus Himself condemns) includes all sex outside of marriage.

This issue, therefore, is about obedience to God and His Word: don't let anybody tell you otherwise. What should concern us about many younger Christians today, therefore, when they accept homosexuality, is that they have really given up the Bible as the Word of God. Our attitude about homosexuality is just one indicator of what is our true authority in our lives.

Many will come claiming to be Christians, claiming to speak for God. Do not be fooled: you shall know them by their fruits. If even a bishop, even your local bishop or head pastor, should come to you and say that God condones homosexuality or that God condones any sin that God has clearly said He detests—do not believe him. Yes, we all sin, but beware of those who call sin righteousness and who call God a liar.

"Beware of false prophets, who come to you in sheep's clothing, but inwardly they are ravenous wolves. You will know them by their fruits."

So how should we respond to all of this? What does this mean to those of us who believe God and His Word over the words of sinful men?

First, God is still on His throne. In spite of the evil that men do (and we do it every day), God is still in His heaven. He still reigns. God is still God, and His holy will shall be done—with or without us. This, and only this, is our assurance against any evil.

Second, thank God that there is a place to go. Let me assure you that in the Reformed Episcopal Church, for example, things *are* different than in most of The Episcopal Church. Every one of our bishops, every one of our seminary professors is required to uphold the Bible as the Word of God and to uphold the traditions of the Church. Any bishop or priest who rejected the Word of God in the REC would be looking for another church the next day. And, Reformed Episcopalians are on the same side as the vast majority of Anglicans worldwide (especially if you count only the ones who actually go to church!) Many others in other churches have also maintained the true faith, even while others have forsaken it.

Third, you must never become complacent. It would be easy for us to be self-righteous, thinking that because we are in the Reformed Episcopal Church (or whatever church you're in) that we have room to boast, or that we are safe. But it was complacency, doing nothing when men did evil, that caused the ruin of the Episcopal Church in the first place. Should I, or any other minister of the gospel, or any other person professing to be a Christian, claim a right to sin or claim any standard that contradicts God and His Word, it is your Christian duty to speak up and set us straight.

Never, never, become complacent about God or about sin.

Finally, what about ourselves? My admonition to never become complacent means especially *don't become complacent about your own sin.*

Paul says in Ephesians 5:14, *"Awake, O sleeper, and arise from the dead, and Christ shall give you light."* The time for slumber is past: the time to awaken to God's call upon your life is now. My exhortation to you today is that you make every effort to heed the warnings of Jesus Christ. Learn from the tragic lessons of others before you.

Remember, that several verses before Jesus teaches about false prophets and knowing men by their fruits, He also said: "For with what judgment you judge, you will be judged." Just as you are commanded to know them by their fruits, so shall others know you by your fruits. Do you remember when David squawked and fumed when the prophet Nathan told him about the rich man with many sheep who took the one sheep of the poor man? David advocated that the man be put to death. And then Nathan turned to him and said, "Thou art the man."

You and I are the man. We are the ones who stand as sinners before God. The same question that every sinner in the world has to face is staring you in the face this morning: and that is, "Am I living as Jesus Christ would have me live?"

We have spent perhaps more than enough time examining the sins of others. The real question for you this morning is, "When the world looks at my fruits, what do they see?" For just as surely as we can look at the fruits of others and see that something is not right, others may look at your life or my life and wonder about our fruits.

A good tree, one rooted in Christ, watered by the Living Water and fed by the Bread of Life, will produce good fruit, the fruit of obedience to God.

And to *all* who are trapped in sin this morning, *of whatever kind,* God offers the promise of forgiveness through His Son. But He offers it only to those who are truly repentant and intend to lead a new life, walking from henceforth in His commandments. Make peace with God, while there is still time. Kiss the Son, lest He be angry, and His wrath is kindled.

Brothers and sisters in Christ, *"Beware of false prophets, who come to you in sheep's clothing, but inwardly they are ravenous wolves. You will know them by their fruits."*

But remember: they will also know *you* by *your* fruits, which are some of the best arguments for God and His holy kingdom that God has ever devised.

Prayer:

Grant we beseech thee, Almighty God, that the words which we have heard this day with our outward ears, may, through thy grace, be so grafted inwardly in our hearts, that they may bring forth in us the fruit of good living, to the honor and praise of thy Name; through Jesus Christ our Lord. Amen.

(From *The Book of Common Prayer*, p. 49)

Points for Meditation:

1. If people judged you by the fruits of your life, what would they say and think?
2. Are you guilty of a double standard—of judging the sins of others more harshly than you treat your own?

Resolution:

I resolve to seek to bear good fruit today by confessing my sins and by asking the Lord where He would have me plant, water, fertilize, or prune today.

Matthew 8:1-13

Have you ever met someone who had a commanding sense of authority? An authority so great that everyone around silently took notice and responded to the mere physical presence of this person?

When I first began my career as a teacher my senior year in college as a student teacher, it became quite clear to me that I did *not* have *It*: that indefinable authority that certain teachers seem to have. I had not yet developed the sense of self-confidence, or sense of presence, or The Look.

A few weeks into my student teaching, I was doing a lab in a physical science class. I thought I was doing a pretty good job. I was explaining things to the kids, hopping from lab table to lab table, keeping an eye on things—or so I thought. The next day I learned, from the assistant principal, that he had caught two of my students in the hall, who had apparently escaped from my class during my lab.

I must have been a source of concern and amusement for my supervising teacher, Mrs. Colleen Holmes, for she seemed to have plenty of authority. I began student teaching halfway through the year, and by that time Mrs. Holmes had those kids whipped into shape. I was amazed when I sat in the first day in her class, and the kids were all sitting straight in their chairs. No one ever talked: I wasn't even sure *I* was allowed to! No one moved, no one even fidgeted. She made it look a million times easier than it was, because she had this sense of authority. (For the record, it took me about two days for the kids to figure out they could walk all over me!)

We all understand authority in our lives, even if we sometimes resent it. Someone has the right or power to direct the life of someone under him. We've all had parents or other adults whose authority was so strong you could smell it. Authority is a part of the created order: life wouldn't even make sense without it.

Behind this human authority is an infinitely greater authority, from which all authority is derivative. No human authority exists by itself, by its own authority. The fact is that God is in charge of all things, and this includes your life.

You may *think* you're in charge...but you're not. You couldn't create yourself, and you can't preserve yourself, not without what God first provides. Sometimes you can't even control your own body, thoughts, or feelings.

When I used to teach Government, I taught that there are two kinds of authority—positional and personal. As I became a wiser and better teacher, I tried to achieve the miraculous: to have both kinds of authority in relationship to my students. Some teachers tried to have only personal authority and became too much of a friend to their students. Others cared only about having the positional authority, the right to tell others what to do.

In Matthew 8, the centurion certainly understood positional authority. He says, "*I am not worthy. For I am a man under authority, having soldiers under me*" (v. 8).

He was a man with authority over 100 Roman soldiers. He knew what it was to order men around and to be ordered around. And so, he made this wonderful analogy—he saw that his own authority proved the greater authority of God. Too often, man is tempted to look at his authority over creation or the animals and think that he is God. With the continuing, almost magical advances of technology, this delusion is perhaps even greater than before.

But God has the ultimate positional authority. I shouldn't have to spell this out, but here goes. God is, well, *God*. It's a mistake to think that we are like God, or that God is as we are, only maybe like a Superman. He's not our buddy and equal: He is the Lord of Lord and King of Kings; the Maker of Heaven and Earth; and God Almighty!

So what authority does God have in your life? A God who created all things—including you. A God who knows all things. A God who has always existed. A God who is everywhere.

He has *authority* over every area of the universe, to the outermost reaches of the universe, so far away even the Hubble telescope can't detect it. He has authority over every area of your life.

And your job...is to acknowledge the authority of God.

It's not enough to have only positional power. We could serve God because He is a very powerful tyrant or because He's a big bully. But God also has personal authority, because of His character. When I taught the first group of seniors at All Saints Episcopal School in Tyler, TX, who wanted only to cut up in class and make the classroom a hell for their teachers, it wasn't my positional authority that won them over: they wanted to rebel against that.

I made it a point to sit with them at lunch. I responded to them as real people in the classroom. I showed them that I was really on their side. By the end of the year, I had gained a personal authority with them, and they became more willing to do what I asked them to do.

God's authority concerns not only His position or power, but also His person, or who He is. What authority does God have in your life? A God who is the definition of goodness. A God who is holy and perfectly just. A God who is merciful and gracious. A God who is True and Beautiful. A God who loves you.

So how can you adequately respond to such a great God? What can we mere humans do to acknowledge the God whose positional and personal authority over us is without limit? If you begin with God's greatness and authority, then you must continue by responding with humility. If you want to be great in the Kingdom of Heaven, learn to be the servant of all. Authority in God's Kingdom comes through humility, by bowing before God and recognizing that all authority belongs to Him.

The centurion's servant could never have been healed by the centurion himself. All of the broken and sick things in life we most want to be made better are things we cannot fix ourselves. And, therefore, we come to God's authority because of His power, but also because of His love (personal authority).

You should come with obedience. Every time you cheerfully obey, no matter how it feels, you are acknowledging the authority of God and you give Him glory, the very thing He has created you to do.

True power comes from recognizing God's authority in your life, and not by asserting your own. The astounding thing is that the Almighty God with the ultimate positional authority of Heaven came to serve in humility on earth. Even more astounding: He shares His authority with you, for you are to reign with Him.

He shares His life with us through the Church, through His Word, through the Sacraments, and through His Spirit. And He gives His authority and life to those who unite themselves to Him. By identifying ourselves with His authority, we gain authority to speak the truth, to live the truth, and to be called the sons of God.

What is all of this, our response to God's authority?

Is it not *worship*? What is to be *your* response to a God who has the ultimate positional and personal authority and comes to give Himself to you?

Worship, in the iridescent spectrum of ways in which worship should fill our lives!

Prayer:

We praise thee, O God; we acknowledge thee to be the Lord.

All the earth doth worship thee, the Father everlasting.

To thee all Angels cry aloud; the Heavens, and all the Powers therein;

To thee Cherubim and Seraphim continually do cry,

Holy, Holy, Holy, Lord God of Sabaoth;

Heaven and earth are full of the Majesty of thy glory.

The glorious company of the Apostles praise thee.

The goodly fellowship of the Prophets praise thee.

The noble army of Martyrs praise thee.

The holy Church throughout all the world: doth acknowledge thee;

The Father: of an infinite Majesty;

Thine adorable, true and only Son;

Also the Holy Ghost, the Comforter.

Thou art the King of Glory, O Christ.

Thou art the everlasting Son, of the Father.

When thou tookest upon thee to deliver man: thou didst humble thyself to be born of a Virgin.

When thou hadst overcome the sharpness of death, thou didst open the Kingdom of Heaven to all believers.

Thou sittest at the right hand of God, in the glory of the Father.

We believe that thou shalt come to be our Judge.

We therefore pray thee, help thy servants: whom thou hast redeemed with thy precious blood.

Make them to be numbered with thy Saints, in glory everlasting.

O Lord, save thy people: and bless thine heritage.

Govern them, and lift them up for ever.

Day by day, we magnify thee; And we worship thy Name, ever world without end.

Vouchsafe, O Lord, to keep us this day without sin.

O Lord, have mercy upon us, have mercy upon us.

O Lord, let thy mercy lighten upon us, as our trust is in thee.

O Lord, in thee have I trusted; let me never be confounded.

Amen.

(The Te Deum)

Points for Meditation:

1. What are some areas of your life where you do not acknowledge God to be your Lord? What is one area where the Lord is most asking you to humble yourself before Him?
2. Which kind of authority (positional or personal) is the primary way in which you think of God? What's one way you could more properly acknowledge His other kind of authority?

Resolution:

I resolve to submit to the Lord in the one area in which He has specifically asked me to submit today.

Matthew 8:14–27

"Teacher I will follow you wherever You go."

"Lord, let me first go and bury my father."

I am a disciple of Jesus Christ.

That's who I am.

I have many other identities and roles, but this is my most fundamental one: I am a disciple of Jesus Christ.

It amazes me that Jesus makes this so clear—that we are His disciples—and yet many, if not most Christians, don't really see themselves that way. Instead, they see themselves as Christians. Well, I consider myself a Christian, too, but unfortunately that word can mean just about anything these days. It should mean *Christ*ian, a little Christ, a disciple of Jesus Christ. But it may also mean "Jesus was a good teacher except when he disagrees with me" or "Of course I'm a Christian—what else would I be?"

But what is a disciple? It's one who has dedicated himself to follow a master. As disciples of Jesus Christ, we have pledged ourselves completely to *the* Master. That is who we are.

And so I like it when my Master plainly commands me, saying, *"If anyone desires to come after Me, let him deny himself, and take up his cross, and follow Me"* (Matthew 16:24).

But I also like it when He teaches me about being a disciple in less plain ways that make me have to think about what it means to be a disciple. And so here in Matthew 8 we get what appears to be a less direct teaching from the Master about being a disciple. Maybe Jesus' teaching in Matthew 16 is more direct and forceful because Peter has confessed Him as Christ and He has begun to openly teach that He must go to Jerusalem and suffer.

But here in Matthew 8, Jesus' teaching on discipleship is more subdued. And sometimes this is exactly what we need in order to hear better.

The first disciple that comes to Jesus boldly proclaims: "Teacher, I will follow you wherever You go."

To which we expect (as I expect this disciple expected) Jesus to say something like, "Bravo! Well done, old chap. Now let's do get on with this business of redeeming the world together, shall we?"

O.K. Well maybe none of you quite expect Jesus to say something like this. O.K., maybe I don't really either. But I do expect Him to applaud such a bold and forthright expression of a willingness to follow Him.

But He doesn't. Instead, the Master, the Teacher, tests His disciples, so He says, *"Foxes have holes and birds of the air have nests, but the Son of Man has nowhere to lay His head."*

That's nice, Jesus. But what's that got to do with the price of tea in China? This answer catches us off guard, as so many of Jesus' answers do. He catches us off guard, because we expect Him to openly applaud such a faith-filled answer. Of course, He doesn't. We're also upset because of what His answer implies. His answer points to how He lives. Since the disciple has just made a proclamation that he'll follow Jesus anywhere, Jesus returns the favor and shows just a little of what the life of the Master is like. The truth is that in His life of service, and especially of suffering, the Son of Man did not find rest in this life. There's something about redeeming the world of sin and suffering from sin and suffering that necessitated suffering on the part of the Master.

The problem for us disciples is that since we aren't above the Master, what He experiences is what we experience (which is only fair, since what we experience is what He experiences: all in all it's a spectacular trade!) We don't hear the response of this particular disciple, but there's a good chance it's not what he wanted to hear.

Often, it's not what we want to hear, either. We want to hear that once we sign on the dotted Jesus line then everything will be groovy. We want to have no more wind and no more waves in our lives. We want to be carried to the skies on flowery beds of ease (from "Am I a Soldier of the Cross?")

Maybe this discipleship business is trickier than I thought!

What about the other disciple in this story? He's got a pretty good excuse, don't you think? "Lord, let me first go and bury my father."

Now what could be wrong with this? That's an important thing to do. In fact, I've heard that one of the most sacred obligations of a Jew was to begin each day with the prayer (the Shema), "Hear, O Israel, the Lord our God, the Lord is one, and you shall love the Lord your God with all your heart and with all your soul and with all your mind and with all your strength." This was regarded as the most important thing a Jew did each day. And yet (I've heard), that when a man's father died he was so obligated to bury him that this duty came even before the recitation of the Shema, and also that it might be a rather extended affair.

And yet when this man pleads that he must go and bury his father before he can follow Jesus, what does Jesus say? "Oh, that's O.K. You know what they say: 'First things first.' I've got all the time in the world. I wouldn't want to appear too radical and turn you away. Maybe it's better to ease you into my kingdom— you know that camel's nose in the tent thing. I'll be patiently waiting for you outside, meekly knocking to enter into your door. You do promise to listen to me, don't you? Don't you?"

Oops! Wrong sound clip! What Jesus actually says is: "Follow Me, and let the dead bury their own dead."

Ouch! Really, Jesus, don't you think you can catch more flies with honey than with vinegar? So much for the subtle approach. Jesus only *appeared* to me to be speaking less directly about the cost of discipleship here, as compared to Matthew 16. Oh no! Jesus has sucker punched me! He's not really playing nice after all: He means business.

Oh well, I might as well reveal my weirdness in all its glory to you now. If you've read *Give Us This Day* this far, you know that sometimes I can see things in, uh, *different* ways. I have this mental image of Jesus that recurs to me every now and then. I call it "Steamrollin' Jesus." In this image, I see Jesus riding on a yellow Caterpillar steamroller. He's about 20 to 30 feet away to begin with, and I notice that He's got the traditional long hair, but in place of the traditional toga and sandals He's wearing a red plaid shirt, jeans, and some cowboy boots (and sometimes a feed cap). Just as I begin to wonder at all this—SPLAT! He comes over to me, running me over with His steamroller! I look up, having become a crumpled mess on the floor and being now one with the earth into which I've been ground, and muster just enough energy to see Jesus looking back at me. Only He's *smiling* at me. And as He smiles, He raises his forefinger to His temple and salutes me with it. And then He goes on His merry way, and the film ends.

There—I feel better for having shared this. I receive this image sometimes when I feel that Jesus has "steamrolled" me in life. Matthew 8 is one of those times. I thought He might go easy on me, but He doesn't.

If you, like me, were looking for an easy road to discipleship, then you'll have been disappointed. You might feel like Jesus has steamrolled you. Or maybe you think that Fr. Charles is the one who's steamrolled you. "He always seems so intense!" (And this, from the man who just brought you the image of "Steamrollin' Jesus.")

Like me, maybe you've figured out that Jesus leaves you with no place to hide. Look—do you want to be His disciple or not? If the disciple in Matthew 8 wasn't even allowed to bury his father before He chose to follow Jesus, then you aren't allowed to first "get your act together" or "find a place of peace" or "just get out of this mess" or allow yourself to get out of the habit of following Him.

There are no excuses. None. Follow Him today. *Now*. I mean it!

But just in case there are a few who are weak (I know there's at least one—and he's the one writing this!)—see what Jesus says to you next. When you feel like Jesus' call to be a disciple has steamrolled you, you're like the disciples in the boat in a storm (which is the very next story in Matthew 8 after His discussion of the cost of discipleship).

You cry out to the Lord, "Lord, save me! I'm perishing! If I follow you and give up everything, then I'll have nothing left. It's too hard!"

To which Jesus says, "Why are you fearful, O you of little faith!" And then He calms the wind and waves in your life. And then He reminds you that His calling you to be His disciple isn't to harm or limit you but to free and heal you.

And then you say "_____."

Well, what *do* you say?

Prayer:

Father, I abandon myself into your hands;
do with me what you will.
Whatever you may do, I thank you:
I am ready for all, I accept all.
Let only your will be done in me,
and in all Your creatures—
I wish no more than this, O Lord.
Into your hands I commend my soul;
I offer it to you with all the love of my heart,
for I love you Lord,
and so need to give myself,
to surrender myself into your hands,
without reserve,
and with boundless confidence,
For you are my Father. Amen.

(Prayer of Abandonment accredited to Fr. Charles de Foucald)

Points for Meditation:

1. What keeps you back from fully dedicating your life to the Lord? What fears do you have? What temptations do you have?
2. What are the blessings that you have experienced by being a disciple of Jesus Christ?
3. Meditate on how Jesus has brought much of His blessing in your life through the things that have been most difficult. How does this change your perception of trusting His difficult call to give up yourself to Him?

Resolution:

I resolve to listen to the Lord and follow Him in the one way He is asking me to follow Him today.

Matthew 9:1-8

It's curious in today's passage that Jesus doesn't just say, as He sometimes says: "Your faith has made you well," but says instead: "Your sins are forgiven you." It's interesting, of course, because in Jesus' mind there is a connection between the paralysis of this man and his sins. From this, we might understand three related points that Jesus wishes us to hear today.

First, bodily sickness is sometimes caused by spiritual sickness. It could be that God is judging us or that, if we are His children, He is disciplining us so that we might come back to Him. It could be that the sickness in our soul has gotten into our hearts and minds and therefore makes the body sick. Modern medicine is becoming more and more aware of how spiritual and mental sicknesses may manifest themselves in bodily sicknesses.

It's also important to realize that even if our bodily sicknesses aren't always directly caused by our spiritual sickness, ultimately they are derived from sin. This is because the world, as a result of sin, including the world of the body, is fallen and decays as it was not created to.

The second point we might learn from Jesus' pronunciation is that God cares about all of you: body and soul. Jesus could have gone around making a severe distinction between the body and the soul, proclaiming that people's sins are forgiven without also healing their bodies. Instead, we find Him ministering to both body and soul. Sometimes, He heals the body and makes no direct mention of healing the soul; sometimes He ministers to the soul and doesn't directly address the body. And sometimes He ministers to both, as in this passage and in the Feeding of the 5000.

It's interesting also to remember that the Greek word *sozo* means both "to heal" and "to save."

The third thing we might learn from Jesus' pronunciation to the paralyzed man is that sin is the real problem in our lives. This is clear from His confrontation with the scribes. In the next section, verses 9–13, Jesus continues to show that He is ultimately concerned with spiritual sickness.

"Those who are well have no need of a physician, but those who are sick...For I did not come to call the righteous, but sinners to repentance" (vv. 12–13).

Today, you are the paralytic, and you are the tax collectors and sinners. In fact, we all are, for "none is righteous, no, not one." You are the one who is paralyzed by your sins, which keep you from the life and health that God desires for you. You are the sinner who needs to repent from your sins.

Jesus, the Great Physician of the Body and Metaphysician of the Soul, has diagnosed your sickness: you have a terminal case of sin that will end in eternal death if untreated. But, Jesus has also prescribed the remedy for your terminal illness: faith in Him demonstrated by repentance from your sins.

I want to conclude by looking at verse 8, which is the punctuation mark on this episode. "Now when the multitudes saw it, they marveled and glorified God, who had given such power to men." Verses 1–7 are intended to teach us about our sinfulness before God, as well as God's power and mercy in forgiving us our sins. But verse 8 teaches us about the response to God's forgiveness we should have today.

This story of Jesus' healing was written for our learning. From this story of the paralytic man made whole you are to learn about Jesus and your proper response of repentance, and about marveling and glorifying God. What response would you have if someone you knew who had a physical problem were instantaneously healed from it? It would be to marvel and glorify God.

But you are to place yourself into this story even more immediately and personally. *You* are the one who is to be healed by Jesus. Although Jesus' healing in your life today may not be as physical or dramatic as was the paralytic's, it's no less a marvel. Jesus turns to you today, if you believe and repent, and says, "Son, be of good cheer; your sins are forgiven you."

Unlike the paralytic who was healed once, you are healed every day. No matter how many times you sin against God, He forgives you, as long as you repent. Every day when you come before the Lord to ask forgiveness, Jesus performs His daily miracle in your life. As with the Israelites, we need to make sure we don't despise this daily miracle, just because it happens every day.

They ate the manna, the bread of heaven. But, when we turn to Jesus and confess our sins, we eat Jesus Christ, the Bread of Heaven, and our daily bread.

As one who is sick and in need of healing, rush to the One who can heal you and perform the miracle of forgiveness one more time.

If you do, the prognosis is good—no—it's G-r-r-reat!!, for Jesus Christ says to you: "Son, be of good cheer; your sins are forgiven you."

Prayer:

Our Father, who art in heaven, hallowed be Thy name. Thy kingdom come. Thy will be done, on earth as it is in heaven. Give us this day our daily bread. And forgive us our trespasses, as we forgive those who trespass against us. And lead us not into temptation, but deliver us from evil. For thine is the kingdom, and the power, and the glory, for ever and ever. Amen.

Points for Meditation:

1. As you consider your sins today, meditate on and marvel at the greatness of God's gift of forgiveness.
2. Meditate on the power of God to forgive sins. What response should His forgiveness of your sins provoke from you?

Resolution:

I resolve to come to Jesus today, confessing all my sins. I further resolve to glorify God when I accept His forgiveness.

Matthew 9:9-17

A few years ago I was on flight back home from Atlanta to Little Rock and for the first time experienced a flight delay due to mechanical difficulties. My twin brother Danny was with me and has happened to have had experiences like this more commonly, so I thought maybe his bad aeronautic luck rubbed off on me. It turned out that the plane was held up by single screw being loose on one of the wings (which, naturally, reminded me of the TV show called *The Twilight Zone*, and in particular, the episode in which actor William Shatner portrayed a man who hallucinated that there was a gremlin on the wing of the plane, mischievously destroying the wing).

My point is that a single screw held up the flight, and none of us could move on until it was fixed. There was something that must be taken care of before we moved on.

In the same way, repentance is something in our lives that we must take care of if we are going to move on to a true relationship with God. Before we can arrive safely at our destination of being in the arms of God, we must take care of the dangerous obstacle of sin in our lives.

In Matthew 9, Jesus calls Matthew, five chapters after He called the four fishermen. There's something unusual about the calling of Matthew: in fact, several things. Unlike the fishermen, who were called in pairs, Matthew is called by himself. While the profession of James, John, Peter, and Andrew was that of a fisherman, Matthew was a tax collector. But a tax collector is not just a tax collector. If you've read the Gospels very often, then you know that "tax collector" and "prostitute" were stock categories of people known to be sinful. The Pharisees make this clear in verse 11, when they ask Jesus' disciples: *"Why does your Teacher eat with tax collectors and sinners?"*

Jesus' answer is classic Jesus:

"Those who are well have no need of a physician, but those who are sick. But go and learn what this means: 'I desire mercy and not sacrifice.' For I did not come to call the righteous, but sinners, to repentance" (v. 12).

What's especially astounding about this call is that the person recording this passage about Jesus' calling sinners to repentance and about the call of Matthew the sinful tax collector is none other than Matthew himself! It's intriguing to think about writing a Gospel of Jesus Christ and then coming to the part where you're called by Jesus!

The call to repentance is very real and personal: it certainly was in Matthew's life!

The fact is that Jesus calls *sinners* to be His disciples, not those who are righteous, and so in the Gospel story, Jesus calls not only fishermen but a *tax collector*. In fact, Jesus calls *nothing but sinners* to Himself. And sinners, a tax collector among them, are the ones to whom He entrusted his Gospels and now entrusts His Church.

Jesus calls sinners to Himself. It's the essence of the Gospel, but somehow when I see it in Matthew's life I realize the wonder of it in my own. *You and I* are the tax collectors, the sinners, who Jesus is calling!

In order to call us, Jesus first spends time with sinners. First, He called Matthew. Then, when they were together at the table, other sinners came and sat down with Jesus and His disciples. How did they get there? In one way or another, Jesus called them. Some He called by a direct command, such as Matthew and the four fishermen. Others, He called by His teaching, and yet others by His miracles. Some came because of the testimony of others, and, of course, there is His own welcoming presence among them. If He hadn't been willing to spend time with them and to get into their lives, then very few would have responded to His call.

Which reminds me of a Good News/Bad News story. You've all heard good news/bad news stories, right? Here's one for you:

Gallery Owner:	I have some good news and some bad news.
Artist:	What's the good news?
Gallery Owner:	The good news is that a man came in here today asking if the price of your paintings would go up after you die. When I told him they would he bought every one of your paintings.
Artist:	That's great! What's the bad news?
Gallery Owner:	The bad news is that man was your doctor!

The Gospel, the story of how God saves man, is a Bad news/Good news story, and for that reason it's a comedy and not a tragedy. As one preacher has said: "I can't save you until I've lost you first."

The bad news is that each and every one of us is a sinner who, apart from the grace of God, is dead in his sins and deserves to spend eternity apart from God. But, the good news is that God calls sinners to Himself.

But, that's not the end of the story. You've heard the phrase: "What if they threw a party—and nobody came?" What if God threw the greatest party in the world—the banquet feast of His Son—and nobody came? It's not enough that God calls sinners: sinners must make the choice to come to Jesus, if they are to be saved.

When Jesus called, Matthew came. We don't hear the whole story, but I'm sure Matthew knew his own sins and knew that he could not become a disciple of Jesus without repenting of his sins: the first words of Jesus' public ministry were, *"Repent, for the kingdom of heaven is at hand"* (Matthew 4:17).

Matthew, if he wanted to come to Jesus as a sinner, had to confront his own sin, confess it before His Lord, and follow Jesus. Notice that he left his tax booth to follow Jesus. He turned from his old way of life, and that's true repentance, for repentance is turning in deed and action from your previous sins.

The wonderful thing is that, like Matthew and the fishermen, God is calling each of you to Himself. But, the only way to come is through true repentance from the sin in your life.

There is a sinner I know who felt awful inside, but he didn't know why. He made himself and others miserable, and sometimes he didn't think life was worth living. He knew he should repent and went through the motions, and in some ways truly meant it. But, he effectively deflected true repentance. Finally, he turned completely to God and His mercy and acknowledged that he himself was the main reason he was miserable. He had been carrying this burden of guilt for years, and it had made him a very unlikable person. But, after he had fully confessed, from the heart, his countenance changed. His face became brighter, and he felt as if he were flying! I counseled him to repent every day and to not return to his old ways.

. . .

Jesus Christ is calling a world full of sinners to Himself. And it's your job to respond by coming to Him with true repentance. It's not the repentance that's to be feared: it's the sin! Jesus is calling *you*, a sinner, to Himself today.

Prayer:

Lord Jesus Christ, Son of God, have mercy on me, a sinner. Amen.

(called *The Jesus Prayer*)

Points for Meditation:

1. Do you confess your sins on a daily basis? What would be a good daily time for you to do this?
2. Get quiet for a few moments and listen for the voice of the Lord. Do you hear Him calling to you? What is He saying?

Resolution:

I resolve to listen for the voice of my Master today.

Matthew 9:18–35

So many wonderful choices today! Do I want to be a ruler whose daughter is raised from the dead, a woman whose twelve-year flow of blood is healed, a blind man who sight is restored, or a mute and demon-possessed man who is healed?

How 'bout I get to be all of them!

In a way, I do, because the point of each of these healings is more about Jesus Christ and who He is revealed to be than it is about me. The miracles of Jesus, in fact all parts of the Bible, are first and foremost about Jesus Christ. And today, the Scriptures teach me about a God made man who has power over disease, demons, and even life itself! Only after I understand Jesus can I understand where I am in today's lesson.

I feel as if my bold adventure in writing *Give Us This Day* has been a life lesson in how to interpret the Scriptures. Now I have to begin to look and listen to God's Word in new ways to keep hearing what He wants me to hear. I also have to find the balance between trying to stretch the New Testament out on a procrustean bed so that every passage fits exactly into my life, down to every literal detail, and the other extreme of simply pooh-poohing what Scripture says.

So here we go again. On the one hand, I want desperately to have faith and be healed from every infirmity I have. The Scriptures seem to suggest that if only I had faith, I would be healed from whatever troubles me: *"According to your faith, let it be to you"* (v. 29). On the other hand, I know that I and other faithful Christians aren't always healed. I remember that even St. Paul was not granted that the thorn in his flesh would be removed. Even the Son of God was denied His fervent, sweat-as-blood soaked prayer in the Garden.

And so there must be another way: a holding of the two hands together in prayer. I choose both to have faith *and* to accept that I won't always be healed. The truth is that sometimes I will be healed from my troubles, and other times I won't. Do I have true faith only in the times I'm healed? No! I will have faith both when God heals me and when He doesn't, so that in all things I put my trust in Him. Ironically, it is often in *not* being healed that our faith is demonstrated.

Maybe we should step back a moment and examine the nature of faith. Is faith only faith when the desire of the faithful one has been granted? In that case, was the faith of Abraham null and void because he didn't receive all his promises immediately? Was Paul's or Jesus' faith really faith*less*ness, since their prayers "weren't answered."

You can see that this gets us nowhere fast. Isn't faith a trust in God and His goodness, *regardless* of how things turn out? If so, let me show you how an unanswered prayer might demonstrate a remarkably strong faith.

First, let's assume that the poor slob whose prayer "isn't answered" is, in fact, praying for what he needs. Let's assume further that when he asks, he truly believes that God *can* deliver him and *will*, if it pleases Him. Already, we can see faith in work in such a man.

Now here comes the tricky part. What if God doesn't deliver that man? What are our options? We could posit that the man had no faith, but as we've already seen that isn't always the case. Here's another point: after how much time has passed can we say that God hasn't heard and answered the prayer? Some prayers, such as healing, may be open-ended for quite a long time. Furthermore, is it necessary that every prayer be answered affirmatively? If that were the case, then we'd have to infallibly know what was good for us, so that God would always give us what we asked for.

The only other option is that we must sometimes ask for things that aren't in our best interest. Yes, it would be good for God to heal each and every one of us from every problem we've ever had. But, God doesn't, so He must have something better in mind. This is the way faith thinks, because its basic instinct is to trust in God and His goodness over and against what the flesh and the world might naturally affirm as good.

This is faith in action: to trust in God, *even when, especially when*, sight doesn't affirm God or His goodness.

Let's return to our unhealed man. What might happen if he were healed quickly and easily every time? Given our fallen nature, it would be easy for us to go on our merry way, forgetting God and thinking that we were owed this healing. But what about the unhealed man? If he keeps his faith in God, in spite of not being healed, what great faith that man has!

Faith, once again, trusts in God and His goodness; therefore, faith waits humbly and patiently for the Lord, and it accepts whatever the Lord grants. Faith believes that as long as it trusts in God, whatever the answer is will be something God gives him out of love and goodness.

In this way, whether the prayer is "answered" or not, the prayer of faith is always answered, because God will honor the one who is faithful to Him: "He has filled the hungry with good things." What the prayer of faith ultimately wants is what the Father wants. And that's the whole point of prayer and faith: that we may be united to the will of the Father, regardless of what that will is.

This isn't always the case, mind you, but the saint who has faith in trouble and is not healed may be the saint with the greatest faith of all. He may be one, like Paul and Jesus, whom God loves in a special way. God must believe that ones with faith such as these have a faith so strong that they can withstand a loving "No" from the Father. They are the ones who are driven moment by moment and day by day to the One who can sustain them in their spirit, even if their flesh is decaying. These are the ones who are called to share in their Master's sufferings, as He first suffered for them.

Such a saint may also be the saint who has more than his fair share of prayers "answered" as well! This is because he is one who is learning to trust the Father in all things, and so he finds favor with his Lord.

And so I vow to be faithful to God, to have and to hold Him from this day forward, for better for worse, for richer or for poorer, in sickness and in health, to love and to cherish, for death will not part us.

Prayer:
Lord Jesus Christ, Son of God, have mercy on me, a sinner! Amen.

Points for Meditation:
1. How have you accepted God's "No"s in your life? Is it possible that He intends to bless you through them but you haven't realized it?
2. Meditate on these words from Mother Angelica: "Faith asks, knowing the Father hears us. Hope waits for His reply. Love accepts that reply with joy."

Resolution:
I resolve to ask God for faith during difficult times when He seems to be slow in answering.

Matthew 9:36–10:15

When I was a kid, one of the shows we loved to watch together as a family was *Mission: Impossible*. We loved the way that the Impossible Mission Force were always in some Eastern European country in which they used fake Eastern European accents and the way there were always vehicles that said "Statz Polizei," (i.e., "State Police").

We loved the way that everything was choreographed perfectly, down to the mandatory latex mask one of them would use to pretend to be one of the bad guys.

We especially loved the beginning of the show. Jim Phelps, the leader of the Impossible Mission Force played by Peter Graves, would pull a reel to reel cassette tape recorder out of a car or safe deposit box and begin listening to it. His boss would begin to explain the nature of the latest mission by saying, "Your mission, should you choose to accept it..." And then he would carefully explain what the Impossible Mission Force was being asked to do.

Like the Impossible Mission Force, you, too, have been given an assignment, a mission. Here's how Jesus Himself presents your mission in this morning's lesson from Matthew 9:

"When he saw the crowds, he had compassion for them, because they were harassed and helpless, like sheep without a shepherd. Then he said to his disciples, 'The harvest is plentiful, but the laborers are few; pray therefore the Lord of the harvest to send out laborers into his harvest.' And he called to him his twelve disciples and gave them authority over unclean spirits, to cast them out, and to heal every disease and every infirmity" (vv. 9:36–10:1).

This commission of His to go out and do His will on earth as it is in heaven, which we pray for every day and which He issued here in Matthew, is also the last commission He gave to His disciples. Your mission, therefore, is the mission of the Son to obey the will of the Father; to continue the ministry of Jesus which He continues through us; and to make disciples of all the nations, teaching them to obey the will of the Father as well.

This mission seemed like an Impossible Mission to the disciples. Who were they to heal every disease and infirmity and to cast out demons?

Our mission, to obey the will of the Father, to make disciples, and to teach them to obey the Father, also seems like an Impossible Mission. But, here is where our reality must part from the fiction of the TV show, *Mission: Impossible.* Our mission is a possible one because it is not our mission but that of Jesus Christ. With Him, all things are possible, for all authority has been given to Him, and He shares this authority with us. Secondly, we are not told, "Your mission, *should you choose to accept it...*"No, we are not told, we are *commanded*—"Go and make disciples" and "Go into the harvest."

In Luke's account of the sending out of 70 and their return, the 70 returned with joy because of what they'd seen the Lord do through them. It was important that they shared what they saw God doing with others.

Jesus' response was also important, for when they returned with their report He said, *"I saw Satan fall like lightning from heaven."* (Luke 10:18)

When we obey and go into the harvest and labor, then we will see Satan fall like lightning from heaven. For when we obey, the Kingdom of Heaven comes, and Satan must flee.

In June 2008 I went on the first mission trip of my life, taking a group of teens from St. Andrew's Episcopal Church in Fort Worth, along with a group from All Saints Episcopal Church. Those of us who went from St. Andrew's and All Saints were commissioned by our churches and by the Lord to go in His Name to Belize and minister. In Belize, the harvest is plentiful. There is much work to be done. Jesus has compassion on the people of Belize because they are harassed and helpless and like sheep without a shepherd.

When we got to Belize, I had the distinct sense that God had already been there—and so He was. In Belize, we saw Satan fall like lightning from heaven, because we saw God at work there.

The young people we took saw Him as they labored with their hands and wood, like their Master, the carpenter. They saw God at work in learning to work together as a team with others to help put up a building. That building soon became a completed library and computer lab for the 450 kids who go to Holy Cross Anglican School.

Others saw God when they assisted the teachers and filled in for them and gave them a break. It was difficult work: without the teacher being active, the kids quickly began to spread all over the room. Some of the girls also saw God by cleaning dishes for a few hours one day. I don't think they were too thrilled to be doing it, but they learned the meaning of service and what the women at

Holy Cross went through every day, six days a week, with no vacations. I think they learned compassion.

 I had quite a few encounters with God myself, as I saw Him at work. It was thrilling to see our youth serving and learning. All of us saw God at work in the lives of Vernon and Frances Wilson, who established Holy Cross School just a few years ago. Vernon and Francis taught all of us what God can do with just two people obeying Him. Because of their faithfulness, mission team after mission team is now coming to serve in San Pedro, Belize. Through their work at Holy Cross, they are helping to transform the educational system of the entire country!

One night, I was talking to a man with dreadlocks who played reggae music and called himself the Lyrical King who told me that a man he was talking to wanted to talk to me.

The first words out of this man's mouth were: "I just got out of prison. What should I do?"

From there, I had an opportunity to tell the man, whose name was Russian (which he pronounced "Roo-shon"), about God and that he needed to find a church. We talked a long time, and I prayed with him. I also gave him some of our leftover pizza and my Bible, which he carried with him everywhere the next few days. He told me that he had been praying that God would lead him to someone to talk to—and God led him to me.

The Sunday we were there, I was privileged to preach at the Holy Communion. It was the first communion service they had had there since December!

Sunday, after church, I was walking on the beach, still wearing my collar, and someone on the beach by a wall in front of a cemetery called out, "Father!"

I went over and asked the man, whose name was Oscar, how he was doing. He said, politely, "I'm doing good." He paused a second and then added, "I'm not doing good. Three years ago I had a good job, a car, a wife, and kids. But, I lost them all."

I asked how.

"To alcohol," he said. He said that he prayed to Jesus but that He never answered, which gave me an opportunity to talk to him about God's love and about his responsibility. I talked to Oscar for about 20 minutes, prayed with him, and told him that he must find a church to help him. He had three friends sitting in front of the cemetery with him, in various stages of inebriation. For the next two days

I stopped by to talk to all the guys on the wall in front of the cemetery every time I happened to pass by and saw them.

And so I'm here to tell you that when we were in Belize we saw Satan fall like lightning from heaven, because we saw God working to establish His kingdom—in Belize, and in our lives.

It was, as the people of Belize like to say, "Unbelizeable!"

What made these things possible?

1. We spent time praying and readying our hearts to serve God and see Him in Belize.

2. We left behind our normal routines and riches, our media and our expectations, and went as servants, ready to do whatever was asked of us.

3. Every evening we'd gather together to pray and to share with one another the answer to three questions: What was good that day? What was challenging? and Where did I see God at work today?

But, Fort Worth—and wherever you live—is also the harvest, and your town is the harvest for you. Jesus has compassion on the people of your city because they are harassed and helpless and like sheep without a shepherd. Belize is just a more dramatic version of what happens daily here in my town and in your town—if only we would see. God is there at work every bit as much as He is in Belize—if only we would stop and see it.

The Possible Mission for all of us is to obey the Lord when He sends us into the harvest to do His will, and to look for Him and where He is at work. To do this, we'll all need to do the same three things we did to help us see God in Belize.

1. Prepare to see Him. Get and keep the heart of a servant.

2. Get rid of distractions. Don't let your weekly routine become an excuse for not seeing God. Don't get so addicted to your conveniences and gadgets and leisure that you lose the heart of a servant. Make time to see God every day.

3. Share God with others when you see Him at work, for He comes to you every day and in many ways.

Mission: Impossible was a memorable TV show because it was filled with heroism and adventure. One of the great contributions to Western civilization made by the late night comedian, Conan O'Brien, was his discovery that even the most ordinary and mundane daily activities could be made to seem exciting and adventurous if the *Mission: Impossible* music is played while you're doing it. In a similar way, the Christian life is to be lived as if the *Mission: Impossible* music is playing in the background!

Your Possible Mission—and you *should* choose to accept it—is to listen for the Lord's command and to go and labor in His Kingdom. Your Mission each day this week is to share with at least one other person where you saw God and where you saw Satan being cast down.

The harvest is truly plentiful, but the laborers are few. Therefore, pray the Lord of the harvest to send out laborers into His harvest.

Prayer:

Heavenly Father, we pray, according to the words of your Son, to the Lord of the harvest to send laborers into his vineyard. We earnestly beg you to bless all those who love You fervently and who gladly and courageously spend their lives in service to Your Son's Church under the guidance of the Holy Spirit. We pray that their lives may always be centered on our Lord Jesus and that they may be devoted sons and daughters of God in making You known and loved, and that they may attain Heaven. Teach us all to look for and find You every day, and having found You, to share You with others. We ask this though the mercies of Your only begotten Son, with whom You are blessed, together with Your all holy, gracious, and life creating Spirit, now and ever and forever. Amen.

(Adapted from a Roman Catholic prayer for Vocations)

Points for Meditation:
1. Practice looking for God today, even in small things. Keep a list throughout the day. Where did you see Him? Were you surprised in any way?
2. Make a point to share where you saw God today or recently with one (or more!) person. What do you notice about this person's reaction? Did he find your sharing the Lord encouraging?

Resolution:
I resolve to look for God today and to share with at least one person where I have seen Him today.

Matthew 10:16-31

I feel like Jonah running away. I saw what today's lesson was in Matthew 10 and ran smack dab in the middle of the difficult sayings of Jesus. I thought about talking only about verses 30 and 31—they seemed pretty safe.

Whenever Jesus spends time with His disciples, He gives them a radical call: to deny self, to give up the world, and to give up *everything* for Him. The original call that Jesus gave to the first disciples meant that they had to leave their jobs and homes, follow immediately, and trust only in Him.

In Matthew 10, He calls them again, this time to proclaim Him to others and to act in His name. This is the same radical call He gives to each of you, as His disciple. This doesn't sound so radical does it? What could be so dangerous about simply saying, "I'm a Christian, and I'm here to offer you God and His love"?

Here's how Jesus proclaims His call to us, in verse 27: "*Whatever I tell you in the dark, speak in the light, and what you hear in the ear, preach on the housetops.*"

What is this preaching from the housetops, and why does Jesus give such dire predictions about persecution that will accompany this action? For those whom Jesus sent out, preaching from the housetops meant that they were to preach in His name, heal diseases, and cast out demons.

But, there would be resistance and persecution: Jesus Christ is an offense to those who are perishing and don't want to give up themselves to God. He's an affront to the idea that "I'm O.K. and that all religions, beliefs, and behaviors are the same," and He's a challenge to the kingdom of man that resides deep in each human heart.

And so Jesus warns His disciples in verse 16, saying, "*I send you out as sheep among wolves.*" In verse 17, He tells them that they will be delivered up to synagogues and councils and scourged (as He would be). "*You will be hated by all for my name's sake,*" He plainly states in verse 22.

How's that for rallying the troops? How did they respond to this difficult call, knowing what they would face? They faithfully preached from the housetops, especially after the coming of the Holy Spirit.

Acts 2:36 (Peter): "*Therefore let all the house of Israel know assuredly that God has made this Jesus, whom you crucified, both Lord and Christ.*"

Acts 3:16 (Peter and John, after healing a man): *"And His name, through faith in His name, has made this man strong, whom you see and know."*

Acts 4:20 (Peter and John, when commanded not to speak in name of Christ): *"Whether it is right in the sight of God to listen to you more than to God, you judge. For we cannot but speak the things which we have seen and heard."*

The end for almost all of the apostles was martyrdom.

But, what does preaching from the housetops mean for us? Jesus' meaning isn't literal, but it also isn't meaningless. Preaching from the housetops means making Jesus Christ known to the people in our lives. It might be best to think of making a small start. Why not proclaim Jesus Christ to your spouse and your kids? Why not preach Him to your brothers and sisters in Christ? They need to hear about Him and have Him in their lives every day.

Once we broaden the concept of "preaching Jesus" from the housetops to include all that we might say about Jesus to all who have ears to hear, our job becomes much larger, more glorious, and more comprehensible. Instead of "preaching Jesus" being only the words that will get someone to say the Sinner's Prayer, preaching Jesus is any time we proclaim Him and His Kingdom *to anyone*. In fact, the number one place that Jesus Christ is proclaimed or preached is in the Church, among believers!

When we practice this, then maybe we'll be encouraged to preach Jesus to other people we know well. Every once in a while, when we are filled with Christ in our ears and hearts, we'll want to preach Him to acquaintances or strangers, some of whom do not know Him.

What can we expect if we truly preach from the housetops? You won't be delivered up to council or synagogues, and it's not likely you'll be thrown into prison. But, you may have people look at you funny. Friends or work associates may back away from you a little bit.

What, then, will make us want to preach from the housetops? Here's something for starters: *"Therefore whoever confesses Me before men, him I will also confess before My Father who is in heaven. But whoever denies Me before men, him I will also deny before My Father who is in heaven"* (vv. 32–33). What motivates some men may be the stick: that Christ will deny me if I deny Him. But what motivates me much more is the divine carrot: that if I preach Him from the housetops, He'll announce and proclaim me in a higher place—Heaven!

What will make us preach Jesus Christ from the housetops? It's knowing that He has and continues to faithfully proclaim us to the Father in Heaven. What makes me want to preach Him is that He lives within me. Finally, one day, I hope to hear (even in this life) those most blessed of words: *"Well done thou good and faithful servant"* (Matthew 25:21, 23).

-------------------------------- • --

Prayer:

Father, I thank You that I can approach Your throne room with confidence because Jesus Christ, my High Priest, proclaims me before You day and night. I praise You, Jesus, because You made the good confession on my behalf. I ask You Spirit, that You might be for me the Spirit of Christ that I may want to follow my Master in all things, especially in preaching the Truth from the housetops. Amen.

Points for Meditation:

1. Who are some people God is asking me to speak to Jesus Christ about? Remember: it can be someone who is already a Christian. How might I speak about Jesus Christ to this person? (There are many ways of doing this.)
2. What keeps me from more boldly preaching Jesus? Is it fear? Or is it that I don't know Him well enough and am not passionate enough about Him?

Resolution:

I resolve to preach Jesus Christ intentionally to one person today.

Matthew 10:32–11:1

"Behold, I send you out as sheep in the midst of wolves" (v. 16).

"Whatever I tell you in the dark, speak in the light; and what you hear in the ear, preach on the housetops" (v. 27).

"And do not fear those who kill the body but cannot kill the soul. But rather fear Him who is able to destroy both soul and body in hell" (v. 28).

"He who does not take his cross and follow after Me is not worthy of Me" (v. 38).

"He who receives you, receives Me" (v. 40).

As I reflect on the second half of Matthew 10, both yesterday's lesson and today's, I see several important truths converging, truths represented in the verses I quoted above. Here's what I see:

1. Jesus sends us out to do what He did and preach what He preached. We are His representatives here on earth.

2. We will face opposition if we do what He did and preach what He preached. This is because we are truly united to Him and participate in Him.

3. If we are not willing to bear what He bore and take up our cross and follow Him in all things, we're not worthy of Him.

I talked yesterday about some of the things that will motivate us to follow Jesus and obey Him. In a strange way, I find the cost of the cross highly motivating. But it isn't for the sake of suffering or misery by itself that I'm motivated: it's that I've come to realize that there is no Christ without a Cross. There's no way around it: no Cross, no Christ.

But, rather than wail and moan over the coming persecution and suffering, I welcome the Cross of Christ when it comes into my life. It's one of the ways I know I'm a Christian: one willing to pick up his cross and follow Jesus. Why? Because Jesus and His Cross is attached to my own personal cross, and His Cross is none other than the way of life.

I'm not too crazy about the suffering part of the Cross: I'd just as soon have Jesus without it. But I know that to be united to the one who bore my sins and the painful penalty for them I must participate in that painful redemption that is the Cross. I also know that with the Cross comes the Resurrection, and with my every cross comes my own resurrection, sometimes even in this life.

What motivates me about the Cross is that it is the point at which God and I meet every day.

You all remember how Jesus Christ carried His cross. His Cross wasn't just His Cross: it was yours and mine. He carried your Cross for you when you couldn't carry it. And now He's asking you to carry His cross. And *this* is the Cross of Jesus that He has asked you to carry: that you, His disciple, become like Him, the Master; that as He died for you, so you die to yourself for Him; that as He gave up His life for you, so you give up your life for Him; and that as He faithfully confessed you before His Father, so you would faithfully preach Him from the housetops.

We are called to be Simon of Cyrenes, only we're not forced to carry a cross by the Romans: we've been *asked by the Master* to carry *His* Cross.

Prophets often have strange visions. Well, I've had one. Oh, it wasn't a vision like Ezekiel's, of strange spinning wheels and creatures with multiple heads and wings (much as I'd like to see that).

My vision is this: that when I say we are to carry the Cross of Christ, I'm not just saying that we should carry His Cross, as if it's simply a physical object outside of Him or us: I'm saying that we are to carry Jesus Christ Himself, and that He *is* our Cross. I see a picture, but it's not of me carrying the Old Rugged Cross, as if it were just a rough piece of wood, from which I might imagine I get a few splinters every now and then.

No, I see all of us together carrying the image of Jesus Christ within us, individually and together. It's *through* us that people will hear and see God—or not at all. For Christ, through the Holy Spirit, truly lives in us!

We are Christophers: "Christ-bearers." This is what it means to be a "Christian"—to be a bearer of Jesus Christ, *who is our Cross to bear.*

If we do this, we will be persecuted to some degree, and we will suffer. When we boldly proclaim Jesus Christ, some people will come after us. In *Mere Christianity*, St. Lewis said the following about bearing Jesus Christ:

> "But above all, He works on us through each other. Men are mirrors, or 'carriers' of Christ to other men...But usually it is those who know Him that bring Him to others. That is why the Church, the whole body of Christians showing

Him to one another, is so important...(p. 190) The Church exists for nothing else but to draw men into Christ, to make them little Christs. If they are not doing that, all the cathedrals, clergy, missions, sermons, even the Bible itself, are simply a waste of time. God became Man for no other purpose. It is even doubtful, you know, whether the whole universe was created for any other purpose" (p. 199). [3]

But, praise God He does not ask you to answer this call alone. All of the pronouns in this passage of Matthew referring to the radical call to discipleship—*are in the plural*—not the singular. You (*plural*) are being sent out among wolves and you (*plural*) are to preach Jesus from the housetops. Jesus didn't just send you to preach from the housetops: He sent His army, the Church.

And so we carry the Cross of Christ *together*, as His Body, filling up in our flesh what is lacking in the afflictions of Christ. We do this for the sake of His Body, which is the Church, of which we became ministers according to the steward-ship from God which was given to us. We fulfill the Word of God, the mystery which has been hidden from the ages and from generations, but now has been revealed to His saints!

Hear what Jesus our Master says to us this morning: "*He who does not take his cross and follow me is not worthy of me*" (v. 38).

He is telling you and me, "I am your Cross to bear, and through me, you will carry my life of salvation and be a blessing to everyone you meet. And if you confess me before men, I will surely confess you before My Father in heaven."

---

3   C.S. Lewis, *Mere Christianity* (San Francisco: HarperSanFrancisco, 2001).

Prayer:

Lord Jesus, who willingly bore my cross for me, help me to hear Your command today to carry Your Cross for you. By Your grace, enable me to have the strength to accept and pick up whatever it is today that You have sovereignly prepared for me to bear. Remind me that in so doing I am bearing not only my cross but also Yours. May I see You and be with You through this daily cross, which I gladly pick up today for You. Amen.

Points for Meditation:

1. How can you take up your cross today so that you may follow Jesus?
2. What price might you have to pay for faithfully preaching Jesus Christ, that is, proclaiming Him through every part of your life?
3. How might you be a Christ-bearer today?

Resolution:

I resolve to find one way today to be a bearer of Christ and His Cross.

Matthew 11:2–19

"Are you the Coming One, or do we look for another?" (v. 3)

It seems like a clear and straightforward question. I don't know why, but I expect a clear and straightforward answer, you know, something like: "Yes, I am Jesus, the Messiah, the Coming One, the King of the Jews, the Son of God, Yahweh. Any other questions?"

But, as He almost always does, Jesus surprises me. What He actually says is, *"Go and tell John the things which you hear and see: the blind see and the lame walk; the lepers are cleansed and the deaf hear; the dead are raised up and the poor have the gospel preached to them"* (v. 4).

That's an odd answer. Jesus doesn't say anything about Himself—or does He?

What He doesn't say is what I want or expect Him to say, or, at least, not *how* I want Him to say it. What are John the Baptist's followers to think of Jesus' answer? He doesn't answer directly who He is but tells them to tell John the things which they have seen and heard. Apparently, seeing and hearing what Jesus did should make us understand who He is.

Who is it that can make the blind see and the lame walk, cleanse the lepers and raise the dead, and preach the gospel to the poor? I think you have your answer. The intriguing thing is that it was the things John had heard in prison about the works of Christ (verse 2) that made him inquire into the person of Christ to begin with.

There's something here: I can smell it. There's something important here about Jesus and how God works in the world, and I want to know about it.

One of the explanations I've heard about why Jesus answers John so obliquely is that He knows that if He openly proclaims Himself to be the Messiah, the King of the Jews, then Herod might want to hunt Him down. This was true not only about Herod but also, perhaps, the Pharisees and scribes. So Jesus has to reveal Himself obliquely.

But, maybe there's another reason as well. When I consider my life and this world, I feel like John the Baptist may have felt. I ask to see God, and the answer I usually get is something like the answer Jesus gave John. What I mean is that I don't get the obvious answer, "Here I am, my son. I will make myself as bright as the sun to you and as near and obvious as your own hands. I will fill you with the best feelings today and will make life easy on you. You will hear my voice loud and clear when I speak to you, and I will stand before you and have my glory and goodness pass before you."

What I get instead is a small, still voice telling me to go out and seek God today. I have heard about Jesus, and He is telling me that I will find Him today in what He does, just as He told John. But, there's a twist: I won't see the blind see or the lame walk today. The lepers will probably not be cleansed, and the deaf may not hear. The dead will most certainly be raised (in some manner), but I won't see it.

God makes us look for Him every day: He doesn't waltz in, announce Himself, start throwing miracles around like confetti, and sit back and wait for everyone to be overwhelmed and believe in Him.

No, one of the things God wants from me today is faith. He wants me to see Him in the small things and believe in Him through the invisible things. He wants me to prove faithful to Him today by going out and working for my manna. Faith will not walk to me on its own, as if I'm not supposed to be an active participant in this faith business and this work of finding God on earth. I'm at the center of this activity because God wants to involve me in His work!

What I want is the Land of Cockaigne. What God gives me is a heaven-filled earth. (Here's Breughel's *The Land of Cockaigne*. [Look closely at the egg on legs!]) http://www.abcgallery.com/B/bruegel/bruegel116.html)

I'm supposed to go out every day and find my daily bread, for which I first must pray, because God wants to involve me in His story, His life, and His work. I cannot be a passive spectator, or else I will remain an atheist or agnostic or merely part of the inanimate setting. I must actively seek Him, which means looking and listening for Him.

One other implication of this looking and listening is that as a Christian I must be involved in doing God's work, even as I eagerly seek Him each day. As I look and listen for Him, I must be so involved in His life and work that He can use me to help others see and hear Him through His works. Remember: it was what John had heard about the works of Christ that caused him to inquire about Christ. And remember that Jesus' answer about Himself was for John's followers to tell John what they had heard and seen.

As I participate in the work of God, two miraculous things happen. First, others are enabled to see and hear God. This is true both for the things I do and the things I say. After all, one of the works of Jesus by which He is demonstrated to be God is that the poor have the gospel preached to them.

But, something else miraculous happens as well. As I participate in God's work, *I* am the chief person who gets to see and hear God! We don't see and hear God so much from the outside but from the inside, from a life that has become one with His life.

Haven't you noticed this before? If you sit around and wait for God to come to you, He sometimes delays, but if you actively go out and seek Him, He has a miraculous way of showing up! When you sit around and seek God only by yourself, He seems to be a shadow. But, when you share Him with others, through what you say and do, and others share Him with you, the shadow becomes substance, and the hazy black and white is turned to Technicolor.

We are not merely auditory or visual learners about God but instead learn in a multi-sensory, multi-faculty, whole-person way.

God could simply tell us who He is. But, we might not believe Him. But, when He *shows* us, by involving us in His story, His life, and His work, then we truly begin to see and believe—and so do others!

Prayer:

Father of light, in You is found no shadow of change but only the fullness of life and limitless truth. Open our hearts to the voice of Your Word and free us from the original darkness that shadows our vision. Restore our sight that we may look upon Your Son who calls us to repentance and a change of heart, for He lives and reigns with You for ever and ever. Amen.

(Roman Catholic prayer for 2nd Sunday in Lent)

Points for Meditation:

1. Where could you look for God today, perhaps in places you haven't been looking?
2. How can you look and listen for God today by your words and deeds or the words and deeds of someone in your life?

Resolution:

I resolve to cultivate an attitude today of actively looking and listening for God.

Matthew 11:20-30

"Come unto Me, all ye that travail and are heavy laden, and I will refresh you" (v. 28).

Those who are used to the traditional Book of Common Prayer will recognize this verse as one of the four Comfortable Words that are said by the priest to the congregation after the General Confession of Sin and Absolution.

And so, after hearing the difficult words of Jesus earlier in the chapter and in chapter 10, and bearing my own cross this day, I'm ready for the Comfy Words. I'm ready to hear, "Come to Me, all you who labor and are heavy laden, and I will give you rest." I want to hear more, and so I make the mistake of continuing to read. And what do I hear? "Take My yoke upon you and learn from Me."

Huh? What's this about a yoke? That sounds like something heavy, it sounds like something hard to do. It sounds suspiciously like, *"He who does not take his cross and follow after Me is not worthy of Me"* (Matthew 10:38) and *"If anyone desires to come after Me, let him deny himself, and take up his cross, and follow Me"* (Matthew 16:24).

I suspect that there's a cross lurking somewhere around this promised rest. And there is, so let's go right for it and embrace it, for there's no use denying it or avoiding it. There truly is a yoke to take upon you, as Jesus says, and that yoke is the cross of Christ. But, what is this cross to me?

It's an instrument of the punishment for my sins. It's the instrument of death by which my Lord and Master and God was crucified and died. And so it's a painful reminder to me of my own sins and of the suffering my Savior bore for me.

But, there's something else. This cruel instrument of death is also the most common and famous symbol of Jesus Christ and Christians. Why would that be? There must be more to this cross than simply suffering and death.

This cross is also the holy place and time at which my God took my sins upon Himself, and so it's transformed for me into the Tree of Life, the place and time at which my Master gave His life for mine.

And so this cross must also become my cross, for on it I am united to Jesus Christ, both in His death and in His life. It is my cross as well because on it the old man in me must be crucified and put to death so that the new man may live in me. On this cross, as my Lord gave Himself up for me, I must now give myself up for Him. And so I must take up this cross daily, for it's how I take Him up.

It is a cross, it is a yoke, and it is something to bear. There are times when I don't feel like bearing it. But, that's only because I've forgotten the proper way to carry it, and that's *with* Him, and not by myself.

It turns out that this yoke is indeed easy, and my burden is light because He is with me carrying it with me, if only I'll let Him. Once I allow Him to carry it, my life becomes light again because it turns out that I'm really the source of my own burdens after all. *I'm* the reason that life is so heavy, because I interpret my life apart from Him and try to live it without Him. And *that* is a hard and heavy thing!

But, when I take up His yoke, which is His cross, which is Him, I find rest. Rest from my worries and rest from my fears. When I give up myself and take Him up, I remember my eternal destiny, which is to be with Him, and I remember that I can be with Him right now, if only I'll take up His yoke.

When I take up His yoke I find rest because I can finally rest from myself and all my labors. I am constantly doing things by myself and for myself, and that makes my life heavy. Even as a Christian I find myself constantly laboring and groaning with toil, mostly because I think that it's up to me to keep the yoke of the Law. But, when I learn from Him to give myself up to the Father, I find rest for my soul again.

Let me explain it to me this way. There is, indeed, a weight, a cost, to giving myself up to God. It's not that this weight or cost ever goes away in this life. But, when I take on the yoke of Jesus, it becomes light, as His labor for the Father must have been light, even when it was objectively heavy.

It's like the burden a husband would feel if he were carrying his unconscious wife in his arms as he fled from their burning house. She might be heavy in his arms, but he would not interpret her as a burden or as heavy. Why? Because love makes even the heaviest burden light.

And that's how we are to feel when we take Jesus Christ and put Him on us, who is our spiritual armor and our new skin.

"Come to Me, all you who labor and are heavy laden, and I will give you rest" Jesus says. "Take My yoke upon you and learn from Me." Give up the yokes you have chosen to place on yourself, and put Jesus Christ on today instead. No matter what that human yoke is, it's time to give it up for the yoke of Christ, the yoke of love for which you were created.

Is it a yoke of money and worry? Is it a yoke of not feeling good enough or moral enough? Maybe it's the yoke of worldliness: that you are so consumed by your To Do Lists that you never have time for the yoke of prayer and coming to Christ. Maybe it's the yoke of guilt that needs to be removed or the yoke of past pain. Whatever your personal yoke is, take it off today and take His yoke upon yourself instead. For His yoke is easy and His burden is light, because He is in them, and He makes them so.

Some have said that when Jesus says, "My yoke is easy," He means "My yoke fits well." His yoke fits well, because you are a Christian, and His yoke is your yoke. You could even say that we are yoked together with Jesus, sharing His cross, sharing His labor, and most importantly of all—sharing His life.

Now—where's that yoke? I'm ready to take it upon me.

Prayer:
Father, I come to You today, accepting Your love that sent Your only-begotten Son into the world that I might not perish but have everlasting life. I take on myself today Your Son, Jesus Christ, who is the propitiation of my sins and my advocate before You each day. I come to You today, Father, through Jesus Christ, seeking the rest that only He can give me. Amen.

Points for Meditation:
1. What human yokes are you bearing today?
2. What might you do to come to Jesus and replace that yoke with the one He wants to give you?

Resolution:
I resolve to find one way to take off all my other yokes today and to put on Jesus Christ instead.

Matthew 12:1–13

What are we to do with the Sabbath? Jesus actually has some things to say about the Sabbath, although mostly He teaches about it indirectly.

This is a question that has vexed Christians for 2000 years. At one extreme, Christians have insisted that there is just about nothing we can do on the Sabbath, except go to church services. No work, no card games, no dancing, no reading of novels, no temporal pleasures, no parish gatherings called "church-ales," no sports! It reminds me of a sign I saw once on a piece of property near Tyler, Texas meant, presumably, to chase away trespassers. On a white board in crude red letters was written:

"No hunting
   No fishing
      No nothing!"

At the other extreme we have contemporary attitudes toward the Sabbath. There's still a consensus that Christians should go to church on Sunday, but even that is eroding to some degree. Business as usual, get out of church as quickly as possible to go to the greener outdoor temple of 18 holes, and spend as much leisure time as possible because today is mine.

The idea of the Lord's Day, or the Christian Sabbath, is just one of many Christian doctrines that's overdue for a re-examination.

I want to begin with two basic assumptions, and then work from there. My first assumption is that God has hallowed time and set apart special or holy times. He is the one who created in six days and rested on the seventh day, a principle upon which He established the Sabbath in the Mosaic Law and a principle which He has never revoked. God has hallowed the Sabbath, although for the Christian the Sabbath is no longer the 7th day but is now the 8th day or the day of the new creation, the Lord's Day.

This is because Sunday, the Lord's Day, is the Day of the Resurrection. The first Christians worshiped together as the Church on Sunday for this reason, something they've been doing for 2000 years. So there is, in fact, something special about Sunday.

My second assumption is that the primary thing that Christians have done on Sunday that makes it special is to celebrate the Resurrection. A corollary to my second assumption is that the primary way Christians have celebrated the Lord's Day from the beginning was to celebrate the Eucharist or Lord's Supper. (This is well-established by church history: it is not my invention or that of the Roman Catholic Church.) In fact, this coming together as the Body of Christ to receive the Body and Blood of Christ and be fed by Him and made into Him is the most important thing we do each week.

Even for churches where weekly communion is not the norm, the weekly coming together as the Body of Christ to worship Him and celebrate the Resurrection is the most important thing you will do this week.

But, what happens before the 10:30 service, and what happens after 11:45? These are questions that few Christians ever think about. I'd like to suggest a few things, based on my prior two assumptions.

Traditionally, since the Lord's Supper was weekly, Christians spent part of Saturday evening and Sunday morning preparing themselves to meet with God and partake of the Body and Blood of Jesus Christ. There would be a time of examination and a quieting of the soul. Often, no food would be taken on Sunday morning until after the Body and Blood of Christ were consumed. A confession of sin would be made, as well as a reconciliation of any broken relationships and a preparation of the body and soul to meet God with fear and reverence.

How do *we* traditionally prepare for our worship services? Get up at the last possible moment, throw the kids in the car, and pile into the pew the way the Simpsons pile into their couch at the beginning of every episode.

How do we leave the service? We may spend a few moments making a few social connections, but then it's time for lunch and getting onto the real business of our many hours of Sunday leisure (let's not forget the Cowboys game or tee time!)

I've often wondered how long the half-life of the average sermon is, as one marker of our approach to worship. When I was at St. Andrew's in Fort Worth, the priests were expected to spend many hours each work preparing the sermon for the main Sunday morning service. What's the half-life of the sermon in the soul of the average parishioner? In science, the half-life is the time it takes for half of a radioactive substance to decay into its non-radioactive relative. Colloquially, the "half-life" of something is used to mean how long that thing effectively exists.

For most Christians, I'll wager that the sermon is effectively forgotten by the time the church service is over. A few hardier Christians may have a few pieces of sermon confetti drifting through their minds by the time the service is ended. How many of us actually *do* something with the sermon once we've left the church building and gotten into our cars?

Does what we have heard and experienced on Sunday morning, and not just the sermon, have a lasting effect on us? Will it, if we rush immediately from it and treat the final "Amen" as a punctuation mark that ends our participation with the Lord that week?

If we are really fed by Jesus Christ in our worship service, why has He fed us? Aren't we supposed to do something with that divine energy and life that He so graciously gives us? Since Sunday is a feast day, even during the fasting season of Lent, I take it that Sunday is a good day to feast. But, are we feasting because Jesus has risen from the dead and raised us with Him into heaven, or because now the remainder of the sacred weekend is ours to do with what we will?

The Son of Man is Lord of the Sabbath, and that means something.

Jesus Christ rose from the dead on Sunday, the Lord's Day, and that means something, too.

When we partake of the Holy Communion, we feed upon Jesus Christ, and that means something.

The Lord made the Sabbath for man and created it good. Let's use it in a way that would be very good for both our bodies and our souls.

Prayer: (A Prayer Before Entering a Church)

As for me, I will come into Thy house, even upon the multitude of Thy mercy; and in Thy fear will I worship towards Thy holy Temple.

O Lord, hear the voice of my humble petitions, when I cry unto Thee; when I hold up my hands toward the mercy-seat of Thy holy Temple. We wait for Thy loving-kindness, O God, in the midst of Thy Temple.

Be mindful of the brethren who are present, and join together in prayer with us now: Remember their devotion and their zeal. Be mindful of them also who upon good cause are absent: And have mercy upon them and us, according to the multitude of Thy mercies, O Lord.

We bless Thee for our Godly Princes, ordained ministers, and for the founders of this Thy holy habitation.

Glory be to Thee, O Lord, glory be to Thee; glory be to Thee, because Thou hast glorified them; for and with whom we also glorify Thee.

Let Thine eyes be open, and Thine ears graciously attend, to hear the prayer which Thy servant prayeth in this place, wherein Thy Name is called upon.

Woe is me, I have sinned against Thee, O Lord, I have sinned against Thee: O how evilly have I done; And yet Thou hast not requited me, according to my sins.

But I am ashamed, And turn from my wicked ways, And return to my own heart, And with all my heart I return to Thee, And seek Thy face; And pray unto Thee: saying, I have sinned, I have done perversely, I have committed wickedness; Lord, I know the plague of my own heart, and, behold, I return unto Thee with all my heart, and with all my might.

And now, O Lord, in Thy dwelling place, the glorious throne of Thy kingdom in heaven, hear the prayer and supplication of Thy servant. And be merciful unto Thy servant, and heal his soul. I dare not so much as lift up mine eyes unto heaven, But standing afar off, I smite upon my breast, And say with the publican, God be merciful to me a sinner. To me, a greater sinner than the publican, be merciful as to the publican. The earnest desire of man shall be to Thy praise, and the continuance of that desire shall hold a festival to Thee. Amen.

(From the Private Prayers of Lancelot Andrewes)

Points for Meditation:

1. What are some ways in which you could better prepare for the Sunday worship service?
2. What are some ways you could use the Lord's Day (after worship) more profitably?

Resolution:

I resolve to prepare more adequately for the Sunday worship service this week.

Matthew 12:14–30

This Jesus is a mystery!

He must have especially seemed a mystery to the first century Jews who encountered Him. He does miracles that make people believe in Him, but when people demand a miracle, He doesn't do one. He does spectacular, divine things, and then He warns you not to tell anyone about what He's done—as if you could contain it within in you, as if people aren't going to hear anyway, as if one who is God doesn't want everyone to know just yet.

He heals and teaches in a way that only God could do, but He comes as a servant and not as a King. And yet He says that He's a King with a kingdom, and one that He says is in our midst! He does and teaches good, and for this He is persecuted and hunted down like an animal.

This Jesus is a mystery!

And here He is 2000 years later, again demanding that we make sense of Him, demanding that we take a stand: for "He who is not with Me is against Me, and he who does not gather with Me scatters abroad" (verse 30).

It won't do to answer the way that most modern people answer the mystery of Jesus: that he's a good teacher and good man who teaches basically what all other good teachers and religions teach. This simply isn't true. No other teachers, except for His disciples, dare to say that He is fully God, as He Himself claimed to be and demonstrated Himself to be. Neither Confucius nor Buddha, neither Mohammed nor the Dalai Lama have healed miraculously or turned water into wine or fed 5000 with so little food or raised someone from the dead or been raised from the dead themselves.

I know who Jesus is: He is the Son of God, God incarnate, and the Savior of the world. And yet He is still a mystery to me.

I believe that He is God Almighty; I believe that He performed the miracles that are recorded of Him; I believe that He has power over disease and nature and demons and even life itself. I've read and heard all of these accounts of Him.

And yet there are times when He seems to hide Himself from me as well. There are times when, in spite of what I know, He seems to not want to make Himself known to me. There are times when I seem worn down by life or exhausted or blah beyond the point of feeling.

These are the times when I myself am the mystery: one who has a deep faith in my Lord Jesus and yet can't really sense or experience Him.

"Where," I ask "is the power and the glory of the Strong One who has bound the evil strong man and entered his house, and the One whose kingdom came with the glory of angels and miracles?" Why is there still suffering, and why do I still sin if the Holy Spirit dwells within me? How can men be both so beautiful and so ugly? On and on the mystery drones, like some freak out jam session from an over-bloated 1968 psychedelic rock album.

I become as the blind and mute man in Matthew 12. In this chapter, the blind and mute man is brought by others to Jesus to be healed, and he finds healing. In this chapter of my life, I will bring myself to Jesus to find healing once again. This is my advantage over the blind and lame men in the Gospels: they have to wait for others to bring them to Jesus, but I can come to Him any time I want.

Even, especially, when I can't see or feel Jesus, I can come to Him and ask Him to heal me, to show Himself to me once again.

And I know that He will do it. But, precisely because He has already driven the evil strong man out of my life I have the confidence that even if He chooses to reveal Himself to me slowly that He will show Himself to me in His time. And I know that even in my most blind, deaf, and dumb moments He will not abandon me. I know that He has the power over my every disease and weakness, over my blindness and numbness, and over my life. And if He chooses to hide Himself and help me in invisible and intangible ways, I'll be content with that, for I know Him, even when He hides Himself in the shadows of the earth and in the dark places of my life.

I know what to do, for I know *who* this mystery is. I *know* Jesus, mysterious though He is. Therefore, even, *especially*, at my darkest, weakest moments, I will seek Him and His healing.

Knowing Him, I choose, as well, to trust whatever it is that He gives me today. Even if it seems like too little to me, I know that He will give me exactly what I need, if only I ask Him.

Here I am, Lord, though I can't see you or feel you very well today. Here I am, a mystery even to myself. Here I am. Be merciful to me, and hear my prayer. Give me what I need today: give me Yourself, and I will be happy.

Prayer:

Here I am, Lord, although I can't see you or feel you very well today. Here I am, a mystery even to myself. Here I am. Be merciful to me, and hear my prayer. Give me what I need today: give me yourself, and I will be happy. Amen.

Points for Meditation:

1. What are the implications of the fact that the Kingdom of God has already come and that Jesus has already bound the strong man Satan?
2. What is your response when God seems to hide Himself from you? What would be the best response to such times?

Resolution:

I resolve to ask God to loose whatever it is that is binding me today that I might see Him and know Him better.

Matthew 12:31–50

A lot of attention is paid to the Holy Family, especially at Christmas, and right-fully so. Mary, in particular, gets an extra measure of devotion from both Roman Catholics and Orthodox Christians.

And so today I want to talk about the Holy Family, which is the family of God. I can't say that I have a lot of insights into what went on in Jesus' family when He was growing up. I know about the annunciation of Jesus' birth to Mary and the humble and faithful way she received news of the great blessing; about the shepherds and angels that attended Jesus' birth; about Joseph's great obedience through it all; about the magi who came later; and about that one event in the Temple when Jesus was 12.

So it's with great interest that I read that Jesus' family, Mary and Jesus' brothers, show up unexpectedly to see Jesus. With the special reverence that's given to Mary by many Christians, we might expect that Jesus would rush to greet her and show her great public reverence.

But, strangely, we never actually get to hear what Jesus says to Mary: He doesn't really seem all that concerned that she's there. In this story, Mary can wait and is secondary. Secondary to what? That's the beautiful part of this little story, tucked away at the end of Matthew 12. What is it that Jesus is so concerned about that He ignores Mary his mother?

The surprising thing is that *it's us*! It's His disciples!

We might expect Jesus to uncross His legs, bound up to a standing position, and go running to meet Mary, leaving His disciples in the lurch.

But, He doesn't. Instead, He answers the one who told him His mother and brothers were waiting outside to speak to Him by saying, *"Who is My mother and who are My brothers?"* (v. 48) In other words, Jesus is saying that there is something here that at this moment is more important than His mother, even though she's Mary.

And then He stretches out His hand toward His disciples and says, *"Here are My mother and My brothers! For whoever does the will of My Father in heaven is My brother and sister and mother"* (vv. 49b, 50).

What an astounding statement! Do you see what Jesus has done? He's elevated us to the position of Mary! He's placed the will of His perfect heavenly Father above the will of His fallible and earthly mother. This is not to take anything away from Mary or demote her: she's not really the point in this case: *we* are.

Jesus' teaching to His disciples is meant to shock us because what Jesus is, in fact, doing is elevating us to Himself. It's not that I have a low view of Mary: it's that I have a high view of what Jesus does for everyone who is truly His disciple, Mary first, but also us if we do the will of the Father. Just as the Holy Spirit entered into Mary, the Holy Spirit enters into us (I'm not suggesting in an identical way). Jesus has raised us up to be members of His family just as important as His mother.

What Jesus is doing is something as miraculous as what God did with Mary when He brought Jesus to her by the Holy Spirit. What Jesus is doing is bringing us to Himself, and therefore to the Father, that we might be one with Him.

What Jesus is doing is bringing us up to heaven with Him, if we will do the will of the Father. He's telling us that He desires for us to be one with Him as He is one with the Father. How will this happen? The same way that He is one with the Father: by obedience to the will of the Father. That's what He came to do, and that's what we are supposed to be doing.

In this passage, therefore, Jesus brings us into His family—the Holy Family. Imagine if you really were one of Jesus' brothers or sisters in Nazareth! What would it have been like? Wouldn't it have been great! Maybe, maybe not. It didn't do much good to His brothers, who originally didn't believe in Him.

But, we're dreaming far too small. When I say that Jesus is making us members of His Holy Family, I don't mean just Mary and Joseph and James, Joses, Simon, and Judas. I mean that He's making us members of that far greater Holy Family: the Father, the Son, and the Holy Spirit!

What does it take, therefore, to participate in the life of the Holy Trinity, Jesus' Holy Family? That's a question worthy of an answer. It's a dream too magnificent and blessed to dream, except that Jesus has held it out as our potential reality.

"Whoever does the will of My Father in heaven is My brother and sister and mother."

Think about this today: every time you do the will of the Father you are united to the Son and thereby the Holy Trinity. Every time you obey like a son or daughter of God you *are* a son or daughter of God. Every time you do the will of the Father you demonstrate that you belong to Jesus Christ and are a part of His family.

Growing up in the 60s and 70s, I felt very blessed to be a part of the Erlandson family, having two wonderful parents and three wonderful siblings. We enjoyed each other's company and shared many pleasant and profound experiences. I'm also part of an even more blessed family: the family of Jesus Christ! That family extends all the way up to heaven where my older brother Jesus prays for me. It also extends to the hundreds of saints in my family I've met so far here on earth and to the millions that I've never met, whether part of the Church Militant or part of the Church Triumphant.

Today, this is my motivation for obedience. It's not the fear of disobedience and punishment: it's the possibility of participating in my Holy Family, the family of God. I will obey today, not out of fear or even duty, but out of the love and joy that comes from being united to God the Father through the Son and by the Spirit.

"Whoever does the will of My Father in heaven
is My brother and sister
and mother."

Prayer:

O my God, Trinity whom I adore, help me to become utterly forgetful of myself so that I may establish myself in you, as changeless and calm as though my soul were already in eternity. Let nothing disturb my peace nor draw me forth from you, O my unchanging God, but at every moment may I penetrate more deeply into the depths of your mystery. Give peace to my soul; make it your heaven, your cherished dwelling-place and the place of your repose. Let me never leave you there alone, but keep me there, wholly attentive, wholly alert in my faith, wholly adoring and fully given up to your creative action.

O my beloved Christ, crucified for love, I long to be the bride of your heart. I long to cover you with glory, to love you even unto death! Yet I sense my powerlessness and beg you to clothe me with yourself. Identify my soul with all the movements of your soul, submerge me, overwhelm me, substitute yourself for me, so that my life may become a reflection of your life. Come into me as Redeemer and as Savior.

O Eternal Word, utterance of my God, I want to spend my life listening to you, to become totally teachable so that I might learn all from you. Through all darkness, all emptiness, all powerlessness, I want to keep my eyes fixed on you and to remain under your great light. O my Beloved Star, so fascinate me that I may never be able to leave your radiance.

Consuming Fire, Spirit of Love, overshadow me so that the Word may be, as it were, incarnate again in my soul. May I be for him a new humanity in which he can renew all his mystery.

And you, O Father, bend down towards your poor little creature. Cover her with your shadow, see in her only your beloved son in who you are well pleased.

O my 'Three', my All, my Beatitude, infinite Solitude, Immensity in which I lose myself, I surrender myself to you as your prey. Immerse yourself in me so that I may be immersed in you until I go to contemplate in your light the abyss of your splendor! Amen.

(Elizabeth of the Trinity)

Points for Meditation:

1. What are the blessings that result from being part of God's Holy Family?
2. In what ways is God calling you to obey Him that He may make you a part of Him and bless you?

Resolution:

I resolve to obey the Father in the one way He has told me to obey today.

Matthew 13:1-23

How do you think of yourself compared to other people? Would you say that in the grand scheme of things you are blessed—or that life's been a little unfair to you?

Maybe you're in debt, but you're not quite sure how you got there. Maybe you struggle with a physical infirmity, or maybe you're in the middle of a difficult relationship. Your life may seem rather dreary and humdrum compared to those of others, or maybe there's just a certain indefinable ennui or malaise to your life.

There are many scales by which we might measure our lives. By the standard of many of these, if we use them, we will judge ourselves to have inferior lives. We're not as rich or famous as the celebrities that graffiti our lives; we're not as attractive as the beautiful people that ogle us from our sacred screens or the checkout aisle at Wal-Mart, and we're not as successful or happy as we presume other people to be.

But, I tell you we are blessed! Even in strictly material terms, if you're an American reading this in the 21st century, then you're blessed beyond all other men in history. We live longer, have less disease, can travel more freely, have more choices of food and entertainment and employment, and have a greater quality of life, in material terms, than any other people in the history of the world.

I seem to get a lot of respiratory sicknesses, more than my fair share. I figure that if I were born at any time before the 21st century I would have died long ago of a respiratory infection. I'm glad I live when and where I do.

But, that's not what I mean when I say that we are blessed.

"Blessed are your eyes for they see, and your ears for they hear" (v. 16).

This is why I call you blessed today: because your eyes see and your ears hear. Seeing with physical eyes and hearing with human ears is no great trick: the vast majority of humans has been able to do both of these things, even when they differ in just about every other imaginable way. But, blessed are those who see God and hear Him, for He is the source of every blessing, and He Himself is the greatest blessing of all.

"Assuredly, I say to you that many prophets and righteous men desired to see what you see, and did not see it, and to hear what you hear, and did not hear it."

How would you rate your degree of blessedness compared to Noah, Abraham, Jacob, Joseph, David, Isaiah, and John the Baptist? As great and as blessed as they may have been, none of them was as blessed in this life as you are, for none of them saw what your eyes have seen or heard what your ears have heard.

John, at least, saw Jesus, God, in the flesh. But, even John was not blessed enough during his life to see the Resurrection of the Christ or the Ascension. He did not have the fullness of the gospel. The truth is that we are especially blessed today to be able to have the entire Word of God so close to us. Throughout the past 2000 years of Christian history, many Christians have only been able to hear part of the Word of God, and often that Word was shrouded in an unintelligible language.

That Kingdom which the King Himself announced is here among us. The mustard seed has become a great tree. The field has been bought and the treasure obtained; the pearl of great price has been discovered, and we have sold all and bought it.

But often we don't feel like it. We are governed too much by our physical senses, and our spiritual senses grow weak and dim. One of the blessings I experienced when I took a group of teens to Belize for a mission trip one summer was to fast from certain earthly distractions so we could hear the heavenly voice better. We had less of the world with us. Our eyes saw less and our ears heard less because the sacred screens were left home and the magic boxes through which we talk and write and listen were gone. We had fewer choices because we knew we would be doing the work we were commissioned to do.

And so we saw and heard more within the Kingdom of Heaven as the kingdom of earth was subdued. We saw God because we waited and looked for Him, and we heard Him because we listened for Him. We saw Him at work because we accepted His invitation to come alongside Him and work with Him. We continued daily with one accord and worshiped Him on the beach, eating the food that was served to us with gladness and simplicity of heart, praising God and having favor with all the people.

All of this is available to us every day, here in 21st century America, if only we don't allow the material blessings to crowd out the spiritual ones and as long as our physical senses are not so sated that our spiritual senses fall asleep.

To those who have eyes to see there is a throne in heaven and One who sits on that throne. To those who have eyes to see there is One who is like a jasper and a sardius stone in appearance, and there is a rainbow around the throne. Around that throne there are twenty-four elders, clothed in white robes.

To those who have ears to hear, there are thunderings and voices, and the four living creatures are heard to sing:

"Holy, holy, holy,
Lord God Almighty,
Who was and is and is to come!
You are worthy, O Lord,
To receive glory and honor and power,
For you created all things,
And by your will they exist and were created" (Rev. 4: 8b,11).

Those who have eyes see the Lamb upon His throne and hear the new song. They have now been given voices, and so they join the song as the heavenly choir sings:

"You are worthy to take the scroll,
And to open its seals;
For you were slain,
And have redeemed us to God by Your blood
Out of every tribe and tongue and people and nation,
And have made us kings and priests to our God,
And we shall reign on the earth.
Worthy is the Lamb that was slain
To receive power and riches and wisdom,
And strength and honor and glory and blessing!
Blessing and honor and glory and power
Be to Him who sits on the throne,
And to the Lamb, forever and ever!" (Rev 5:9b–10,12,13b)

Those who have eyes to see can see that Jesus Christ is exalted to the right hand of the Father in heaven, from where He rules as Lord of lords and King of kings. We see Him as our High Priest and the Lamb of God, the true Temple made without hands, who intercedes for us before the Father day and night; we hear that He takes our Spirit-interpreted groanings before the Father as sweet incense before Him and offers Himself to the Father; and we know that He blesses us in this way that we might be one with Him and receive all of the spiritual benefits that come from union with Him.

Open your physical eyes, and you may not see it. All you see might be one of the sacred screens in our lives. But, close your physical eyes and open your spiritual eyes, and you will see.

Or best of all: open both your physical and spiritual eyes to see the blessed things which the patriarchs and prophets could not see. And then go and proclaim them from the housetops!

"Blessed are your eyes for they see, and your ears for they hear."

Prayer:
Holy, holy, holy,
Lord God Almighty,
Who was and is and is to come!
You are worthy, O Lord,
To receive glory and honor and power,
For you created all things,
And by your will they exist and were created.
You are worthy, O Christ, to take the scroll,
And to open its seals;
For you were slain,
And have redeemed us to God by Your blood
Out of every tribe and tongue and people and nation,
And have made us kings and priests to our God,
And we shall reign on the earth.
Worthy are you, O Lamb that was slain,
To receive power and riches and wisdom,
And strength and honor and glory and blessing!
Blessing and honor and glory and power
Be to Him who sits on the throne,
And to the Lamb, for ever and ever! Amen.

(taken from Rev. Chapters 4–5)

Points for Meditation:
1. How does your world look to you today when you look only with your physical eyes? How does it look when you open your spiritual eyes?
2. What are some spiritual truths that God wants you to see today that might help you to see things more clearly?

Resolution:
I resolve to open my spiritual eyes and ears today that I might see the spiritual world and be blessed.

Matthew 13:24–30, 36–43

The parable of the wheat and the tares seems so self-explanatory that I know there must be more to it. We all understand that He who sows the good seed is the Son, that the good seeds are the sons of the kingdom, and that the tares are the sons of the evil one. We know as well that the enemy who sowed them is the Evil One himself. We know that in this world there is both good and evil and that there are those who love God and those who don't.

But, what good does knowing this today do me? I want to make two applications that may not be immediately transparent.

First, I want to apply the wheat and tares to my own life. There's a dispute about this passage as to whether the wheat and tares are talking about good and evil people in the world in general or in the church. Rather than boring me with all of the details of this dispute, it's possible that both sides are right. The church is in the world? Shouldn't we expect and don't we actually see both good and evil men in the church? If you don't see this, then you obviously haven't been hanging around your church much lately!

But, isn't it also true that in my own world, the one which is my life, there are both wheat and tares? I know God and His goodness and grace in my life: I know that He has planted me as His good seed. So I can't apply this passage to myself in terms of agonizing over whether I personally am the wheat and tares: God has made me the wheat.

And yet there are tares in my life. Evil creeps into my life from without and from within. Let me talk first about the evil from within. The seeds that the Evil One planted, unfortunately, have produced evil fruit not only in the evil tares out there but also in my life right here.

I hate them! Because I hate them, I want to understand them. I believe that knowing how the Evil One plants tares among the wheat can help me understand the evil that still finds its way within me.

While men sleep, the enemy comes and sows tares among God's wheat. This is just as true of my individual life as it is for the world as a whole. It is when we are spiritually asleep that Satan comes and does his work in our lives. The minute I begin to coast or to think that I've got things made on my own, Satan goes to work. The minute I close my eyes to God and His presence in my life, Satan goes to work.

In one of his famous sermons, Hugh Latimer, the Anglican bishop, described Satan and his work like this:

> "There is one that surpasses all others, and is the most diligent prelate and preacher in all England. And would you like to know who it is? I will tell you—it is the Devil. He is the most diligent preacher of all. He is never out of his diocese; he is never from his cure; ye shall never find him unoccupied; he is ever in his parish; he keepeth residence at all times; ye shall never find him out of the way, call for him when you will he is ever at home; the diligentest preacher in all the realm; he is ever at his plough; no lording nor loitering can hinder him; he is ever applying his business, ye shall never find him idle, I warrant you." [4]

The first defense against the tares and Evil One, then, is to be spiritually awake. Write notes to yourself, tie phylacteries to your wrists and foreheads, get others to remind you, schedule times of prayer and Bible reading, and hold spiritual conversations with others. Drink spiritual caffeine, take spiritual showers, and punch yourself spiritually in the face! Do whatever it takes to stay spiritually awake.

Another principle is that the wheat and tares grow gradually. It's not always visible to me what's taking place inside me. This was especially true when I was younger. One of the most visible cases of the wheat and tares growing together is in the behavior of little children. The tares that we find so cute and humorous in a two year old may become weeds and thorns in the five year old. If we continue to do nothing about it, even after we've seen the tares emerge, they may become the renegade and rebellious life of the teenager.

Because the wheat and tares grow up together organically and slowly, oftentimes the remedy in this life is a slow and organic one. The new convert may want to really lop off his eye or hand because it offends him still, but the more mature Christian realizes this really won't help things and will only hurt in the end.

We must not be too violent in getting rid of our sins or the sins of others. It's not that we shouldn't seek to eradicate them in this life but rather that we should work on them carefully and patiently. Wishing them away in a single heroic moment won't truly conquer my sins, even if it may give me the illusion of power for a brief time. But, it might cause me to take my eyes off the Lord and His means of removing my sins.

---

4   "Sermon on the Plough," delivered 29 January 1548.

I sometimes despair that sins in my life or in lives of my children will ever be eradicated. This despair is almost as delicious to the Evil One as are the sins themselves, and if it will lead me away from my Lord and to myself, then Satan is quite happy to use it.

My sins have grown up organically within me along with Christ, the New Man, and my job is to appeal to Him every day for His way of dealing with my tares.

The second application I want to make from today's parable also involves trusting in the Good One to deal with the tares in my life. The truth is that the Lord has allowed them to continue to exist, at least in part, so that I may manifest the trust and patience that He seeks to have grow in me.

Make no mistake about it: the tares in my life are evil, and I wish them gone as soon as possible. But, I also know that my Lord delights in performing miracles, and His favorite miracle makes changing water into wine look like child's play. His favorite miracle is changing evil into good, just as Satan's only trick is to change good into evil.

The existence of the tares in our lives may be the source of many blessings. They, their motives, and their actions remain evil, but God uses them for good in our lives. Think of how many virtues are exercised and developed because of the evil that exists in the world, how much love has a chance to shine in the darkness, and how strong humility and patience are shown to be in the midst of this crooked and perverse generation.

What zeal to evangelize is provoked in us by the wickedness of the tares of the world, and what patience is revealed to the glory of God because of the existence of suffering!

Precisely because we can't get rid of evil men in the world we must learn to live in their midst, being tempted to be like them without succumbing, returning good for their evil, praying and working patiently for their conversion into wheat. How much like God we are made to be when we live among those who are sinners without becoming like them, even as we return their evil with the love of God.

The greatest blessing of all, to be in the presence of God, is provoked in me by the tares that I see around me. I don't want to be like them, and I don't want tares to grow in my own garden. But, the only way I can avoid them is to rush into the arms of the Sower, who is also my Gardener, that He might continue His good work in me. And the tares in me also make me turn to God in penitence and sorrow, magnifying my desire to be made a more perfect wheat.

While there will be both wheat and tares in this life, in the world as a whole and in your own little world, remember to appeal to the Sower of good seed that He might bring forth His fruit in you, despite, and sometimes because of, the tares of the world.

Prayer:

O God that art the only hope of the world,
The only refuge for unhappy men,
Abiding in the faithfulness of heaven,
Give me strong succor in this testing place.
O King, protect thy man from utter ruin
Lest the weak faith surrender to the tyrant,
Facing innumerable blows alone.
Remember I am dust, and wind, and shadow,
And life as fleeting as the flower of grass.
But may the eternal mercy which hath shone
From time of old
Rescue thy servant from the jaws of the lion.
Thou who didst come from on high in the cloak of flesh,
Strike down the dragon with that two-edged sword,
Whereby our mortal flesh can war with the winds
And beat down strongholds, with our Captain God. Amen.

(The Venerable Bede)

Points for Meditation:

1. What tares have you allowed into your life? Have you been turning to the Lord to help you deal with them?
2. What wheat has God planted in your life?

Resolution:

I resolve to ask the Lord today to help me deal patiently and lovingly with the tares in my life and in the world.

Matthew 13:31–35, 44–52

"The kingdom of heaven is like treasure hidden in a field, which a man found and covered up; then in his joy he goes and sells all that he has and buys that field."

When I and my family lived in Hot Springs, Arkansas, we went one day to visit the only diamond-producing site in the world open to the public—Crater of Diamonds State Park in Murfreesboro, Arkansas. In 2006, the year we went, someone found a 6.35 carat brown diamond. We eagerly packed up our shovels and trowels, buckets and gloves, and went looking for diamonds.

We found no diamonds that day, but at a different mine, my son Charlie and I came away with two large clusters of beautiful, large quartz crystals. The idea of finding buried treasure has a universal appeal to people. It's this image of finding a treasure hidden in a field that Jesus uses this morning to help us understand what the kingdom of heaven, in which we live, is like.

What does your life seem like to you today? If someone had asked you, say yesterday, to describe an image that portrayed your life, it probably wouldn't have been the parable of the hidden treasure. Yet this is exactly what Jesus says our lives are like in the kingdom of heaven.

Imagine that my family and I had gone instead to an empty lot somewhere in Arkansas, and the kids began digging around. Suddenly, one of them, probably Charlie, runs to me and says, "Dad! I found a diamond!" And then he shows me what is clearly a large, white diamond. It appears likely that there are other diamonds nearby.

I happen to know that the lot is for sale. What do you think I might pay for that piece of land? I might go and sell my other possessions to make the purchase possible. I don't have a lot of spare cash lying around, but I'd probably put a lot of things up for sale on eBay. I'd be likely to defer paying my credit cards and even take some cash advances from all my credit cards to buy that piece of land.

This is a picture of our life with God, of life in the kingdom of heaven. You and I have stumbled across the greatest treasure known to man. We've discovered God Himself. We've discovered eternal life and the one who gives eternal life. We've discovered the source of every blessing in this life and in the life to come.

What would you give for such a treasure? What is it worth to you?

If you were told that you had to give one hour of your time every week for such a treasure, surely you'd do it. What if you were told you had to give 10 hours of your time every week? Would it be worth your while? And what if you were told that to receive this greatest treasure known to man that you had to give 10% of your income every year? Would it be worth your while?

The truth is that it's easy to say that we're Christians, but saying that we're Christians isn't enough. To say we're Christians, without showing it to God by our lives, would be like saying we know about the buried treasure in the field but refusing to sell everything to buy the field.

It's not enough to "know" that the field contains the greatest treasure in the world: to obtain the treasure, you must do something. Just being able to say that God is my treasure or that I know that God sent His Son to save the world isn't enough. You have to do something about it.

There is, in other words, a cost to being a disciple of Jesus Christ. But, rather than measuring this cost in terms of money or possessions, God measures it in terms of our very lives. How much of your life are you willing to give to the Lord who has given you everything? (Of course this cost isn't a *payment* for eternal life: that price was paid by someone else!)

To truly follow Jesus Christ costs everything you have because it costs your life. It's a pretty good deal. I give my life to God, and He gives me His life, eternal life with Him, and blessing in His presence forevermore, starting right now.

But, sometimes we forget that we've vowed to give our lives to God. We want God to keep His end of the bargain, while we renege on ours. You promised to give your life to God, if He gave His life to you. He's done what He said He would. What does keeping your end of the bargain involve? What will it cost you? Many people would give all they had if they could find the secret of eternal life, even if that life were limited to a life on earth. But, what will you give for life everlasting in the presence of God, a life that starts now?

Rather than considering the entire cost this morning, I want to make it simpler for all of us. I want to make a suggestion that is bite size, something we can act on today, in considering this great treasure God has shared with us. I want each of you to consider one way in which God is asking you to give yourself more completely to Him. It might involve what people have called time, treasure, or talent.

Time. Maybe you should invest in God and His kingdom by investing time praying, reading His Word, or serving others.

Treasure. God has given you Himself, at a great cost to Himself. Do you give Him a tithe, or tenth, of the monetary treasure He's entrusted to you? Maybe He's even calling you to more!

Talent. God has given you His gifts for His purposes. He has given you life, and He's given you His Body, that you might contribute your life to His Body as well.

. . .

"The kingdom of heaven is like treasure hidden in a field, which a man found and covered up; then in his joy he goes and sells all that he has and buys that field" (v. 44).

Consider investing today in the kingdom of heaven. Consider investing in just one way today in the greatest treasure known to man: God Himself and His kingdom.

Prayer:
Lord, I long to discover the mystery of your Kingdom and live in it ardently in my daily life. May I, with the help of your Holy Spirit, penetrate into this mystery in prayer. Lord, I want to be generous and give up everything for the sake of your Kingdom in my life and in the lives of those souls entrusted to me. You know that I cannot do so on my own. Help me with your grace to be generous. Amen.

Points for Meditation:
1. How might you invest yourself more fully in God and His kingdom today?
2. Imagine life in God's presence in this world as being a great treasure. What does that treasure look like? What response do you have to possessing this treasure?

Resolution:
I resolve to ask myself today what God wants me to give today that I might obtain His treasure, which is more of Himself.

Matthew 13:53–14:12

It just wasn't right, you know. My master was a good man, a great man. It just wasn't right for things to end this way.

All his life he had this burning passion to do the will of YHWH. He had taken the vows of the Nazarite and had kept them his entire life. He took on the mantle of Elijah and willingly subjected himself to the scorn and laughter of the insiders. He was, in fact, the ultimate outsider.

And he was strong. He was a rock when other men would have turned to sand. We all, those of us who followed him, knew that he was a prophet of YHWH, and we secretly wondered if he might not also be more.

He had borne the hardships of the wilderness, and we gladly followed him in his chosen life of self-denial. He was the greatest man of his generation; we all knew that, even if others couldn't see it. He was noble and pure, and in following him many of us found our way back to God.

We knew things were reaching a critical climax, but none of us guessed what would happen next. We knew the constant threats of imprisonment or death, but we all knew that something more had to happen before that could ever happen.

But, we were wrong. We all had our theories about why Herod did it, and knowing Herod, he was evil enough to prove us all right about his wicked motives. Some thought he was a coward and was afraid John would lead us into a rebellion. And there were some of us who were itching for just such a rebellion. But, John made it clear that this wasn't God's way. Others of us believed that it was the Pharisees who were really behind it, especially because of John's association with Jesus. Some of us knew that John had rebuked Herod and that Herod had to put him in prison to save face. We heard rumors that although even Herod knew better, he put John in prison because he was not as strong as the women in his life.

And so it happened that that mighty voice that spoke to our generation and seemed like the very voice of YHWH was quieted, cast into the darkness and silence of the dungeon. That dungeon was like the grave itself, deep in Herod's castle-palace where the light doesn't shine and words don't escape.

And it just wasn't right. Why should he go down to Hades when Jesus and his disciples roamed the earth and feast and drink? Where was YHWH in all this, that our master should be put to death by Herod, who down the road in his palace shouts to the world with his adulterous, murderous wife and his drunken cohorts? Why do the righteous suffer, while the wicked prosper?!

This isn't what any of us expected when we first followed John. He taught us that the kingdom of heaven was at hand, and we believed him. We thought we had seen it. We saw people coming to John to repent and be baptized. We saw people turn their hearts back to God. I tell you, we saw the kingdom!

And then this happened. It shook us to our core. Everything we thought we knew was shaken and seemed ready to fall. Everything that John had done seemed destined to fall away. What would we do then, and where would we go? They always killed the prophets, didn't they? I think John knew what his end would be. But, this time it was supposed to be different. This time the kingdom was supposed to be restored, and this time the people were supposed to be turned back to YHWH and His righteousness.

For a moment, I must confess, it seemed as if everything I knew about the Scriptures and YHWH and John was false. We had all been misled. This life was all that existed, the same world in which evil was as likely to triumph as righteousness.

While John was down there in Herod's Sheol, he sent for me and one of the others to go to Jesus. We had told him before about some of the things we had heard and seen about Jesus because we knew John would want to know. A strange look came over John's face, and we couldn't tell if Herod and the dampness and the darkness had broken him or if he had just received a word from the Lord. I think he knew the end was near. I think he wanted to know that he had been a faithful and good servant. But, he needed to know something to die in peace. He needed to know something in order to make it all worthwhile.

And so he sent us to Jesus. When we found Jesus, we asked him the question straight from John's lips, the question that was burning on all our tongues: *"Are you the Coming One, or do we look for another?"* (Matthew 11:3)

I'll never forget Jesus' answer: "Go and tell John the things which you hear and see: The blind see and the lame walk; the lepers are cleansed and the deaf hear; the dead are raised up and the poor have the gospel preached to them. And blessed is he who is not offended because of me."

Jesus began to teach, and we wanted to hear him some more, but we rushed to John with Jesus' exact words. John soaked them in for a moment, and then he smiled. This was agonizingly unclear to us, but John knew he had his answer. He knew that Jesus was the Messiah.

He faithfully cried in the wilderness; he faithfully prepared the way of the Lord. He preached repentance and the Kingdom of Heaven, and he preached righteousness to Herod.

I don't think it made sense to me until the day we took the body of John and buried it. I don't think I knew until he was gone that he had not failed in his mission, which meant that YHWH had not failed in His promises.

The day that we buried John (feeling like we died with him) and we had nowhere else to go, is the day we followed Jesus. From that day, we began to see the Kingdom of Heaven in ways we had never imagined before.

John's was not the only dungeon which we inhabited: each of us had our own personal dungeons. Life did not immediately become wonderful and perfect, and the wicked were not all cast down in a day. There were still times when I flinched from the awful price of being a disciple, now of Jesus.

But, I never forgot what John had taught me, even though he died in a dungeon, the victim of a lustful and cowardly king. And nothing, not even the cold, mortal reach of Herod or his greater lord, could ever take me away from the Jesus the Messiah and His Kingdom.

Prayer:

O Merciful God, be Thou now unto me a strong tower of defense, I humbly entreat Thee. Give me grace to await Thy leisure, and patiently to bear what Thou doest unto me; nothing doubting or mistrusting Thy goodness towards me; for Thou knowest what is good for me better than I do. Therefore do with me in all things what Thou wilt; only arm me, I beseech Thee, with Thine armor, that I may stand fast; above all things, taking to me the shield of faith; praying always that I may refer myself wholly to Thy will, abiding Thy pleasure, and comforting myself in those troubles which it shall please Thee to send me, seeing such troubles are profitable for me; and I am assuredly persuaded that all Thou doest cannot but be well; and unto Thee be all honor and glory. Amen.

(Lady Jane Grey)

Points for Meditation:

1. What dungeons do you have in your life? How are you tempted to respond to them?
2. How can you remind yourself of what Jesus has said and done so that when you spend time in the dungeons of life your faith may remain strong?

Resolution:

I resolve to seek Jesus in the dungeons of my life and to receive His messengers and reminders when they come to me today.

Matthew 14:13-21

Do you ever find yourself doing some of the most important things in life as if you're just going through the motions? Sometimes the most important things in life have become so common that we stop noticing them. For example, most of the time we don't notice that we have to breathe to take in the oxygen that helps support our life.

And sometimes our daily need to eat food can go unnoticed; after all, every year you live you probably eat more than 1000 meals.

And yet when you think about it, the fact that we stuff things in our mouths, and swallow them and make them part of ourselves is a pretty amazing thing!

Throughout the Bible, food is important.

The fall of mankind, in which sin entered into the world, all came about over the issue of food. How would man sustain himself—by his hand, or by the hand of God?

In one verse taken from this morning's lesson, Matthew 14:19, we see the entire gospel, the good news of Jesus Christ, encapsulated: "*And He took the five loaves and the two fish, and looking up to heaven, He blessed and broke and gave the loaves to the disciples; and the disciples gave to the multitudes.*"

In this verse, through the medium of earthly bread, Jesus Christ brings us the Good News of salvation.

Matthew 14:19 begins with one of the most basic facts of our existence: human hunger. Men are hungry. They need food to live, and yet there is not enough food where the 5000 are to feed everyone. The hunger of the 5000 represents all human need, especially our need for salvation. Our physical hunger reminds us about an even deeper hunger that we all have felt in this life, just as the goodness of food is to remind us of the goodness of God.

What will Jesus do about the hunger of the 5000? He took bread, the most basic food, and from this He fed the many. He used, as He does so commonly in our lives, the ordinary in His miracles. He speaks to us and He feeds us through His creation. This is the sacramental principle in the world by which God takes the ordinary things He has created and blesses them so that they become blessings to us—the very means by which He gives Himself to us. Sometimes food is not just food.

What will God do about the spiritual hunger of humans? What God does in response to our spiritual hunger and need is The Incarnation. The Lord of Creation became part of Creation. He sees our need, He takes the Creation in His hands that He might bless it, and He blesses us through it. He takes man, who has profaned himself, becomes a man, and then blesses this Man that through Him all might be blessed.

But, the Creation is never sufficient by itself. It's limited, and it's fallen. There was not enough bread or fish to feed everyone. In the story of our lives, man cannot take care of himself.

Therefore, Jesus takes the bread and thanks God for it, or blesses it. He takes the bread and transforms it, in this case into more bread. The result is that people are fed. There is no more hunger, and there is even more than enough.

And like the few loaves of bread, we are never sufficient to take care of our deepest needs. And so God took human nature and transformed it: He became the Creation. The Incarnation is God's greatest miracle: God becomes man that He might save man.

Jesus gave the physical bread He had blessed and multiplied to His disciples first. The bread that Jesus provides must now be given to feed the hungry. How good that bread must have tasted! I don't know if any of you have ever participated in a total fast for some time, but it's amazing when you begin eating again how wonderful simple, store-bought, preservative-ridden, bread smells and tastes.

Jesus also gives the Bread of Life, Himself, first to His disciples. He taught the disciples first and gave Himself to them first, and then they go and feed the others who are hungry.

We, too, are His disciples, and God has fed us. But, He doesn't feed us automatically: we're not comatose on a hospital bed, hooked up to an IV and catheter. We must pray for and eat our daily bread when He offers it to us. Jesus' miracle of feeding the 5000 was to teach us.

He did that miracle one time for those people. But, the greater miracle is that as the Word of God the miracle of the 5000 keeps multiplying, and through it God has continued to feed His people for 2000 years. As we read the Word of God, which we are doing today together, we must feed on the heavenly bread, Jesus Himself. That's the sacramental teaching we are to receive today.

We eat physical food three times a day (or four or five or six if you count snacks!) Shouldn't we seek our daily spiritual bread at least as often as this? Shouldn't we relish our times of worship and prayer and meditating on God's Word at least as much as we do our breakfasts and lunches? How good the Bread of Life tastes when we break our fast from God and eat Him again!

We've trained ourselves to be connoisseurs of food. We know fine wines, and have tasted deeply. Why not become connoisseurs of God, who is our heavenly food, so that truly we "Taste and see that the Lord is good"?

After eating and being filled, the disciples give the bread to the others who had come. After being taught, the disciples are supposed to distribute the Bread of Life, Jesus Himself, to all who will come. That's our commission, as it was the disciples', both here and at the end of Matthew in the Great Commission. We also must be disciples who go out and make all disciples. We must not only keep this holy food for ourselves but also bring it to all whom we meet who are spiritually hungry—and that includes everyone you meet.

The Feeding of the 5000 is a picture of how Jesus Christ gives Himself as the Bread of Life: it is the Gospel of Bread.

It would be easy to be fed this morning once, digest the spiritual food, and then that's it. But, why not take every opportunity to see the physical food God gives you as a reminder of His goodness to you?

The best reminder of all, of course, is the spiritual food of the Body and Blood of Jesus Christ which He offers in His Supper.

"And He took the five loaves and the two fish, and looking up to heaven, He blessed and broke and gave the loaves to the disciples; and the disciples gave to the multitudes" (v. 19).

This is the story of our lives, for this is the Gospel of Bread.

Prayer:

Almighty and everliving God, we most heartily thank You, because You feed us
through the Bread of Heaven, Your Son, Jesus Christ our Lord; and You assure
us through Him of Your favor and goodness towards us. We humbly ask that,
having been fed by You, we would go and feed others in Your Name. Through
Jesus Christ, who is the Bread of Heaven. Amen.

Points for Meditation:

1. What are the various ways that you might feed on Jesus Christ throughout
   the day?
2. Have you been strengthened enough by God's heavenly food to begin serving
   others? If not, how might you eat more of this heavenly food to be strengthened to that point?

Resolution:

I resolve to remember God's heavenly food, Jesus Christ, every time I put food
in my mouth today.

Matthew 14:22-36

There are so many encounters that the disciples have with Jesus in such a short time in this one episode that I see myself in this story multiple times. Each encounter, I see a little more of myself and my Lord reflected from the waters of the Sea of Galilee. In fact, what I see this morning is a depiction of how we come closer to Christ in faith and the stages of experiencing Him that we encounter on the way.

In the first scenario, the disciples are in the boat by themselves. They're in the middle of the sea, tossed by the waves, for the wind was contrary. This is a condition I find myself in often. I sense a storm coming in my life, I feel that something's wrong. The world seems contrary to me, and obstacles array themselves against my plans. Often, in such circumstances, I don't see Jesus anywhere around. This might also be the condition of someone who is laboring in life without Christ and isn't even aware of Him at all.

The second case is when the disciples actually see Jesus coming but mistake Him for a ghost. This is an improvement in the condition of the disciples, even if they don't think so at the time. While Jesus comes to bless them, they're probably thinking, "Oh great—first a storm is rising, and now the ghosts come out as well!"

They cry out in fear because they don't recognize Jesus Christ for who He is. This might be like someone who has heard of Jesus Christ or even grew up in a Christian home, but who doesn't understand or believe that He is truly the Son of God. In terms of my life, there are certainly times when Jesus comes into my life and I don't recognize Him. I believe that I am actually in His presence all of the time, but often I don't perceive it.

Seeing Jesus is a tricky business, more of an art than a science. When I am not feeling well physically, I might see the world in grayer terms and miss Jesus. On the other hand, when I'm euphoric because things have gone well, I might easily begin the party without inviting Jesus.

Often, I'm just too busy (or think that I am). The really tricky part about this is that usually I'm busy doing something for Him, whether at church or at home, and I profane these holy things by making idols out of them. There are times when I probably wouldn't even recognize Jesus if He rapped on my office door. I think I'd say (without bothering to look up) something like, "Not now, I'm busy doing the Lord's work, writing a sermon, working on a Bible study, planning youth events for this semester. Can we schedule an appointment?"

Then there are the more blessed times when Jesus makes Himself known to me and speaks to me. *"Be of good cheer! I AM! Do not be afraid,"* He told the disciples (v. 27).

There are times when those who are in the process of getting to know Jesus take important steps forward in their faith walk. Jesus makes Himself known, and they "get" who He really is, and are joyful.

How many times in your life have you been on the water when a storm comes up and, worse yet, something really spooks you? You truly believe that you are going under and that there is little, if anything, you can do about it. You're in a downward spiral, and life seems to be a menacing force.

And then Jesus manifests Himself to you in one of the many ways in which He comes to His brothers and sisters. He tells you to be of good cheer, and you are of good cheer because Jesus is with you. He tells you it is He, and that therefore you should no longer be afraid. Things are now right, because even though the difficult situation exists, so does Jesus, and you know that you can make it with Him.

We should all remember, rehearse, and share such moments when Jesus comes in them, for it's one of the most important ways we remember and share Jesus.

There are times of even greater blessing in store for us at other times. Having seen Jesus and come into His presence, we tell Him that we really want to be sure He is in our lives, and so He tells us to come closer and see. Peter made just such a request, and Jesus said to him, "Come."

And so those who have come to Jesus to see and hear Him are invited to come closer in their lives with Him. Is it really true what they've heard about Jesus? They must now go and find out for themselves.

In my life, Jesus has beckoned me to come closer to find out what He's really like. I ask Him frequently to reveal Himself to me so I can be sure He's in my life. And lo and behold! sometimes I begin to walk on the water, as Peter did. The reason I'm able to go is because there is only one thought in my head at the time—to come to Jesus and be with Him. As I focus on Him, all else grows dim. The other things in my life don't go away, and I'm still aware of them. It's just that they're less significant, all of them: the storms in my life, as well as the bright shiny toys that dazzle my eyes.

But, my life with Jesus doesn't ever stay that way for long. It's not long before I begin to pay attention again to the fact that the wind is boisterous in my life, and fear and anxiety and worry come slouching back into my life. I may end the day with Jesus, reflecting on how I saw Him today, but when I begin the next day, behold! Jesus is gone while my worries remain.

I begin to sink, because I am looking at the sea and the boat and not at Jesus. But, I remember enough of Him to cry out, "Lord, save me!" And then, in His time, He stretches out His hand to me, catches me as I sink, and says, "O you little-faith—why did you doubt?" Getting back into the boat, the wind ceases in my life.

Once again, when I see how good He's been to me and how He comes when I cry out to Him, I come to Him and worship, crying: "Truly, You are the Son of God!"

In reality, I think we're all in various parts of this story at any one time. Some of you may be near the beginning of the story, being tossed by waves and contrary winds, not recognizing the presence of Jesus. Some of you may not recognize Him when He comes to you. Hasn't there been something you've read, something someone said that sure sounded like the voice of Jesus in your life? Or was it just a ghost of your imagination?

Some of us vacillate between moments of walking on the water with the Lord and moments of sinking as we look at ourselves and our lives.

The goal, always, is to look for Jesus and, having found Him, to go to Him. When you are afraid or are sinking, cry out to Him. When He asks you to come to Him, even though what He asks is as unlikely as walking on the water, come to Him. And when He delivers you or comes to you in any way today, come before Him to worship Him as the Son of God.

Make it your goal today to see Jesus, and when you do, to share Him with someone else.

Prayer:

Jesus, I ask that you come to me today and reveal Yourself to me. When I am blind to You, help me to recognize You; when I recognize You, let me come to You; and when I come to You, may I remain with You. Reach out Your hand today, Lord, and take hold of me, that I may look at you and not the things of this world. Amen.

Points for Meditation:

1. Where are you likely to see Jesus today? What are some ways you've seen Him in the past?
2. Where are you in this story today? What would coming to Jesus mean for you today?
3. Make it a point to share an encounter with Jesus with someone today.

Resolution:

I resolve to consider where I am in today's story and to come to Jesus from that place.

Matthew 15:1–20

Here's an interesting experiment that would be fascinating to run: to write down every word that you uttered in a particular day and then examine the transcript.

I wonder what such a transcript would reveal about who you are and about how holy you are.

An even better measure, though even more impossible to use, would be to record every thought you had in your head throughout a given day. Then, if you had certain clips of your day's thoughts played back to you, what would you sound like?

It's an intimidating experiment even to think about, isn't it?

My point is the one Jesus is making today, which is that it is not what goes into the mouth that defiles a man but what comes out of his mouth. While He's talking about the particulars of the Pharisees' insistence on ritually washing the hands before eating (as opposed to the things that come out of their mouths), there is a deeper principle at work. It's not our outward actions that are really what make us impure but our inward desires and thoughts.

The Bible has a profound anthropology, and the biblical writers make it clear that the heart is at the center of our being. It's been said that, "What the heart loves, the will chooses, and the mind justifies." [5]

To which I would add, "...and the body enacts."

We don't just do things, not even when we have moments when we feel like we're just reacting or having a reflex. A common reflex is to get angry and begin to raise your voice. This might be in response to someone cutting you off on the highway, to a poor call in a sporting event, or to someone being belligerent towards you. But, this so-called reflex of anger comes from a heart that allows itself to get angry. There are other possible responses besides anger, you know.

It is the inner man, the heart, that God desires to cleanse, and not the outer man. They say that "cleanliness is next to godliness," and personally I prefer clean people to slobs and those who drool all over themselves or who bathe only once

---

5   Ashley Null, "Interview with Dr. Ashley Null on Thomas Cranmer: Primary Architect of the Prayer Book," Anglican Church League, http://www.acl.asn.au/old/null.html.

a month. But, the "they" who say this aren't the Holy Trinity or even the holy writers of the Bible.

The importance of the inner man is made clear even when we consider the outer actions that proceed from the inner man or heart. If you have a problem with anger, adultery, fornication, theft, lying, or blaspheming, then you know that the way to solve the problem isn't to simply will yourself to stop doing such things. Such efforts are doomed to failure, and they simply compound the guilt. You know that you must change your heart first so that the will is not fighting against the heart, and so that the body and emotions may learn to follow and not lead.

We can apply this principle to ourselves and our spiritual lives. In many cases, we attempt to change our behavior by simply going out and changing. If we're a little more careful, we might muster up all of our will power to successfully cease our undesirable behavior for a short time, only to relapse. But, to successfully change, we must change our desires.

Think of your sinful desires in terms of a sinful appetite, in terms of what used to be called gluttony but which is now the unmentionable sin. We've all known people who took a look at themselves in the mirror and saw that they had allowed themselves to become obese and then decided it was time to do something about it. They go on a diet, exert their will for a while, and either quit or go back to their obesity when they have lost the desired weight and stop their diet.

What went wrong? What went wrong was that the heart was never truly engaged, even if the body and will were put into motion. What went wrong is that we see diets as the weather in our lives when we should see them as the climate of our lives. Weather is what the atmospheric conditions are like at any given moment or any given day, but climate is the long-term conditions of a place. A diet is really what you eat, and so we are always "on a diet". The only question is "Which diet?" What people who diet are really doing is having a poor diet, choosing for a short while to have a good diet so they can then return to the poor diet.

Why? When we put it in such terms, why do we continue to choose what we know to be poor and unhealthy diets? Because we're simply following our hearts. We didn't really desire the new, healthy diet and all that it entails. We don't like fruits and vegetables and whole grains but prefer our food to be white, fast, and fatty. All we really wanted was a way to lose weight and feel good about ourselves so we can go back to the poor but tasty diet again.

This is also the way we are with our spiritual diets. Why don't we read the Bible or pray more? There's a part of our hearts that really don't want to. Why do we have evil thoughts, get angry, lust, plot how to maximize our benefits at the cost to others, lie to achieve our ends or protect ourselves, and covet? Because we want what we want.

We might temporarily stop such thoughts and desires and behaviors, but really, they taste kind of yummy, and trying to stop them feels bad.

So the heart must be changed in order for the mind and the body to be changed as well. In reality, all three must work together, which brings us back to the proper place of external rules and rituals. Jesus isn't saying that there is no place for tradition or rules or rituals, but He is saying that they are only a means and not the end. The end is holiness, which can only come from a heart that truly desires God and His holiness.

But, this raises a profound question for me: how can we get this more holy heart that desires God and His holiness? This is where I see the two natures at work in me. As I'm writing this, I truly desire God and His holiness. I'm truly committed in my heart and mind and body to doing what the Lord wants me to and to not doing what He doesn't want me to. But, I know that sometime today, when I least expect it, I'll be tempted to do what the other will within me, the Old Man, wants to do. I may not even become aware of such slips until after I've made them.

What am I to do? Knowing that God is absolutely sovereign and that I'm rather helpless, I could simply wait for Him to change me. But, that isn't God's way. He wants me involved. He has given me various means of changing my heart, and even when I pick them up and use them, it is all of His grace.

What are these means? First, of course, I must pray. I have to ask: I don't receive because I didn't change my heart enough to humble myself before God and ask Him. I also have to act. When I've prayed, a lot of which is to train my heart to seek God, I need to immediately seek to act according to what I've prayed for. When I'm next confronted with a choice of which diet I want to eat, God's or mine, I must choose God's.

Here's where the outer man and his rules and rituals come in handy. Although they are not the end of holiness and aren't the starting point, they are still essential. I must construct my life in such a way that I am more likely to follow what my newly God-oriented, praying, self truly desires. When I go to the supermarket to do the weekly shopping, I should choose to buy more fruits and vegetables and less white food. I should prepare to *not* eat out some of the times I normally would. I must choose to exercise, even when I don't feel like it.

The funny thing is that through such external actions and rules and rituals, all the time I'm establishing new rituals and subtly changing my desires. When I was a kid, I put a spoonful of sugar on every cereal that wasn't already sugar-saturated. Wheaties, Cheerios, Kellogg's Corn Flakes—they all got the sugar treatment. But today, I find these cereals already have enough sugar and taste better without more of it. After a month of a consistent time to exercise, I find that I desire to exercise because my heart, mind, and body have all come to expect it.

Frankly, this is how *Give Us This Day* got written every day. Over the two years I originally wrote *Give Us This Day* I developed a heart, a new desire to write *Give Us This Day* so that it *felt* wrong to not write it, and I *thought* that it was wrong since it was a primary way I came to God and listened to Him and helped feed others. I truly desired it because it was good for me, and I enjoyed meeting God in it. Even on the days when I didn't feel like writing *Give Us This Day* I wrote it, because through the external rules and rituals it had become a part of me.

Those who study behavior and change understand that if an action is active, public, and effortful, then that behavior is more likely to become a part of the person who does it. This is true both for good and evil actions.

Every time we decide to follow God and His holiness, it's a good idea as well to bring someone along for the ride. Let someone know what you are seeking so they can walk with you and support you and hold you accountable. Other Christians are the best external support for holiness that you'll ever find.

All of this, of course, has implications for the raising of children. We must give them rules and rituals, but the real goal is for them to be inner directed and not outer directed. They must desire God in their hearts, and not just because their parents desire Him. This is what's behind the classic titanic struggle some Christian parents have in dragging their teens and pre-teens to church. The child is still outer directed and doesn't want what the parent wants anymore. Such children have never developed a true heart for God on their own.

Being children, they need a lot of external supports and props to help them love God in the inner man. But, the goal for all of us is to reach Christian maturity, the full stature of Christ, in which we do the will of the Father because we desire it. We desire the will of the Father so much that, like Jesus, to do the will of the Father is our very bread.

What comes out of the heart makes a man clean or unclean. And what comes out of the heart is what is in it. Put God in your heart today through every means available to you.

Prayer:

Lover of our souls,
Come into these cold and empty hearts of ours,
Come to fill them with light, warmth, and love,
With the heavenly music,
With the sound of the eternal harmony,
With the footfalls of the saints that rejoice in Thy bliss;
Thou art Lord of all, Master of suns and stars,
Yet art Thou our Beloved,
The Savior of our souls from death and night.
Come, our Lord, Thou Lover of our souls,
Come to purify and uplift our failing hearts,
Come to impart unto us the eternal joy of those that are in bliss with Thee.
Amen.

(John S. Hoyland)

Points for Meditation:

1. In what ways does my heart desire what it wants instead of what God wants?
2. What rules, rituals, and reminders could I place in my life to direct my heart
    more towards God?

Resolution:

I resolve to meditate on one way in which my heart does not desire what God
desires, to ask God to change my heart, and to take the first opportunity I have
today to seek Him in this thing.

Matthew 15:21–39

Jesus loved the little children, and I think one of the reasons must have been because they are often so humble. How many times have my children come to me or Jackie to ask us for something that they can't get for themselves. "Daddy, can you put on my shoes?" "Mommy, I'm h-o-ongry!"

Of course, most of the time, Jackie and I give them what they need (though not necessarily what they want) without their even asking for it!

This morning's lesson in faith, taken from Matthew 15, reminds us how we must come to God with the faith and humility of a child. The person of faith this morning is a woman, a Gentile, and a Canaanite, and she is our guide, for she manifested three essential characteristics of a truly faithful person: humility, fervency, and persistence.

Her humility is revealed in the way she sees Jesus and the way she sees herself. Believing that He can help her daughter, and worshiping Him (verse 25), she comes to Him with humility. She recognizes as well who she is: a helpless woman who is a Canaanite, or dog.

But, this "dog" utters the most basic and simple prayer of all: "Lord, help me!"

Her humility is matched by her fervency. Her understanding of her need and helplessness, and the power and mercy of Christ, makes her fervent. She doesn't just ask, she *cries* out to Him, not only in verse 22 but also in verse 25. She seeks Him with passion and, having found Him, implores Him fervently.

Humility and fervency might fall short, however, if they were not married to persistence as well. This persistent woman outlasted her obstacles: who she is, the Lord's disciples, people in the way, and the apparent reluctance of the Lord to help her. This woman perseveres, even when the answer appear to be a resounding "No!" The essence of her faith is that she believed, even when she couldn't see what was going to happen. She keeps asking, even when she doesn't immediately get what she wants.

Because of her humility, fervency, and persistence, Jesus answers her and heals her daughter.

What's even more amazing: she's a picture of us!

We're just like this woman. We have no right to come before God. We've all sinned and fallen short of the glory of God, and there is no health in us. And we must approach God the same way she did.

Humbly: Do you know who God is and who you are before Him? Do you freely acknowledge your sin and helplessness and that only God can help you? This is the faith of the Canaanite woman that received the blessing of Jesus. She didn't come on the basis of how good she was or that she was an Israelite and acceptable to God. She had no illusions about who she was and what she deserved. Like her, we need to come humbly before the only one who can deliver us

Fervently: Do you have a passion to come before the Lord each day? We should not be ashamed to cry out to God. We should not be ashamed to weep before Him. We should not be ashamed to pour forth our emotions and our soul before Him.

I'm not saying that we should necessarily do this in the middle of a worship service, but if we can't pour out our souls before the Lord in private, then maybe our relationship with God has grown a little cold (and maybe some of us can do with a little emotion and fervency in our Sunday worship!)

This woman came with passion and intensity because her daughter was at stake. We should come with passion and intensity because *we* are at stake.

Persistently: How easily do you give up in your prayers and life with God? Are you an easy person to shake off and defeat? This woman was truly a dog in one way: she was like a pit bull who had gotten hold of Jesus' leg and was not going to let go. Do you have persistence—do you have faith like this? When you don't immediately get what you want, how do you respond? Like this sinful, outcast, Canaanite woman, we must seek God Himself.

This "dog," this Canaanite woman, was content with crumbs, and yet Jesus, because of her faith, was willing to give her so much more. And if you respond with this kind of faith, with humility, fervency, and persistence, then God will bless you with much more than crumbs. He will give you the very Bread of Life that satisfies the deepest needs of your body and soul.

We've looked at the woman and her response, but what of the main character? Jesus Christ is always the main character in our lives. What is His response?

Draw near to Him, and He will draw near to you. It was because this woman sought out Jesus that He responded to her faith. We need to come before the Lord, to seek Him out every day, in church and out of church.

Jesus also responds by listening. This is why we pray, as this woman implored and begged Him. He may not always respond immediately. There may be obstacles in the way.

But, Jesus will bless those who are faithful. If Jesus so blessed this Canaanite woman, how much more will He bless His own brothers and sisters who seek Him with faith? How much more those for whom he died and for whom He prays?

. . .

BONUS: For those who worship using the traditional Book of Common Prayer, I've marked some of the places in the Holy Communion service of the 1928 Prayer Book where Jesus leads us, through the liturgy, through our own unworthiness before God and to His mercy and grace in giving us Himself. (If you use a different Book of Common Prayer, you should be able to find the corresponding place, and if you don't use the Book of Common Prayer, you may find it a rich devotional resource, as have many others.)

p. 93—"we humbly beseech thee most mercifully to accept our oblations, and to receive these our prayers"

p. 94—"we most humbly beseech thee, of thy goodness, O Lord, to comfort and succour all those, who in this transitory life are in trouble, sorrow, need, sickness, or any other adversity."

p. 107—"Draw near with faith, and take this holy Sacrament to your comfort; and make your humble confession to Almighty God"

p. 108—The Comfortable Words

p. 112—"Take, eat, this is my Body, which is given for you; Do this in remembrance of me...Drink ye all of this; for this is my Blood of the New Testament, which is shed for you, and for many, for the remission of sins; Do this, as oft as ye shall drink it, in remembrance of me."

p. 113—"And although we are unworthy, through our manifold sins, to offer unto thee any sacrifice; yet we beseech thee to accept this our bounden duty and service; not weighing our merits, but pardoning our offences"

p. 114—Lord's Prayer—"give us this day our daily bread"

p. 114—"We do not presume to come this thy Table, O merciful Lord, trusting in our own righteousness, but in thy manifold and great mercies. We are not worthy so much as to gather up the crumbs from under Thy table...[the rest of the Prayer of Humble Access, too]

p. 115—"Almighty and everliving God, we most heartily thank thee, for that thou dost vouchsafe to feed us, who have duly received these holy mysteries, with the spiritual food of the most precious Body and Blood of thy Son our Saviour Jesus Christ..."

Prayer:

I do not presume to come to You today, O merciful Lord, trusting in my own righteousness, but in Your many and great mercies. I am not worthy to gather up the crumbs under Your table. But You are the Lord who is always merciful. Give me therefore, gracious Lord, Your Son Jesus Christ today, that I may feed on Him and that I may evermore dwell in Him, and He in me. Amen.

(Paraphrase of The Prayer of Humble Access from *The Book of Common Prayer*, p. 82)

Points for Meditation:

1. Which of these three do you most need in your life with Christ: humility, fervency, or persistence?
2. What most keeps you from coming more to Jesus today?
3. Re-read this *Give Us This Day* before the next worship service you participate in.

Resolution:

I resolve to focus on coming to Jesus today in one of these three ways: humbly, fervently, or persistently.

Matthew 16:1-12

The Pharisees and Sadducees asked Jesus to show them a sign from heaven. But, Jesus denied their request, saying that they knew how to discern the face of the sky but could not discern the signs of the times. He said that He would give them no sign but the sign of the prophet Jonah.

The truth was that the signs of the Messiah and God's Kingdom were all around the Pharisees and Sadducees, but they were too blind to see them. Even when the sign of the prophet Jonah would be given, Jesus spending three days in the belly of the earth and then being raised up on the third day, they would refuse to see.

I am like the Pharisees and Sadducees in this one regard: Lord, I seek a sign from heaven from You. But, there is a difference. They came to You wanting to justify themselves and testing You that they might war against You and triumph. And so You refused them their proud request.

But I, Lord, come before You this morning, asking as well for a sign. You know that I used to desire signs from heaven in the sky, that I had a secret desire to see the miraculous in my life. These things you have refused me and, in your wisdom and grace, You have caused my faith in You to prosper and grow without such signs.

And still I ask for a sign from you, and yet more. I ask simply that You reveal Yourself to me today in the way that You think best for me. I give up all other demands for a sign, other than that You would give Yourself to me today and reveal Yourself to me. I know that You are wiser than I am and that you know me and know what's better for me than I know myself.

Sometimes I am prone to become discouraged or fatigued in my following You, and so I seek to be refreshed. One of my favorite things that You say to me is what You tell me in the Holy Communion service, when You say (and I believe): *"Come unto Me, all ye that travail and are heavy laden, and I will refresh you"* (Matthew 11:28).

You know how I travail, and You know the weight and force of my burden, and what I ask of You is that You would refresh me. I could seek refreshment from other sources; I could seek my rest in food or drink, or entertainment or sports, or in human company. But, I know that You are the Giver of every good gift and that when I come begging to You I will not be sent away empty-handed.

I miss Your presence in my life. I miss You because I'm not as close to You as I'd like to be and can't find the strength or vision to come any closer. I miss You because even when You do come to me I'm like the Pharisees and Sadducees in their blindness.

I don't ask anymore that You come to me from the clouds of heaven, with a flash of light and a thunder of voice, but I do ask that You come to me today. Give my eyes strength of vision to be able to see You when You come and purity of heart to be a mansion fit for Your presence.

Help me to wait and look for you in the small things of life, since they are so much more prevalent than and compose so much more of my life than the big things, and since You delight in hiding Yourself in small and humble things.

When I wake in the morning, let me see You in the renewed life You give to me. When my senses have been turned back on, let me see You in the colors of the day. At work, may I see you in the people I serve and work with, and may I see You in the minutiae of my labors. When I am at home, may I see my house as Your house.

The sign that I seek from You, Lord, is not something outside myself that will come and go like the glory of fireworks. There is no lack of Your presence or its signs in the world, but there is a shortage of those who can see You. I desire something deeper and more eternal and constant. What I desire from You, Lord, is the transformation of my being. I myself am the sign of Your presence with me, a changed life that is able now to see and hear You and willing now to obey when I hear.

I seek a sign from heaven today from You, Father, knowing that it will come among the common things of the earth. Show me the sign of Jonah the prophet today, the Resurrection of Your Son, my Lord. As I see His Resurrection and partake of it, resurrect me from my slumbers that I may see and praise You again today.

One thing have I desired of you, Lord, that I will seek: to dwell in Your house all the days of my life, to behold Your beauty, and to inquire in Your Temple.

Prayer:

Day by day, Oh dear Lord,
Three things I pray:
To see thee more clearly
Love thee more dearly
And follow thee more nearly. Amen.

(St. Richard)

Points for Meditation:

1. What are the various ways in which God might show Himself to You today, if you were watching for Him?
2. What are some of the ways that the Lord has "given you a sign" of Himself in the past?

Resolution:

I resolve to seek to see God in the small things of my life today.

Matthew 16:13-28

One thing's for sure: contrary to what atheists would have you believe, heaven will definitely not be boring!

I say this because even in this life God constantly desires to show us new things and take us to the next level. I've discovered that I went through three phases of watching the *Batman* TV show made in the 60s. When I was a little kid, I wanted to be Batman. I had a Batman cowl, a Batman TV shirt, the coolest electronic Batman game, and once I even had a bowl of Batman ice cream that I remember as being different psychedelic colors. I liked Batman because he was a hero. When I was a little older, I thought Batman was a show for little kids and not nearly as good. And when I became a young adult, I saw all sorts of campy things that made the show enjoyable again.

I'm constantly discovering new levels of reading the Bible, and one of my not so secret missions in writing *Give Us This Day* is to learn to see things I haven't seen before.

We do get bored, even with God, in this life. But, contrary to this life, in heaven we'll give up ourselves and complacency and toys, and we'll want to go to the next level that God is willing to take us to.

As a teacher, I always want to take my students to the next level that they are ready for and desire. Jesus, being the perfect Teacher, takes His disciples, particularly Peter, to a dramatically new level today, not once, not twice, but four times.

In His first teaching, Jesus tests His disciples to see what they already know. It's not clear in the Gospels exactly how clearly He had taught His disciples the answer to the all-important question He's about to ask. Often, He seems to prefer teaching by example and by leading His disciples with parables. He begins by asking an easier, warm up question that establishes a context for the all-important question and implies a distinction between those who answer this question in different ways.

"Who do men say that I, the Son of Man, am?" (v. 13b) They tell Him that some say John the Baptist, some Elijah, and others Jeremiah or one of the prophets.

And then Jesus asks part two of the question: *"But who do you say that I am?"* (v. 15b)

It's interesting that Jesus asks all of the disciples, but it's Peter who answers. Peter's justly famous answer is: *"You are the Christ, the Son of the living God"* (v. 16).

Jesus immediately calls Peter blessed, but not in exactly the way we might expect. Why does Peter answer, and not the others? It could be because he's always the impetuous one. But, Jesus has a different answer. He calls Peter blessed because flesh and blood has not revealed this to him but the Father in heaven.

Peter gets an 'A' on this assignment. This was not merely a test of Peter's ability to memorize: he had to demonstrate some original (even if it did come from God) thinking about who Jesus was. He made explicit what had been implicit: he had internalized what Jesus had been teaching.

Most of us teachers would have been overjoyed and stopped there. But, not Jesus. He pushes Peter further, and in his second teaching plants some seeds. Continuing with His theme that revelation and salvation are from God, Jesus announces to Peter that he now has a new name: Peter, or "Rock" (maybe even better—"Rocky"). On this Rock, Jesus will build His church. Furthermore, Jesus will give him the keys to the kingdom.

But, these are things that hadn't happened yet to Peter. The same God who revealed that Jesus was the Christ and the Son of God must also have foretold these things about Peter. Jesus was greater than Peter first imagined Him to be, and now Peter is told that he will also be greater than he imagines himself to be.

We know how Peter's story turns out and who he turns out to be. But, take a look at the very next story of Peter, and imagine that it is this person about whom Jesus says He will build His church.

The third lesson Jesus teaches is when His teaching takes a dramatic new turn. Now that the disciples, led by Peter, understand that Jesus is the Christ, the Son of the Living God, Jesus wants to take them further. "From that time Jesus began to show to His disciples that He must go to Jerusalem, and suffer many things from the elders and chief priests and scribes, and be killed, and be raised the third day" (v. 21).

Now that the disciples have understood that Jesus is the Messiah, He must show them who the Messiah really is, and so He begins to teach about the Suffering Servant. It was difficult enough to get the disciples to understand that He really was the Messiah, the Son of God, but now He has more to teach.

But, this teaching doesn't seem to fit with what the students have just learned. Say it ain't so! Peter, the star pupil, gets up and takes Jesus aside and rebukes the Master! *"Far be it from You, Lord; this shall not happen to You!"* (v. 22b)

Peter's feeling was understandable. If Jesus were the Messiah, why would He have to suffer many things, and then be killed (Peter probably never even heard the part about being raised on the third day!)? It just doesn't seem fair. Don't you think Jesus was maybe a little hard on Peter? Couldn't He have corrected Peter more gently? Why is He suddenly such a hothead?

"Get behind Me, Satan! You are an offense to Me, for you are not mindful of the things of God, but the things of men" (v. 23).

He sounds like me to my kids sometimes. I hope for and envision great things for them; I love them and teach them and pray for them. But, when they act in ungodly ways, I sometimes let them have it!

It's hard to feel exactly what Jesus must have felt and know exactly how Jesus said these scathing words. But, surely without knowing it, Peter was speaking the Satanic line. Jesus knows Satan. He's wrestled with Him before, in the temptation in the wilderness, and here He sees him again. Maybe He knows that an even greater temptation will come when the hour comes for Him to be betrayed and delivered to the Jews. Maybe, for a moment, He's genuinely tempted to take the easy path to messianic glory, and He knows He must resist, even if the words come from his own familiar friend in whom He trusted. Peter, in spite of his profession of Jesus, is still following the things of men, and not the things of God.

Jesus uses this temptation to continue His dramatic new teaching, and so He now presents his fourth teaching for today. Not only will the Messiah suffer many things and be killed, but His disciples also must be willing to suffer for Him. Usually, we read this astounding verse, verse 24, knowing that Jesus will die on the cross and be raised from the dead. But, how must it have sounded to the disciples *before* they had seen the Crucifixion and Resurrection?

Not only will this Messiah suffer and die, but those who want to be His disciples and follow Him must deny themselves, take up their crosses, and follow Him. But, He's just told us that He will suffer and then die. This Jesus is not only greater than any of the disciples imagined; He will also suffer more and appear defeated. Peter, who heard such blessed pronunciations of who God had called him to be, now heard about his own need to suffer.

As with Peter, Jesus is calling you to the next level of faith in and commitment to Him. He's asking you to come to the next level of love in your relationship with Him. While still in this life, this next level will require that you give yet more of yourself to Him, and this will be a painful process. Neither you nor I have completely denied ourselves that we might follow our Lord. We are all still too mindful of the things of men.

But, by taking up your cross, Jesus is calling you to the same blessings He offered Peter. Come, sit at the Master's feet a while today. Listen to Him as He tells you what He wants you to learn and to do next.

And stay tuned: you ought to be here for tomorrow's lesson! Same Bat time, same Bat channel.

Prayer:
O Lord Jesus Christ, draw me by Thy love that I may deny myself, and, taking up my cross daily, may follow after Thee, until I am like Thee and with Thee where Thou art. Amen.

Points for Meditation:
1. What is the next lesson that the Master is trying to teach you?
2. In what ways have you been acting like Peter, as God's adversary? In what ways are you resisting the Lord's teaching and leading?

Resolution:
I resolve to listen to my Master today until I have heard His next lesson. Having heard it, I resolve to put it into action in one way today.

Matthew 17:1–13

All of the life of Christ is one piece, like the tunic which He wore to His death and for which the soldiers cast lots. His Transfiguration is therefore of a piece with His Incarnation, Crucifixion, and Resurrection.

In the Incarnation, when God was made man, the glory of the Lord, the glory of Jesus, was revealed. We saw it with the angels and the shepherds and, later, the wise men. The glory of the Lord shone through Jesus' entire public ministry, in his preaching, teaching, and healing, and here in the Transfiguration, for one brief moment, we see Him in all His glory.

And then it's back on the road to Calvary and the Cross. The Transfiguration is a foretaste of the glory to come, but that glory will come more fully only *after* the Cross. At the Cross, the glory of the Father in redeeming mankind was revealed; it was made even more clear and glorious to all by the Resurrection. In the Transfiguration, we (along with Peter, James, and John) see, however briefly, the glory of Jesus. This is who He really is, and we are privileged to see it for this brief, shining moment.

What strikes me today, like a brief but brilliant bolt of lightning, is that the Transfiguration of Jesus Christ is also my own transfiguration, the transfiguration of the human race, and, indeed, of the cosmos! God is all-glorious, whether I see Him or not. His glory is simply who He is: I AM. And yet He's invited me to be a witness to, and even a participant in, His glory.

It would be all fine and good that God has revealed Himself in all His glory, but what good would that be if we were still in our sins? What good would it be to see the true God in an unmistakable, almost blinding way, only to have Him return to heaven and strand us, still rotting and decaying in our sins? This is why the Transfiguration must lead to the Cross and the Cross to the Resurrection. And we participate in each of these through Jesus Christ.

This means that we, like Jesus, must also be transfigured. The Greek word used for transfiguration is "metamorphao," from which we get our word "metamorphosis." The change God effects in us is indeed a metamorphosis, only a much greater one than that of a caterpillar to a butterfly. In fact, the metamorphosis in us is, as it was for Christ, only a completed revelation of what God has already done for us.

The exact nature of this Transfiguration which God takes us through is often misunderstood. Sometimes, for example, our conception of heaven is seriously messed up! We view it as something totally different from earth, something superhuman to the point of incomprehensibility. Therefore, we can't think much about it, and it doesn't penetrate into our earthly lives. Because it's entirely future and has little relevance to us or little impact on our lives.

But in Matthew 16:28, the verse right before the passage about the Transfiguration, Jesus says that some of the disciples will see the Son of Man coming in His kingdom. His kingdom, therefore, must be present *now*. The Transfiguration follows immediately after this; it is the demonstration that the Kingdom of Heaven is here now. I find hope in this, and glory. It cures me of my malaise that is induced by thinking sometimes that Jesus is here with me *less* now than He was at the Transfiguration.

Jesus is here more than ever before: His kingdom is growing progressively and steadily, and it is progressively being revealed to all men. The Kingdom of Heaven is here now, and it is within each one of us because Christ is in us and His rule extends to us, who are His body. So this process of Transfiguration in men has already begun, and we are already in the process of being revealed to be who we truly are.

But, glory doesn't come to us totally and at once. First, there is the suffering of this earth. We see through a glass darkly the fullness of things to come. But, as with Jesus (and we must always look to Him for our example) we know that after the suffering there is glory to come: the glory which Jesus displayed at the Mount of Transfiguration is the same glory He is progressively displaying in us. We too will be manifested as sons and daughters of the light: slowly and partially here in this present life, but finally and dramatically in the life to come.

"Beloved, now we are children of God; and it has not yet been revealed what we shall be, but we know that when He is revealed, we shall be like Him, for we shall see Him as He is"(1 John 3:2).

The trick is in looking for those moments of transfiguration in this life, in which God reveals Himself to us as He will in heaven. The trick is in looking for those moments in which we are transfigured, however, briefly, into what we shall one day be.

When you look at yourself, what do you see? Do you see a weak or aging, a balding or an expanding body? Do you see a terrible sinner or merely an average, ordinary human? Or do you see a new creature, redeemed and being transformed into the likeness of the Son of God? Is your daily life a random collection of moments of experience that just seem to happen one day after another, or are your moments infused with the anticipation of seeing and being with God in whatever you're doing at this very second?

When you look at the Church, what do you see? Do you see only the shallowness or faddishness or sad divisions that mark parts of the Church? Or do you see the Body of Christ filled with the glory of God, the New Jerusalem that has descended from heaven?

In this life, we can't live on the Mount of Transfiguration 24/7. It just isn't going to happen. But, you may be amazed where you might find this Mount in this life, if you seek the One who dwells there. And when you do find yourself there, in the presence of Moses and Elijah, and Peter, James, and John, remember who you really are: you are one transfigured by Jesus Christ!

Prayer:

Father, thank You for making me one of your children and translating me from the kingdom of darkness into Your glorious kingdom of light! Show Yourself to me today that I might behold Your glory, and in Your light see myself. Protect me from the Evil One and the false images of Your holy ones that he seeks to plant inside me. Today, let me see You as you are that I may be like You. Amen.

Points for Meditation:

1. What moments of transfiguration have you experienced before?
2. Close your eyes and probe your heart. How do you see yourself? How *should* you see yourself?

Resolution:

I resolve today to meditate on who Jesus Christ has made me to be and to look for moments of transfiguration.

Matthew 17:14-27

"Why could we not cast it out?" the disciples ask, concerning the demon they had failed to exorcise.

"Because of your unbelief...However, this kind does not go out except by prayer and fasting."

This is an intriguing passage for many reasons. Let me clear up a confusion or red herring right at the beginning. When Jesus says that if we have faith we can actually move mountains, how many of us really believe He's promising us the power of mega-levitation? Commentators are united in believing that Jesus is not speaking literally, and many believe he was referring to a saying of the day or merely using hyperbole.

The truly intriguing thing is that there seem to be degrees of belief. Didn't the disciples know who Jesus was to some degree, and didn't they truly have some measure of faith in Him? Yes, He often chided them for being little-faiths, but they did have a measure of faith. Certainly, they were able to cast out demons in Matthew 10, where Jesus gives the disciples power to cast out unclean spirits. These are the men who followed Jesus when He said, "Follow me."

So I think that there are degrees of faith. It's possible to truly know who Jesus Christ is and believe in Him and yet have such a weak faith that little progress is made in the spiritual life and life seems like a range of mountains arrayed against us.

I'm also intrigued by the fact that although the disciples cast out demons earlier, they were unable to cast this one out. On the one hand, Jesus says it's because of their lack of faith. But, He later says that this kind of demon does not go out except by prayer and fasting. There must be something about prayer and fasting that allows for greater power to exorcise demons; there must be something about prayer and fasting that increases faith.

What do prayer and fasting have in common? Both of them require humility. To pray means you must acknowledge yourself to be too weak to accomplish the good that you want to see done. It also means giving up being in charge, as well as giving up your time and energy. To fast means to choose to go without something you need so that you may be brought closer to God. Both prayer and fasting, therefore, are related to love, the giving up of oneself for another.

We don't have many details in this story, but it seems likely that the disciples had attempted to cast out the demon by their own power. Maybe they remembered how easy it was earlier, when Jesus had given them power to do it. Maybe Jesus gave them an extra measure of grace at that point to demonstrate *His* power over the demons. And maybe the disciples had assumed that Jesus would always give them this same measure of grace and that they wouldn't have to seek God to exorcise this demon.

Or maybe that's just me speaking. That's the way it goes in my life a lot of the time. Sometimes things seem to work by themselves, even though I know it's only by the grace of God. And sometimes they're a lot harder, but not due to any difference in conditions that I can discern. Life with God is an unpredictable one, I find, and I think God uses this unpredictability to keep me coming back to Him.

Sometimes I pray and turn to God, and He blesses me with "success" in apparent ways. Other times I pray and turn to God, and He seems to say "No" and withhold blessings. Sometimes I don't pray and things seem to go O.K. Other times I don't pray and things go horribly.

When I pray to God and all seems right with the world, I should keep doing what is working: praying and turning to God. When I pray and things don't go so well, I should persevere and cry out all the more and seek the presence of God more. When I don't pray and things go well, I should remember God's grace and come back to thank Him, and I should begin praying. And when I don't pray and things go horribly, then I know I must pray.

I find, therefore, that in three out of four of these cases, I'm tempted to stop praying or turning to God. When I pray and God is clearly merciful and blessing me, I'm tempted to give up prayer and enjoy His fruits without Him. When I pray and things are still hard, I'm prone to become discouraged. And when I don't pray and things go well, I'm deluded into thinking they'll always be good without Him. But, when I haven't been turning to God and things go horribly, then my heart is pierced, and I know it's time to turn to Him again.

It's as if God has created this feedback loop so that even when we fail Him, sometimes *most* when we fail Him, He brings us closer to Him. Isn't that just like God: that even our times of unfaithfulness can become a means of blessing, if only we would turn back to Him? If only we had the faith and faithfulness of a mustard seed, we could move mountains.

Where God wants us is with Him, in prayer and in life. How blessed are those who are so constant in their faith that for better for worse, for richer for poorer, in sickness and in health, they continue to turn to the Lord for all things. Fasting is one of the ways we can remember our poverty when we go without God and our hunger for Him. And if we will not fast from ourselves at certain times, then God Himself will impose fasts on us, if that's what it takes for us to have faith and to make that faith grow.

Consider your life today. Where are the mountains that you would like to move, and where are the demon-possessed children in your life? How have you been attempting to move these mountains: on your own, or with prayer and fasting?

Prayer:

O Father, who does not change when all else changes and who does not forsake me when I forsake You, I thank You that when my faith is weak and I wander away from You that You send me messengers to wake me up and guides to lead me back to You. Give me a clearer vision of Your light and a greater hunger for Your presence so that I will not desire to be any place else but with You. Increase in me faith, love, and humility that I might magnify Your name and glorify You by turning to You. Amen.

Points for Meditation:

1. Where are the mountains that you would like to move in your life? How have you been attempting to move these mountains: on your own, or with prayer and fasting?
2. Where are you in your prayer life with God right now?

Resolution:

I resolve to return to a life of prayer today and to consider fasting, if the Lord is leading me back to Him in this way.

Matthew 18:1-14

See what concern Jesus has for little ones in Matthew 18!

"Assuredly, I say to you, unless you are converted and become as little children, you will by no means enter the kingdom of heaven. Therefore, whoever humbles himself as this little child is the greatest in the kingdom of heaven. Whoever receives one little child like this in My name receives Me" (vv. 3–5).

"Whoever causes one of these little ones who believe in Me to sin, it would be better for him if a millstone were hung around his neck, and he were drowned in the depth of the sea" (v. 6).

"Take heed that you do not despise one of these little ones, for I say to you that in heaven their angels always see the face of My Father who is in heaven" (v. 11).

"Even so it is not the will of your Father who is in heaven that one of these little ones should perish." (v. 14).

. . .

First, a word to parents—your children, while they are still in your household, are the little ones that Jesus is talking about. Your obligation, as a Christian to whom Jesus Himself has entrusted these little ones, is to make them disciples of Jesus Christ. Your main way of showing your love for God and love for neighbor, after showing this love to your spouse first, is to serve your children by lovingly disciplining them in the life and way of Jesus Christ.

But, when you divorce or pick spouses who you know will not devote themselves to this task, you are not shepherding these little ones. When your work or social life or leisure becomes more important than your children, then you are leading these little ones astray. Remember—the angels of your children, on behalf of your Christian children, always see the face of God—and so must you!

Guard the children in your life!

But, the little ones to whom Jesus refers are not only the children among us—*all of us* are little ones. We are all to become as these little children, remember? And so we are all little ones: there is only one who is truly great among us, and He came to serve, not to be served.

Once we broaden the category of "little ones" to be all the people in our life, our lives suddenly become much more complicated, but also more exciting and glorious. We don't have to look far to find these little ones in our lives, even if our lives aren't filled with children as mine is. Everyone in your life is a little one, and therefore everyone is to be served in the way that Jesus commands.

Now it's obviously not possible to serve deeply everyone who comes into your life. But I think we're all smart enough to figure out who some of these little ones are. Here's a way to deal with this commandment to love the little ones in our lives, even when we can't always readily identify them. Make it your ambition to serve *everyone* who comes into your life in the ways that Jesus commands.

First, make sure you're not leading others into sin by your words or actions or example. This is most obviously the case with children, but it's amazing how much our sense of right and wrong is governed by the examples of those around us. The closer you are to someone, the more your example will lead him. Every object in the universe exerts a gravitational pull on every other object. Sometimes these gravitational pulls are insignificant: a dust mite on planet Earth doesn't attract a speck in space very much, and I don't have much to do with the 1.3 billion Chinese people on Earth. But the larger and closer an object is, the more it exerts a gravitational pull on those around it. The sun is large and has many objects orbiting it. The size and proximity of a parent to a child exerts a vast gravitational pull, but so do adults who are close to each other. Don't lead others into temptation.

Second, do not despise the little ones in your life. Here's where we might focus the "little ones" to mean those who are poor in spirit. Don't despise those who are a little different or don't fit in. I observed once at a church camp a boy who didn't fit into the larger group very well. He was kind of obnoxious and immature; he wasn't into the same things as everyone else; and he wasn't always very nice. But, he had a lot of fine qualities that were overlooked. The other kids, by degrees, day by day, pushed him away further and further. It was really sort of brutal.

Of course, we adults would never marginalize anyone or look down on them because they're different!

Third, and this is the part that strikes me most, go after the little ones who have gone astray. There are a lot of wandering sheep in the Good Shepherd's flock: some of you may have been one of them, and some of you may still be one of them. These are the little ones we are to especially seek out. No one decides to leave the Good Shepherd's flock in an instant. First, there is the little misstep that's not corrected. Then there's the bolder step away from the Shepherd. Only after a considerable period of wandering away is one of His sheep lost.

The strange thing is that often there are other sheep around who have witnessed this straying sheep but say or do nothing about it. It's not the will of your Father in heaven that one of these little ones should perish—and He's asked *you* to do something about it when you see it. For the amazing thing about the Good Shepherd is that He's commissioned the sheep to also be shepherds, and I'm not talking only about pastors.

Most of us have opportunities every day to say something to someone who is straying or getting lost in some way, even in little ways. How often do we look on, notice it, and then go on our merry way?

Remember: these, too, are the little ones whose angels see the face of God! These, too, are the little ones that the Father does not wish to see perish. So look around you today: where do you see the little ones? What can you do today to point them back to the Great One?

Prayer:

Grant me, O God,
> the heart of a child,
pure and transparent as a spring;
> a simple heart,
which never harbors sorrows;
a heart glorious in self-giving,
> tender in compassion;
a heart faithful and generous,
which will never forget any good
or bear a grudge for any evil.

Make me a heart gentle and humble
> loving without asking any return,
> large-hearted and undauntable,
which no ingratitude can sour
and no indifference can weary;
> a heart penetrated by the love of Jesus
> whose desire will only be satisfied in heaven.

Grant me, O Lord,
> the mind and heart
> of thy dear Son. Amen.

(Translated from the French by George Appleton)

Points for Meditation:

1. Who are the little ones in my life?
2. If you are a little one, how might you seek to come closer, back to your Good Shepherd?

Resolution:

I resolve to identify one little one in my life (it might be me!) and find one way to redirect him back to the Good Shepherd.

Matthew 18:15–35

Growing up in Champaign, Illinois until the age of 10, I had a pretty idyllic, "Leave it to Beaver" childhood. I remember thinking sometimes that life wasn't all that good. The sources of my "suffering"? The teasing of my siblings, the Green Bay Packers team losing a game or the Chicago Cubs not winning the division title, and losing a spelling bee in school that I thought I should have won.

But when I compare what I thought was suffering to some of the things some of my students have suffered: shattering divorces; neglecting parents; broken relationships; sometimes even abuse—what I thought was suffering doesn't even compare.

In the same way, we sometimes make too much of the ways that people offend us. But, when we compare them to the size of how we have offended against God, we find that the offenses against us aren't that large after all. And that's the point of this morning's lesson from our Lord: considering the magnitude of the sins that God has forgiven us, we are to forgive the small amount that others have sinned against us.

As Christians, we are to live in the Kingdom of Heaven. This means that we are governed by the Rules or Laws of Heaven. And in the Kingdom of Heaven, things work differently than in earthly kingdoms. We pray, rightfully: "Thy will be done, on earth as it is in heaven." Through Jesus Christ, heaven has been brought back down to earth...that earth might be brought back up to heaven.

The process of salvation is one of man being made like God and re-created to live in His presence in union with Him forever. Man is to be reborn into the image of Jesus Christ, the perfect man. And so it is that as God has forgiven you, you are to be made like God and forgive those who have sinned against you. The starting point is the forgiveness of God. If we start here, the rest is easier. And if we start with others' trespasses against us? We may never make it to the part about God's forgiveness.

God is the master who has forgiven you much. How much He's forgiven us is something we always underestimate. It's hard for us to even understand the existence of our sins, much less how terrible they are against the one who is God. I think a lot of Christians believe they make it through most days without sinning. Wrong! That just means you may not be very sensitive to the sins in your life.

This blindness to the sin in our lives is just one more measure of how much we have offended God.

Only if we understand the magnitude of our debt to God, first understanding how grand and glorious He is, can we understand how much we have been forgiven.

This forgiveness of sins, however, isn't automatic. If it were, we'd have to be universalists and say everyone goes to heaven and receives God's blessed presence regardless of what they believe or do. In the parable, the servant had to ask to be forgiven, and so must we. God's forgiveness comes only through the means He has offered—the life of His Son. To be forgiven, we must accept salvation through Jesus Christ, which means acknowledging our sins and seeking forgiveness from God. If we truly accept God's forgiveness, offered only through His Son, then we must be made like the Son.

When someone's wronged you and seeks forgiveness, do you think they truly seek forgiveness when they won't look you in the eye? When they say it without feeling, or with obvious resentment? Then why would we expect God to truly forgive us, when we don't come with a truly penitent heart and with humility?

But, Jesus takes us even further into the heart of God. It's not enough merely to seek forgiveness: we must also seek to forgive those who have wronged us. In the parable the servant also had to forgive: when he didn't, he was punished. Forgiveness by God is mysteriously dependent on our forgiving others. Forgiving others is therefore not optional: it's proof that we have been forgiven and have received the new spiritual life that comes only through forgiveness by God through His Son.

The main point of the parable, therefore, is to forgive as you have been forgiven. For this reason we find forgiveness, God's and ours, at the very heart of the Lord's Prayer. *"Forgive us our trespasses, as we forgive those who trespass against us."* Prayer, therefore, is a means to become like the Son. If you call yourself a Christian, who are you to accept God's immeasurable forgiveness and then refuse to forgive others their microscopic motes?

Are there some people you have not completely forgiven? You are obligated to forgive them. This is the clear commandment of God: you cannot refuse it.

This forgiveness, which is required for the Christian, is often a process, and one that must be repeated. The 70×7 is not a limit by which we may come to an end of forgiveness but is representative of forgiveness without limit. I, for one, am glad that God didn't stop forgiving me at sin #491!

We shouldn't be discouraged if we have to repeat this action of forgiveness. How often have *you* had to seek God's forgiveness for the same sin over and over? Then we must forgive others this often, from the heart each and every time. Forgiveness is, therefore, sometimes a process or a lifestyle, and not always a once for all thing.

Corrie ten Boom told of not being able to forget a wrong that had been done to her. She had forgiven the person, but she kept rehashing the incident and so couldn't sleep. Finally Corrie cried out to God for help in putting the problem to rest.

> "His help came in the form of a kindly Lutheran pastor," Corrie wrote, "to whom I confessed my failure after two sleepless weeks. 'Up in the church tower,' he said, nodding out the window, 'is a bell which is rung by pulling on a rope. But you know what? After the sexton lets go of the rope, the bell keeps on swinging. First ding, then dong. Slower and slower until there's a final dong and it stops. I believe the same thing is true of forgiveness. When we forgive, we take our hand off the rope. But if we've been tugging at our grievances for a long time, we mustn't be surprised if the old angry thoughts keep coming for a while. They're just the ding-dongs of the old bell slowing down.'
>
> And so it proved to be. There were a few more midnight reverberations, a couple of dings when the subject came up in my conversations, but the force—which was my willingness in the matter—had gone out of them. They came less and less often and at the last stopped altogether: we can trust God not only above our emotions, but also above our thoughts." [6]

And then there is the cost of forgiveness. In the parable, what was sacrificed by the forgiver was a sum of money. In reality, what was sacrificed for forgiveness was the Body and Blood of Jesus Christ. For us, the sacrifice may be our pride, the deliciousness of feeling superior, the anger and bitterness that may feed us, etc.

One of the most incredible movies I've ever seen is *To End All Wars*, which is based on a true story. In World War II a Scottish regiment is captured by the Japanese and put to work constructing a 400-mile long railroad. They are treated brutally and harshly: many die. Two views of how to deal with the situation emerge. Major Campbell, governed by revenge and hatred, wants to escape and kill their captors. However, following the example of a POW named Dusty, Ernest Gordon (another POW) starts a secret school and spreads the explicitly

---

6   Corrie Ten Boom. As quoted in sermonillustrations.com, http://www.sermonillustrations. com/a-z/f/forgiveness.htm.

Christian gospel of forgiveness. One by one, the other POWs follow Ernie's teaching of forgiveness. In spite of the fact that Dusty himself is brutally murdered (actually crucified), the POWs learn to forgive their enemies and to sacrifice for one another. This astounds the Japanese and gives hope and life to the POWs where they did not have it before.

These POWs had to give up their pride and their anger, and their revenge and hatred. But, they gained their souls, for in learning to forgive, they became like God Himself.

If you are having trouble forgiving, remember how much you have been forgiven. But, if you have learned to forgive, then blessed are you, for you are acting like God, and are a child of God.

Prayer:
Our Father, who art in heaven, hallowed be Thy name. Thy kingdom come. Thy will be done, on earth as it is in heaven. Give us this day our daily bread. And forgive us our trespasses, as we forgive those who trespass against us. And lead us not into temptation, but deliver us from evil. For thine is the kingdom, and the power, and the glory, for ever and ever. Amen.

Points for Meditation:
1. Is there anyone in your life whom God is asking you to forgive?
2. Have you asked for and accepted the forgiveness of God in all things?

Resolution:
I resolve to completely forgive and receive forgiveness today, as God directs me.

Matthew 19:1–15

Jesus' teaching on divorce seems so hardcore to us modern, or post-modern, Christians. I mean in Mark's Gospel He teaches that whoever divorces and remarries commits adultery, and here in Matthew He only adds the exception of sexual infidelity. This isn't a very forgiving or generous attitude towards divorce, is it? I mean, what if my wife and I just happen to drift apart after a lot of years? What if we're incompatible? What if I've had it with her and simply can't put up with her anymore?

I think that one of the problems is that we don't really believe that marriage represents the marriage between Jesus Christ and His Bride, the Church. We don't really believe that marriage is a sacrament that God blesses. We don't understand that when a man and a woman are so joined they become one flesh and one life.

Instead, we treat marriage like a contract—that's why we have prenups, right? What's the difference between a covenant, which marriage truly is, and a contract, which we treat it as? A covenant is put into effect by an oath. You remember your marriage vows, or oaths, don't you? You swore that you would stay married, as one flesh, as long as you both shall live, regardless of your circumstances, whether rich or poor, or sickness or health.

God is the silent third party at every Christian marriage, and when you get married you have also made vows to God. You've told Him that you vow to stay with this other person for the rest of your life. Because such vows mean business and suggest a permanence that is at odds with our supermarket of choices, in the modern, post-modern, world, we get to write our own vows.

It's all about us. The basic premise of this modern contract is that I agree to stay in this relationship as long as I feel fulfilled in it, however I choose to define fulfillment. It's actually a mercenary transaction, and the moment I get a better offer, I'm out of here.

If you truly believe that your marriage is for life, you'll be motivated to work towards making it that way. But, if you think that there's an asterisk by your names or that your names are written in disappearing ink on the marriage certificate, then you've already agreed to be willing to lead a life where divorce is an option. This is the essence of a self-fulfilling prophecy.

It's interesting that the one exception Jesus allows for is sexual immorality, which in a marriage essentially means sexual infidelity. No doubt, sex in marriage is important—it's part of the becoming one flesh, literally and metaphorically. But, sometimes we're too hung up on the sexual. We're taught that everything is ultimately about sex.

The truth is that sexual infidelity is always preceded by other kinds of infidelity. You don't just wake up one morning, see a beautiful woman you don't know, and say, "I think I'll give up 20 years of marital bliss for a few hours of a really good time." How many smaller infidelities must have led up to a single decision to commit adultery?

No woman wakes up one morning, after 20 years of marital bliss and says, "Honey, I think I want a divorce." Usually, there is a fairly long period of growing apart, although in some cases there was never much of a true relationship to begin with, which is its own problem for which there is culpability.

In a way, I think we groom ourselves for divorce. The romantic relationships that a lot of Christian young people have are a series of intimate relationships that get shattered. The pattern seems to be to draw close, become intimate, and hope and pray that the inevitable break up doesn't come, and then wonder why it did and why it hurts so much when it does come.

What we don't understand is the nature of the covenantal, marriage relationship that God has created. For this reason, parents who divorce often underestimate the devastation that divorce wreaks on their children. When I had some of my high school seniors write their spiritual journeys, I was moved to tears by some of their accounts of the terrifying effects of their parents' divorce on them. No wonder they couldn't concentrate in school or didn't care. No wonder that a lot of postmodernity is about being homeless and that teens today often feel abandoned.

In light of the devastating impact that divorce has on the "little ones" of Jesus, Jesus' blessing of the children in verses 13–15 is positively chilling!

What's missing from all of this is Jesus' understanding of marriage. "But, what can an unmarried man really know about marriage," some may say. But we forget that this man, who is also God, is married to His people, the Church. I think Jesus is fully aware of how difficult His teaching on divorce is. Remember: it comes after He has now begun to teach His disciples that the Bridegroom must soon give up His life for His Bride. Jesus' teaching on divorce comes after His teaching on the cost of discipleship and the necessity of denying self.

This is what marriage is really about: it's about love. It's about the kind of love that the Bridegroom has for His Bride. It's about the sacrifice that Christ makes for His Church. Only if a man and woman set out to serve each other in love, as their Master served them, will they have a sure foundation for a lasting marriage.

The same applies to any relationship that any of you are in, whether married or not. Think about a difficult relationship you have now or have had before. How would that relationship be different if you set out to relate to that person with nothing but love, regardless of what you got back in return? How might that relationship be better and more wonderful if you unilaterally chose to repay evil with love? How many more put downs and criticisms might you absorb if you put on love, and how many fewer criticisms and naggings would you commit if you put on love?

What if both of you set out to serve each other in love? What kind of relationship would be possible? No one said it would be easy. Maybe your spouse or person you have a relationship with (it could be a difficult sibling, for example) isn't exactly a jewel. Maybe you feel like you were dealt a rotten hand (of course, if you're married, then it's a hand you dealt yourself).

But, consider the deal that Jesus got! He didn't exactly end up with the pick of the litter, and yet how He loves His Bride!

Jesus' teaching about divorce is indeed hard, but it's hard because marriage is to be made of the hardest substance known to man: love.

It's hard because marriage is a picture of the marriage of Christ and the Church.

And it's hard because marriage is the most amazing, intense, and powerful way in the world for two people to practice taking up their crosses and denying themselves in love for the love of the other.

Prayer:

O God, who hast so consecrated the state of Matrimony that in it is represented the spiritual marriage and unity betwixt Christ and his Church; Look mercifully upon these thy servants, those married couples I know, that they may love, honor, and cherish each other, and so live together in faithfulness and patience, in wisdom and true godliness, that their homes may be a haven of blessing and of peace; through the same Jesus Christ our Lord, who liveth and reigneth with thee and the Holy Spirit ever, one God, world without end. Amen.

(From The Solemnization of Marriage from *The Book of Common Prayer*, p. 303)

Points for Meditation:

1. How might you be more loving towards a difficult person in your life or towards your spouse?
2. In what ways have you not been faithful to your spouse, or to someone close to you?

Resolution:

I resolve to find one way to show love to the person closest to me in my life (my spouse, if I have one).

Matthew 19:16–30

Questions are an important part of life. At their best, they demonstrate a vivacious curiosity and engagement with life. My twin brother Danny from an early age demonstrated a tenacious curiosity about things, a trait that has not abated as he and I have now arrived at the half-century mark in life.

As a teacher, you realize that questions search out the heart. What does a student understand, and what is he thinking? Jesus was a master at asking deep, probing questions that must have stung the hearts of those he questioned.

In today's lesson from Matthew 19, it's the rich young ruler who asks the questions this time. He rightly begins with the most important question: *"What good thing shall I do that I may have eternal life?"* (v. 16b).

This is a profound question and a great place to start, even though his motive may have been to justify himself.

Jesus, the wise Master, doesn't tell the rich young ruler everything at once but probes the heart of the young man. Being the Master, his answer surprises some of us. We expect Him to give the pious answer, "Believe in me, and you will have eternal life." His answer is twofold. The second part of the answer shocks some of us, because the implication is that we must, indeed, do something to inherit eternal life and are not merely passive spectators. Jesus says, *"If you want to enter into life, keep the commandments"* (v. 17b).

But, hidden before this second part of the answer, Jesus wisely plants the seed of directing the rich young ruler toward answering the question of who Jesus is, implying that since He is good, and God alone is good, then He, Jesus, must be God. But, He doesn't press the point here but instead merely plants the rich seed of faith.

The rich young ruler must have been very pleased to hear Jesus' answer that you must keep the commandments to inherit eternal life because he could honestly say that he had kept these commandments. Or at least the ones Jesus mentions, and at least the letter of the Law.

Jesus, however, doesn't let the rich young ruler off the hook but instead peers more deeply into his heart. If the rich young ruler were playing the game, "Who

Wants to be a Millionaire?" he might have made it up to the $1,000,000 question. But, there's just one more thing—the Final Answer.

In His first answer, Jesus listed all of the last 6 of the 10 Commandments, the ones that deal with loving your neighbor as yourself. But look again—He's left one out!

The young man (perhaps he was quite earnest) says, "*All these things I have kept from my youth. What do I still lack?*" (v. 20) It takes guts to ask this question. He could have rested on his obedience to six of the Commandments, but either through a kind of humility or an incredible pride, he wants to go further. And Jesus takes Him further, to the truth. At this point, Jesus has already perceived what is lacking in the rich young ruler, and in an indirect way He comes back to the missing Commandment, the one He had left out earlier: "*Thou shalt not covet*" (Ex. 20:17).

By asking the rich young ruler to sell what he had and give it to the poor, Jesus smashes the final idol of Mammon, which takes the various forms of greed and covetousness. Although seemingly perfect in other ways, the rich young ruler walks away still rich materially, but also spiritually bankrupt. All of the illusions the young man had of his own perfection have been shattered, and he's left to shuffle off sorrowfully, still clinging to the ball and chain of his great possessions.

Like the rich young ruler, Jesus won't let you settle for the easy and incomplete answer because easy and incomplete answers to the most important question one can ask are dangerous to your mortal soul.

Let's look at the meaning of Jesus for each of you.

What this story *doesn't* mean is that everyone must sell everything and give it to the poor. Jesus never commands us to do that. What it also doesn't mean is that therefore the story must be merely figurative. We might try our turn at asking questions and ask, "Did Jesus *really* mean for the rich young ruler to sell all he had?" If He didn't, then He likely won't ask us to do anything so difficult either. But, to ask such a question is to be deceived by the Satanic kind of question that twists the "Thus says the Lord" into "Did God really say?"

What the story *might* mean for you is that you should sell some of what you have and give it to the poor. It is, after all, hard for rich to enter Kingdom of Heaven. Just a few verses later, Jesus says: "*Assuredly, I say to you that it is hard for a rich man to enter the kingdom of heaven. And again I say to you, it is easier for a camel to go through the eye of a needle than for a rich man to enter the kingdom of heaven*" (vv. 23–24).

What pointed words, especially after the rich young man has just walked away sadly from Jesus!

And we are all rich, comparatively. Maybe some of us are called to be St. Francis of Assisi or St. Bernard of Clairveaux, who gave up their earthly wealth for a life of spiritual wealth.

The story *might* mean, "Be willing to sell if God asks you." Of course, it's very unlikely that God would ask directly, isn't it? And we wouldn't even know unless we were seriously willing to entertain the possibility that God was calling us to this.

But, what the story *must* mean is that we must not just be *willing* to sell all but *actually* sell all we have to obtain eternal life. Isn't this the meaning of the parables of the pearl of great price and of the buried treasure? This selling of all we have is not literal, just as the cutting off of our hands and eyes to enter the Kingdom is not literal. But, it is real, nonetheless.

Whatever stands between you and God, don't just be *willing* to get rid of it— DO IT! This was the attitude and action of the original disciples. Just a few verses after the story of the rich young ruler, in verse 27, Peter says, "*See, we have left all and followed You.*"

This is the cost of discipleship: to forsake all for the sake of Jesus. Jesus asks you to forsake mother and father, if necessary. He asks you to give up all your earthly riches, if necessary. He asks you to offer up your entire self to God as a living sacrifice, because this is necessary.

There are many things in the way of God for some of you. Maybe it *is* money, in which case, if God is telling you that money is a problem then go and read this passage again—and see what God is calling you to do. He just may be asking you to lighten the burden of your great riches (which many of us would see we have, if we weren't always comparing ourselves to those who are even wealthier).

Maybe it's your possessions. Does the sheer bulk of your possessions and caring for them crowd out time and room and energy for God? Maybe it's the comforts of this life. This is one of the greatest riches of living in America: having a comfortable life that doesn't demand much of us. But, are you too comfortable to follow Jesus; are you too comfortable to take up a cross as He did, to give up all and follow Him?

Maybe what Jesus is asking you to give up is the leisure time that you want to have for yourself. If your attitude is that you're off duty as a servant of the Lord once you finish your day job, then maybe you should re-examine your priorities.

On the other hand, it might be the various "demands" of your lifestyle that Jesus is asking you to give up. If, for example, your giving your child "everything," such as a good, college prep education, athletics, music lessons, and social events, is crowding out eating family meals together and family devotions, time at church or your youth group, or a life where there are moments of prayer and meditation, then maybe your Lord is asking you to give up at least one of these for Him.

Whatever stands in the way of you and God—and each of you probably has some idea of at least one thing that threatens your relationship with God—sell it! Get rid of it, for the sake of Jesus Christ, for the sake of His kingdom, and for the sake of your eternal soul!

When the Master asks you to do something for Him today, don't walk away sadly, unwilling to give up that which keeps you from Him. Instead, obey with cheer and joy, knowing your Master is good and desires to bless you.

Prayer:
Grant, Almighty God, that I, by Your grace, may today be that which You would have me to be and to do that which You have commanded me to do, listening to the voice of Your Spirit in my life. May I leave no sin unrepented of today, sparing least of all that sin which is costliest for me to give up, that I might come to that greatest treasure, Your Son Jesus Christ, in whose name I pray. Amen.

Point for Meditation:
What might be one thing that Jesus is asking you to give up for Him? How might this thing be an obstacle to greater faith and devotion? What would it take for you to begin giving this thing up, even in a small way? How might you need to restructure your life to do it?

Resolution:
I resolve to give up one thing today in my life, that I might see more clearly God and His will for my life.

Matthew 20:1–16

"That's not fa-a-a-a-a-ai-rrrr!"

That's the traditional complaint of the child, isn't it? As adults, we tell our children that life isn't fair, expecting them to meekly accept this, while we secretly fret and fume about life not being fair in the adult world.

At stake in today's parable from Jesus is the fairness of God. The fairness of God is routinely assailed, even if sometimes in indirect ways. Some directly shake the fist at God, exclaiming, "Why have you done this to me!" Others look at the disasters they themselves have made of life and declare it unfair and that they never get any breaks. Even among Christians, we sometimes believe that we've gotten the short end of the stick, even if we aren't exactly willing to state exactly Who it is that must have given us that short end.

The truth is that if you expect a life with a 1-to-1 correspondence between what you deserve and what you get, then you'll all be sadly disappointed. The key to understanding all of this, of course, is in figuring out what it is, exactly, that we deserve. One way of measuring things is to say that since we all start out equally we should all end up with the same things. Another way of measuring would be to say that since we all don't start out with the same things, then life, or the One who created it, must be unfair.

There is even a major movement in politics that involves the attempt to level the playing field so that all are equal. Advocates of the forced redistribution of wealth often assume that the rich must be immoral and that the poor must be deserving. On this basis, the powers that be attempt to make things "equal," not only in opportunity but also in outcome, regardless of the moral choices made by those involved.

My favorite illustration of this is Kurt Vonnegut's story, "Harrison Bergeron," whose title character is superior in looks, intelligence, and physical strength to just about everyone else. He is thus compelled to wear an ugly mask, headphones that blare loud noises so he can't think, and a hundred pounds or so of weights to reduce his unfair strength. This is the world we sometimes ask for when we so humbly proclaim life "unfair."

I myself once fell prey to such covetous thinking. I never really thought life was unfair, and I knew I'd been given a lot. But, I wasn't particularly happy. I had low self-esteem and secretly believed that I didn't seem to measure up to everyone else. Being an introvert, it also seemed as if the world were laughing and throwing a party but that I wasn't invited. I wasn't exactly covetous of the gifts of others, but I bordered on it, because I would compare myself to others who I felt were superior in some way. I wanted what they had, and not what God had given me.

Many of us have wished that God had made us someone else. But, He didn't. And the question is, "Is God unfair for making you how He made you?"

Well, is He?

Let's begin with a few rock solid assumptions we can make. Number One, God is good. Do we all believe that? If so, then we can move to assumption Number Two, which is that God is just and fair. He will not give you something you don't deserve (Well, almost. We'll get to an exception in a minute).

This leaves us only with the option that we are the ones who are unfair to unjustly accuse God. To the degree that we're dissatisfied with what "life" (meaning "God") has given us, it's a dissatisfaction of our own making. Remember, God is good and fair, so we have no right to complain. There are two possible reasons for our dissatisfaction. The first is the sin in our lives. We might think life is not good because the sins in our life keep us from God and under the thumb of guilt. If this is the case, we know what our response is to be: repentance. A lot of the "misfortunes" in our lives are actually self-inflicted and are the natural consequences from foolish financial, relationship, or other choices we ourselves have made. How can we blame God for these?

The other reason we may be unhappy about our lot in life is because we simply don't like what we've been given. Most of the time, there's nothing wrong with what we've been given; it's just that we feel entitled to more. We're like many American kids who are picky eaters and when they're served certain foods or dishes they turn their noses up at them and refuse to eat them. I'm routinely amazed by how consistently kids and teens will throw away perfectly good, even delicious, pizza crusts, all so they can eat more of the good stuff on the other end of the slice.

Actually, in our turning our noses up at what God has given us in this life as our daily bread, we're like someone who's starving to death but still refuses to eat the pizza crusts that are offered to him.

The issue is what we have versus what we think we are owed. So let's set the record straight. If you really want to play The Fairness Game, then here goes. What does God owe us humans? Let's see: having rebelled against His love and goodness, knowing that He can't dwell with sin and that the penalty for sin is death—we deserve death from Him. So if we want God to give us what we deserve and only what we deserve, if we really want to play the game of "That's Not Fair!" then we can choose death.

But, thank God that He doesn't always give us what we deserve. This is the meaning of His grace, which is commonly defined as "unmerited favor." In other words, God is not only good to us: He's *better* to us than we deserve. Instead of being merely "fair," God is loving and gracious. He gives us the good things we don't deserve: Himself, and with Him eternal life.

Therefore, the next time you feel like pouting because you think someone's getting ahead of you or that life isn't fair, remember what you really deserve, and remember the grace and mercy of God. Begin with the assumption that while life may not be fair, God is good, and that's what's truly important.

And if God is good, then you should accept what He brings into your life. Not what your sin has brought, but what He has brought. Even when bad things happen to you that are not a result of your sin, consider the goodness of God and His mercy to you. Consider that He just might mean it as a way of leading you closer to Him, because that's what He really wants.

Finally, there's at least one good antidote for "That'snotfairitis": it's thankfulness. Instead of looking at what you don't have that you would like (even if you don't deserve it), look at the good things God *has* given you. You'll be surprised by how many good things He's given you. He's given you the best thing in the world which you totally don't deserve—He's given Himself to you through His Son.

Prayer:

Almighty God, Father of all mercies, we thine unworthy servants do give thee most humble and hearty thanks for all thy goodness and loving-kindness to us, and to all men; we bless thee for our creation, preservation, and all the blessings of this life; but above all, for thine inestimable love in the redemption of the world by our Lord Jesus Christ; for the means of grace, and for the hope of glory. And, we beseech thee, give us that due sense of all thy mercies, that our hearts may be unfeignedly thankful, and that we show forth thy praise, not only with our lips, but in our lives; by giving up ourselves to thy service, and by walking before thee in holiness and righteousness all our days; through Jesus Christ our Lord, to whom with thee and the Holy Ghost be all honor and glory, world without end. Amen.

(The General Thanksgiving from *The Book of Common Prayer*, p. 19)

Points for Meditation:

1. Have you been grumbling toward God in any way? In what ways do you think life is unfair to you? How might you allow God to change your heart?
2. Make a list of good things God has given to you and practice rehearsing them whenever you're tempted to grumble and complain.
3. Consider the mercy and grace of God—and give thanks!

Resolution:

I resolve to give thanks to God today and to not allow myself to complain.

Matthew 20:17–34

Have you ever wanted to be great?

That's been a dream of mine ever since I was little. One of my earliest ways of obtaining glory was to become a great football player. As kids, we used to play football at a strip of field at Kenwood Elementary School in Champaign, Illinois, only a block away from our house. I used to be very fast and quick (Mr. Outside), while my twin, Danny, was good at bulling his way through defenders twice his size (Mr. Inside).

Because I was fast, especially in long distances compared to my peers, I also wanted to be the world's record holder in the mile. Jim Ryun was my hero, and he held the world record in the mile from 1966 until 1975, at 3 minutes 51.1 seconds. But, every year I ran, more of my peers seemed to be as fast, and I knew it was all over in 7th grade when a stupid sprinter almost caught me in the mile during P.E. class. The best mile I ever ran in my life was a 5:26.

I'll spare you my pathetic foray into politics but feel I must make mention of my desire to obtain glory by becoming a famous writer. I've always wanted to write, ever since I was in second grade. In fifth grade I started on a novel about a fictitious family that sounded suspiciously like my own, except that the twins were not named Danny and Charlie but Danny and Danny (this way, there was comedic material in the confusion of names, as well as a way for me to exempt myself from the stupid things the kids in novel did). Somehow, my first novel, *Tomorrow is for No One*, never found a publisher, much less make me a famous novelist.

There's a part of me that still wants to be great. But, if not as a football player, miler, politician, or writer—then as what? Maybe there's another way to think about human greatness.

Who are the great men and women of history?

We might think of people like Julius Caesar, Hannibal, Charlemagne, Napoleon, George Washington, and Abraham Lincoln. Some might more naturally think of people like Albert Einstein, Louis Pasteur, William Shakespeare, Beethoven, or Picasso. We might think of world leaders or even some of the heroes of the Bible.

But, Jesus' teaching on greatness calls into question the standard by which we measure greatness. Greatness, in our common understanding of greatness, comes in a number of different varieties. We call some great simply because of the magnitude of their accomplishments. Julius Caesar and Napoleon are generally considered to be "great," based on the magnitude of their dreams and successes. As grand as their achievements are by certain standards, there's a part of us that realizes that world conquest and domination is not a good measure of greatness. We know this because we would stop short of calling Adolph Hitler great, in spite of his incredible achievements.

Some are great because they have nearly superhuman powers: Michael Jordan, Tiger Woods, Usain Bolt, and a host of other athletes we idolize. Others are great because they're excellent at what they do: Bill Gates, Warren Buffet, and the scientists, writers, composers, and artists such as those I listed above.

All of these are great in their own way. All of them will pass away with this earth.

But, today Jesus offers wannabe great men like me a way to achieve true and permanent greatness. The funny thing is that it's 180 degrees away from the normal paths to human greatness. Normally, greatness begins and ends with *me*. *I'm* great because *I've* done this. It's all about me and what I've done and the attention that people pay to me.

Not so in Jesus' kingdom. *"Whoever desires to be great among you, let him be your servant. And whoever desires to be first among you, let him be your slave"* (v. 27).

As many times as I've read, heard, and meditated on this passage, it still jars me. Not as much as it used to, but it jars me, because it's so contrary to everything the world tries to teach me. In fact, to most people it will probably sound nonsensical. How can being a servant—or *slave*—be a path to greatness? It all depends on how you measure greatness. If your goal is to have everyone bow before you and serve you, then serving is a lousy path to greatness. But, if your goal is to be like God and to share in His far greater glory, then this is *the* path to glory.

I find great encouragement in this passage. I completely acknowledge how difficult this path is. There are times when I silently serve and almost begin to think to myself, "What a waste of my gifts and talents!" There are times when it seems as if no one recognizes the many sacrifices I make to serve others. I'm taken for granted, ignored, overlooked, and underappreciated.

I'm still not too crazy about it when the Lord asks me to serve in a capacity in which I know I'm not very good, but the truth is that I've sort of grown to like it. There's something contagious about serving, something more mysterious and profound than mere human glory.

In fact, in my more lucid moments I realize just how joyful and glorious serving is because I realize that by serving I am being like my Master. And that's what I really want, after all. What I really want is for the invisible audience of One to notice me and feel as if I'm pleasing to Him. For what seems like slavery and thankless drudgery here on earth is perfect freedom and laudable worship in heaven.

The Son of Man did not come to be served, but to serve. If I want Jesus, all of Jesus, then I must come to serve Him as He first served me. Everything about His life—from the way He was born, to the beginning of His public ministry and His teaching and healing, to His washing His disciples feet, to His praying for the disciples, to His Passion, to His Crucifixion—screams out SERVICE AND SACRIFICE!

If that is how the King of Glory came to us, then that is how we must go to Him, where we will find greatness. The amazing thing is that He who *is* glory is willing to share that glory and greatness with me. I can have no true greatness and glory of my own, but because of the humility of God who became man and the sacrifice of the Cross, I have been offered true greatness and glory. But, I have to share it, which in this case, is just fine with me.

Do you want the greatest glory and greatness of all? Then learn to be the servant of all. The greatest glory and most glorious greatness you could ever hope for is the glory and greatness of Jesus Christ. By serving Him, as He first served, and by serving Him by serving others, you are united to Jesus Himself. And where is He? In the glory of the Father, at His right hand in heaven.

That's what serving does, you know. Heaven and earth are usually invisible to each other, and sometimes this clouds our minds. On earth, serving in humility looks like an invisible and thankless way to Nowheresville, while in heaven it is a visible and glorious sharing in the life of the Son. On earth, human greatness and success look great, but in heaven, it is often an invisible and insignificant thing. Human greatness is often invisible in heaven because often it has more in common with the Other Place than it does with Heaven.

I don't need anything else today. I can still keep my dreams, if I want to, but I've now got all I need. All I need is to figure out where the Lord wants me to serve today, for if I do this, then He shall call me great. And great I shall be!

Prayer:

O Father, whose service is perfect freedom, help me to seek not to be served but to serve; help me to know the joy of laying down my life for You that You may raise me up. Show me where it is that I should serve today, and help me to serve with joy and gladness. May I serve with diligence and devotion, remembering that it is You I serve in all I do. Unite my service to Jesus my Lord's that I may share in His greatness today. Amen.

Points for Meditation:

1. How much do you desire greatness? What are the ways that you've been trying to achieve it? Are they God's ways?
2. How has God served you today? Perform your daily tasks today as if you are serving God, and remember the greatness He promises you!
3. Do you go to church more to serve or be served?

Resolution:

I resolve to eat my daily bread today, serving however the Lord asks me to serve, that I may share in His greatness.

Matthew 21:1–16

Ignaz Phillip Semmelweis was born in 1818 into a world of dying women. The finest hospitals lost one out of six young mothers to the scourge of "childbed fever". A doctor's daily routine began in the dissecting room where he performed autopsies. From there he made his way to the hospital to examine expectant mothers without ever pausing to wash his hands. Dr. Semmelweis was the first man in history to associate such examinations with the resultant infection and death. His own practice was to wash with a chlorine solution, and after eleven years and the delivery of 8,537 babies, he lost only 184 mothers—about 1 in 50.

He spent his life lecturing and debating with his colleagues. Once he argued, "Puerperal fever is caused by decomposed material, conveyed to a wound...I have shown how it can be prevented. I have proved all that I have said. But, while we talk, talk, talk, gentlemen, women are dying. I am not asking anything world shaking. I am asking you only to wash...For God's sake, wash your hands!" But almost no one believed him. Doctors and midwives had delivered babies for thousands of years without washing their hands, and no one was going to change them now![7]

"Wash me!" was also the anguished prayer of King David.

"Wash!" was the message of John the Baptist.

"Unless I wash you, you have no part with me," said the towel-draped Jesus to Peter (John 13:8). Without our being washed clean, we all die from the contamination of sin. For *your* sake, wash.

God's Temple is holy. When Moses was instructed to build the first tabernacle, he was given blueprints by God, written by finger of God. *"According to all that I show you, that is, the pattern of the tabernacle and the pattern of all its furnishings, just so shall you make it."* (Exodus 25:9) When David prepared to build the Temple that Solomon would build, he said, *"the Lord made me understand in writing by his hand upon me, even all the works of this pattern"* (1 Chronicles 28:19).

As you entered the Temple, you moved through progressively more holy places until the Holy of Holies was reached, which only the high priest could enter,

---

7   Adapted from Boyce Moulton, sermonillustrations.com, http://www.sermonillustrations. com/a-z/c/cleansing.htm.

and he only one day a year. Aaron and the priests were consecrated to serve at the tabernacle, all of the furniture was consecrated, and if you even so much as touched the Ark you would die. All of this teaches us something about how holy God is and about how holy we must be.

And so it is that Jesus comes in Matthew 21 to cleanse His temple. Why? What went wrong? To participate in the annual festivals, an annual Temple tribute of exactly ½ shekel had to be paid, and paid in only the Sanctuary or Galilean shekel. There were Palestinian, Persian, Tyrian, Syrian, Egyptian, Grecian, and Roman shekels all circulating, but this tax had to be paid exactly, and in the right kind of money. Where in the world could a visitor from far away find the right coin?

Not to worry, it just so happened that Jewish tax collectors and money changers had just the coin you need—for a certain price, of course! The necessary animal sacrifices had to be made and paid for as well. What? You don't want to lug your animals all the way from home? Not a problem. Have we got the goat for you! What's that you say? You need to have the animal inspected by a priest? Let Sacrifices R Us be your one stop Temple shop. Guaranteed kosher!

Every step of the way, there was a transaction and a tidy profit to be made by those selling merchandise and changing money. Keeping in mind the noisy bartering and arguing that must have taken place in this Middle Eastern scene, we can imagine why the Master was so livid at what was taking place in the House of God.

So Jesus, the Master, set about to clean His Holy House, the Temple, and He did it violently, with a righteous anger. He must have really cared about holiness!

Today, *we* are the Temple of the Lord, His Body, and the holy Church. God's Holy Spirit lives in His people, but only if they are holy.

And so Jesus cleanses His Temple today as well. Just as the Temple in Jesus' day was polluted and needed to be cleaned, His Temple today is polluted and needs to be cleaned. So Jesus needs to cleanse His Temple again, so that He can inhabit it again. Once again, we have let the Temple go. We have let in the animals and their uncleanness; we have let in the money-changers; and we have allowed God's Temple to be defiled.

There are actually two stories this morning. The first teaches us that the Master's will is done through His disciples; the second teaches that the Master is cleansing His holy temple. Put together, they teach that, "The Master is cleansing His holy Temple through His disciples—through *you*."

First, we see that the disciples are supposed to do the will of the Master. In verse 1, Jesus sent His disciples, and in verse 1 His disciples obeyed. God becoming man, God in His holy Temple, means He has chosen to live with you and work through you! God could snap His fingers and do whatever He wanted. But, He chose to become Man and sanctify Man and to do His will through you. And, the Master's will is that you be holy: that His Temple be cleansed by *you*.

This might seem like a Herculean labor, and, in fact, one of the labors of Hercules was to clean the Augean stables. Augeas, the king of Elis had been given a huge herd of 3000 cattle as a gift from his father, many herds in fact. His problem was that the stables where he kept them had never been cleaned. You can imagine how filthy these stables must have been, as well as how they must have smelled!

Hercules succeeded by diverting the streams of two rivers to clean the stables. How will we clean His Temple? You are to use the Living Water of Jesus Himself, the Master, to clean the Temple. Jesus, and not you or me, is the hero of this story. He has cleansed His temple, and all that we need to do to help Him clean it is to come to Him for washing. "Come once more and seek forgiveness, and I will cleanse you and make you holy," He says. "Come once more and give me your life, and I will give you My righteousness." And then He can use us to bring His cleansing power to others.

In the cleansing waters of baptism, God cleansed His Temple and made you a fit home for Him. At that time, you were made a priest called to guard His holy Temple and to serve in it. In your baptismal vows, you vowed three things: to renounce the world, the flesh, and the devil; to believe the articles of the Christian faith; and to obey His holy commandments. By these things, by your baptism, and by uniting yourself to Christ and His righteousness, you *will* be cleansed!

How well have you been keeping the Temple? If the Israelites of the Old Covenant were supposed to be careful with the temple made of wood and metal, which was destroyed forever, how much more careful should you be with yourself—and with His Church?

Prayer:

Dear Jesus, help me to spread your fragrance everywhere.

Flood my soul with your spirit and life.

Penetrate and possess my whole being so utterly that all my life may be only a radiance of yours.

Shine through me and be so in me that every person I come in contact with may feel your Presence in my soul.

Let them look up and see no longer me but only Jesus.

(John Henry Newman)

Points for Meditation:

1. Review the baptismal service in which you were baptized, if possible, or meditate on the meaning of your baptism today.
2. How well have you been keeping God's Temple, yourself, clean?
3. Is God asking you to help cleanse His Church in any way?

Resolution:

I resolve to return to Jesus today to ask for His cleansing power in my life!

Matthew 21:17–32

"Son, go work today in my vineyard" (v. 28).

Our Father says this to us. God has planted us in His garden, i.e. His Kingdom, and He has called each of you to go and work in His vineyard today. It's a wonderful thing to be planted in God's garden. It's a place filled with every kind of fruit that is good to the eye, good to the tongue, and good to the stomach. It's a place of unparalleled beauty and joy, and you have been placed in it.

But, having tasted the fruits of God's garden and beheld its joys, you're expected to contribute to the good of God's garden and be a participant in its goodness and bounty. It's something that's there for your enjoyment, but only to the degree that you invest yourself in it and labor together with others for the common good and the glory of God. It does not belong to you but to God. It is a garden, and not a self-governing wild orchard. It needs to be tended, or else it will return to weeds and unfruitfulness.

Israel, too, was the garden of God. It was a land flowing with milk and honey, and the Israelites were God's peculiar people, chosen by Him to keep His land. But, throughout their history they played the part of the second son, the one who said he would obey the Father and go and work in the vineyard but in reality refused to. At this point in Matthew 21, Jesus is still speaking to the chief priests and the elders of the people, who had just confronted Him about His teaching and authority. The place where they did this was in the temple, the house of God, which could also be seen as the garden of God.

And so Jesus is warning them that although they speak as if they are obeying the Father, they are actually not. The tax collectors and harlots will enter God's kingdom and garden before the chief priests and elders, for although they initially disobeyed, in time they repented and obeyed.

There's a lesson for each of us here. At various times in our lives, at various times in our day, we may be acting more like the first son, who said he would not obey but did, or the second son, who said he would go but in the end does not.

Aren't there times when, acting like the second son, we've said to the Lord that we will gladly die for Him and move mountains for Him, but when He asks us to clean the latrine or forgive our brother or give up our unit of pleasure for another person, we balk. We have a habit of professing our love boldly for God and then continuing to go on our merry way as if we had not just promised God the moon and the sun.

It can even become like this in that most special of occasions: Sunday morning worship. We may say to ourselves that we go to worship God, but on some Sunday mornings we may not feel like being there. We say that we will establish a holy time each day for God when we can be alone with Him, but when that time comes and the morning is too early or there are too many things to be done or the evening comes and we are in leisure mode, we miss our appointment with God. We hear the voice of God tell us exactly what He wishes for us to do next, and we say, "Yes, Lord," and then fail to do what He's just told us and what we just vowed to do.

But, aren't we also like the first son? Aren't there times when we initially refuse God? We get stuck in our bad habits or patterns and, in a quiet way, refuse the pleading of the Spirit in our lives. We lack faith and refuse to leave our warm, fuzzy cocoon when God calls us out to the adventure of the butterfly. And then, hopefully, at some point, we realize the error of our ways, and we repent.

And that's the difference between the first and second son, isn't it. Their refusal to obey the Father is what the two sons have in common. But, what separates the first and blessed son from the second and cursed son is the place they end up. In our lives, taken as a whole, no matter where we begin, there are only two places we'll end up: in faith and obedience to our heavenly Father, or in pride and disobedience to our heavenly Father.

In our daily lives it's the same thing. Sadly, we will continue to sin in this life. That's an unpleasant fact. But, what distinguishes whether or not we're acting like the first or second son is whether or not we repent. Even the thief on the cross, at the hour of death, had one final chance to repent, no matter what else he had done before. Whether you're hired first thing in the morning or work only the last hour in God's kingdom, the wages are the same: the important thing is to step forward and begin laboring in His garden.

Actually, there's a third, invisible son in the story. He reminds me of my long lost brother Hector. You see, my Dad used to tell my twin brother and I that we were actually triplets and that we had another brother named Hector, who now worked as an elevator operator, I think at Elmhurst hospital: I'm not sure: I lost track of him in the 1960s. (So you see that I come by my weirdness naturally!) This third son is the one who says to the Father "I will obey," and then actually obeys.

Regardless of which of the sons you are today, the point for all of us is the same: listen for the voice of your Father today, and when He speaks, obey. This is the way of the third son Jesus Christ, the Son (who really is my long, lost brother), and all who follow Him in the path of cheerful obedience.

Prayer:

Our Father, who art in heaven, hallowed be Thy name. Thy kingdom come. Thy will be done, on earth as it is in heaven. Give us this day our daily bread. And forgive us our trespasses, as we forgive those who trespass against us. And lead us not into temptation, but deliver us from evil. For thine is the kingdom, and the power, and the glory, for ever and ever. Amen.

Point for Meditation:

What has the Father been asking you to do lately? How have you been responding?

Resolution:

I resolve to listen for the one thing my Father is asking me to do today. I further resolve to say "I will" and to obey when He speaks to me today.

Matthew 21:33-46

I've struggled today with what to write about the parable of the vinedressers, because Jesus' point is about the rejection of the Stone which the builders rejected—and as Christians, we have not rejected the chief cornerstone.

And yet as I gaze more deeply into this parable I see a few things that remind me of my life here on earth. In the first place, I find that I am in a similar situation to that of the vinedressers, who are Israel. The earth is the Lord's garden, and He has placed us in it to tend it, wherever He has planted us. It is all His, but He allows us to live here and allows us to partake of the kindly fruits of the earth.

Furthermore, our Lord has gone off into a far country. Jesus, our Lord, has ascended to Heaven and has left His Church to be the vinedressers of His vineyard. Like the vinedressers in this parable, and like the nation of Israel at the time of Christ, it might occur to us that while the cat's away the mice should play. Since Jesus is not here physically but is invisible to us, as are the Father and the Spirit, it would be easy for us to get off track and begin to act as if God didn't exist and we were not going to meet up with Him again at some point in time.

Maybe you or someone you know has experienced this kind of newfound freedom while in college. While once you were under the watchful eye of your parents, now the world is yours to do with what you will. You know what's right and what's wrong, but now there are more temptations than ever before and no one to watch over you but yourself.

In our lives as vinedressers of the Lord's vineyard, even though the Lord Himself is absent, He sends messengers into our lives. Maybe He sends an event into your life, a "close call" or a "wake up call" that is intended to gently remind you to get back to the work the Lord has given you to do. Maybe He puts someone into your life to say something to you that triggers a return to God. And maybe you ignore the first messenger He sends, and the second one, and He sends more impressive and serious messengers until you return to Him.

Have you ever had the experience in which you slowly drift back into the belief that you've got things covered without the help of God? And then something goes wrong, or something happens that seems to be out of your control or beyond your ability to handle. But somehow, through hard work and a little luck things turn out O.K. and you're now released to go back to trusting in yourself. But, then something else happens that's out of your control. How do you respond?

As with the repentance that we talked about yesterday, we all have episodes where we act as if God is not Lord and we aren't accountable to Him. But, the question is, as it was yesterday, will we return to Him, and will we do it sooner rather than later?

To continue acting as if this world and my life isn't God's is risky. I'd hate to die on a day when I was ignoring God's messengers and was acting as if I owned my life and everything in it. It's risky to spend even a day without God because days have a habit of becoming weeks, and weeks have a habit of becoming months, and months...There's a danger that I might not ever pull out of my nose dive in time. Establishing the habit of ignoring God's voice in my life and the habit of believing my life is my own makes it that much more likely that this is a habit that may form me for life.

But, I prefer to write a different parable for myself today.

"There was a certain landowner who planted a vineyard and set a hedge around it, dug a winepress in it and built a tower. And he leased it to vinedressers and went into a far country. Now when vintage-time drew near, he sent his servants to the vinedressers, that they might receive its fruit. But, one of the vinedressers ignored the servants and refused to hear what they had to say and selfishly began to treat the fruit as entirely his own. Again he sent other servants, more than the first, but this time the vinedresser who had ignored the first group of servants listened to the servants and gladly gave the landowner the fruit that He had asked for. When he received the fruit, the landowner permanently renewed his lease to the vinedresser and allowed him to continue to work for him and partake richly of the amazing fruits of his vineyard all the days of his life."

Prayer:

Lord Jesus Christ, whose bread it was to do the will of the Father and who said, "Apart from me you can do nothing," bless me as I begin the work you have given me. Help me to work with diligence and cheerfulness, and direct me by Your wisdom and power that whatever I do may be a blessing to myself and others and a means of giving glory to Your name. Amen.

Points for Meditation:

1. Have you been like the wicked vinedressers in any way? Have you treated God's kingdom as if it were your own?
2. What kinds of messengers does God seem to send into your life to bring you back to Him?
3. Meditate on how wonderful it is to be a vinedresser in God's vineyard, and give thanks!

Resolution:

I resolve to practice seeing my life today, and all of its details, as something that belongs to God.

Matthew 22:1–14

The Wedding Feast is perhaps the happiest picture of the Kingdom of God that is given in the Bible. We find it portrayed in Matthew 25 and in Revelation 19:7, where we read, *"Let us rejoice and exult and give him the glory, for the marriage of the Lamb has come, and His Bride has made herself ready."* And, Christ's first miracle at the initiation of His public ministry took place at a wedding feast.

In weddings in ancient Israel, first came the wedding itself. The bridegroom wore a diadem and was accompanied by his friends with tambourines and a band (I think maybe it was Led Zeppelin). The party then proceeded to the bride's house, where she was richly dressed and adorned with jewels, wearing a veil which she took off only in the bridal chamber. The wedding was consummated on the first night, but next came a great feast, which lasted for seven days and could even be prolonged to two weeks. The guests were expected to stay during this whole time, and so attending the wedding feast required a commitment and more than leaving a card saying that the gravy boat was now registered at Macy's.

There are two things to keep in mind regarding the wedding feast of the son of the king. First, this is the biggest and best feast of all. Second, only a fool would desire or dare to refuse.

Those who refused the gracious invitation would face ridicule by peers, discipline by the king, and would miss out on the joy of the wedding feast itself.

And so we have Jesus' teaching about His kingdom: it's like the wedding feast of the son of the king. God is the King; Jesus is the Son; and the Wedding Feast is the Kingdom of Heaven. This parable applies not only to the 1st century Jews but also to us.

Historically, the Jews wouldn't come, and, like those in the parable, made excuses for not coming. They wouldn't listen to prophets but instead killed them. In fulfillment of prophecy, in A.D. 70, a Roman army destroyed Jerusalem and the Temple. The response of the Jews to God's invitation and God's ensuing judgment on them are instructive for us, and there are three ways we might respond to God's gracious invitation.

Like the Jews, we might refuse to come and make excuses. We might come but without the proper garments; or we might come dressed and committed. We might, in the first place, make lame excuses. "I've got to go milk my cows and pull some weeds." "I've got to take care of this pressing business." One of my favorite excuses proceeded out of the lips of Gloria, my daughter who was two at the time. When asked why she did something, she thought a minute and replied: "Because I was feezing cold!"

We, too, make excuses. "I'm too busy to worry about God: it (He) can wait." But, if there was ever a thing in your life about which you truly could *not* wait, it is for you to commit yourself to God.

"I'm O.K. the way I am." We make excuses for our sin and minimize them, and thereby make little of the sacrifice of the flesh and blood of Jesus Christ, the Son of God.

"I can come to God anyway and anywhere I want to: I don't need to go to church or worship Him in a particular way."

"I'm so bad that God wouldn't want me." No, you are not worthy, but God will *make* you righteous, through Jesus Christ, if you have true faith.

Some even actively work against God, by persecuting those who follow Him wholeheartedly. Our persecution is still light here in the U.S. But, we're called fanatics and bigots and fundamentalists—and this by others who call themselves Christians!

Like the Jews, our excuses seem to make sense at the time, but how could they possibly justify not accepting an invitation to God's feast?!

There are also those who are not dressed with the proper wedding garments. In Christ's parable, the host had made all things ready. The king desired to have the rules of His feast obeyed, but one man insisted on coming in his own way, in effect, making himself more important than the king. It's likely that the man came in through some other way than the door: "How did you get in without the proper garment?"

Like this man, we might actually come into the Kingdom of God; we might be a member of a church; we might even sit in the pew faithfully week by week... and yet, it is still possible to be like the man who was at the feast without the proper garment. It's possible to be in the church, but not to have entered through the only acceptable door, which is Jesus Christ Himself. There are some in the Church who do not have true faith. There are some in the Church who have entered out of habit, some who have entered for social reasons, and some who have entered on the basis of their own righteousness.

But, the only way one can truly enter into the Marriage Feast of God's Kingdom is to enter through Jesus Christ.

Many commentators believe that the wedding garments are the new life of good works. It's not enough to have been baptized; it's not enough to go to church; and it's not even enough to claim to have faith. One must be clothed with good works that are the proof of our faith.

In Revelation 19:8–9, John records: *"And to her it was granted to be arrayed in fine linen, clean and bright, for the fine linen is the righteous acts of the saints. Then he said to me, 'Write "Blessed are those who are called to the marriage supper of the Lamb!"'"*

The commentator's have it only partially right. We are only righteous and our good works are only profitable if Jesus Christ is our righteousness. And those good works are *His* good works that can't be separated from Him or a relationship with Him. This is the one garment that God the Father will look for when He judges men at the end of all time.

Have you remembered to put on Jesus Christ and *His* righteousness?

What was the King's response to the man without the proper garments? His mouth was stopped: He is "muzzled." He was bound, hand and foot. He was cast out into outer darkness, where there was weeping and gnashing of teeth. There are dire, eternal consequences for those who do not come to God's kingdom—*and* for those who do not come the right way.

Hell is a very real place, and Jesus speaks more frequently and forcefully about the truth of Hell than anyone else in the Bible.

But, thank God that there are also those who come dressed and committed. All of you, if you truly come to God through Jesus Christ and if you truly come confessing your sins and turning from them, will inherit the Kingdom of Heaven and be made participants in the greatest party ever thrown!

If you do hear and accept God's wondrous call to His feast and put on Christ as your righteousness, then you shall be partakers of the greatest feast of all, with joys beyond the greatest joys of earth. All of life is a banquet God spreads for us, although it's not complete or perfect yet. Yet who among you is unable to see the goodness of God, even in this life?

Every good thing in this life is a reminder of what life in God's kingdom is like, even in this life. Every good thing in this life is a reminder of the unspeakable joys of the world to come. The pizza and beer and Monday Night Football; the reflection of the moonlight along a wet, sandy beach; the warmth and cuddliness of a young child the first time you pick him up in the morning...

The Holy Communion! God has even graciously given us the greatest means of all to participate in the Marriage Feast of His Son: it's called the Holy Communion. It's the anticipation of that Great Wedding Feast in heaven, but it's also a participation in that Great Wedding Feast—even now. For right here, in the Body and the Blood, we participate with Jesus Christ. Right here, in the Bread and the Wine, we feed off Jesus Christ, who is our Daily Bread that comes down from heaven. And right here we put on Jesus Christ, as He comes to nourish our bodies and souls.

. . .

Today, you have received an invitation to the Wedding Feast of the Son of God.

"Come to the Wedding Feast of the Son—for all has been made ready!"

Prayer:

Banish, O Lord, both grief and wrath, and then the dumb shall exult in song. Guide us in the paths of righteousness. Gladden our hearts with Your presence and gifts. With the sanction of those present we will bless our God, in whose abode is joy, and of whose bounty we have partaken. Amen.

(From a Jewish Grace after a wedding feast)

Point for Meditation:

1.   What might I do to view God's Kingdom as a Feast that has already started?
2.   What excuses have I been making for not attending the Feast?

Resolution:

I resolve to find one way today to participate in God's Feast, which is life in His Son.

Matthew 22:15-33

We Christians are amphibians: we live in two habitats. We are inhabitants of two universes. We live in the earthly realm and also the heavenly realm at the same time, and often there is tension between the two. Both of today's stories deal with this tension, each in a separate way. Both reveal the wisdom that is necessary for a Christian to be both in this world and yet not of it.

The first story, in which the Pharisees attempt to trick Jesus, is a tale of two kingdoms. In the red corner, wearing the logo SPQR (*Senatus Populusque Romanus* or "The Senate and the People of Rome"), is the heavyweight champion of the world: the Roman Empire. In the white corner, wearing the logo INRI (an abbreviation for "Iesus Nazarenus Rex Iudaeorum" or "Jesus of Nazareth, King of the Jews"), is the challenger, the Kingdom of God. Of course, the Pharisees had an ulterior motive in setting a trap for Jesus by asking the question of whether or not to pay the tax. But, in doing so they highlighted for all time the tension that exists between the kingdoms of this world and the Kingdom of God.

For Jesus, the Roman coin symbolized the tension and even competition that exists between the two kingdoms. When asked about the two kingdoms, the expected answer would have been an Either/Or answer. Either you pay the tax and submit to the Roman Empire (the kingdom of man), or you refuse to pay the tax and join the Kingdom of Heaven. To pay the tax would have seemed to overthrown the Kingdom of God for the kingdom of man, but to refuse to pay the tax would have meant imprisonment or torture or death.

In either case, so the Pharisees thought, Jesus and His kingdom would be discredited.

Not so fast. Jesus asks them to pull out a tax coin. When they do, they're already defeated: they themselves have also played the Roman game, or else why would they happen to have a tax coin? He asks them whose image and inscription was on the coin, and they say, "Caesar's." Now this would have been highly offensive to the Jews. First, they wouldn't have liked the graven image of Caesar on the coin. Second, on some of the coins Caesar proclaimed himself to be both the Son of God and high priest.

And yet, in spite of these things, Jesus can suggest that we are allowed, and even ought, to render to Caesar the things that are Caesar's. Knowing that Caesar was blasphemous and knowing the ungodliness of the Roman Empire, Jesus is generous enough to ask His disciples to live in the Kingdom of Rome and even pay it tribute.

How can He do this? I believe that the answer to that question is only a smaller version of a much larger question that is still a problem for us. How can Jesus, who is the King of kings and Lord of lords, allow the kingdom of man and the kingdom of Satan to still exist? "Why didn't He overthrow the Roman Empire?" is a variation on "Why doesn't He overthrow the kingdom of Satan completely?"

Maybe we, too, are looking for an earthly answer to a heavenly problem. What if it's possible for the Kingdom of God to exist and even advance among the petty kingdoms of men that dominate our lives? Is this so incredible? To me, it's not any more unbelievable than that God, through His Holy Spirit, can inhabit a sinful man like me. This world, as long as it exists, seems to be a mixture of both the Kingdom of God and the kingdom of man, of heaven and of earth. And God has put us here to learn to live in His Kingdom, our true home, even while dwelling in the kingdom of men. I think it has something to do with the Incarnation, in which heaven came down to earth and God came down to man. History seems to be a strange, messy, confusing extension of the Incarnation and of God coming to man in spite of man.

The second story may help make our situation clearer. In it, the Sadducees take their crack at Jesus, and they attack Him along very different lines. They attack the truth of the resurrection and point out its seeming absurdity. But, they can only see the earth and its kingdoms, and from that point of view the resurrection seems to be a lie. Modern science would concur. None of us have ever witnessed a resurrection, and since only the things we can observe are real, then the resurrection must be a myth.

But, Jesus uses their assumptions and attack as an opportunity to open the Kingdom of Heaven to them, even if only for a moment. They are mistaken because they have assumed that this world is all there is. But, if there's a resurrection, then there's also a different kingdom waiting on the other end of it. It's an eternal kingdom and one in which death has no part. It is a kingdom which is invisible and thus impossible to prove. There is no hard scientific evidence for it, and yet the vast majority of humanity has hoped against sight that such an eternal and good kingdom exists after death. Why, if it's so absurd?

The sad truth is that too much of my life is spent thinking like a Pharisee or Sadducee. Too much of my life is spent thinking like this world is all there is and rather stoically bearing all of the injustice, evil, suffering, and disappointment that this life seems to hold.

Yet God has opened the kingdom of heaven to all believers. American culture is ubiquitous and now streams and screams to me 24/7 on my phone, my computer, wherever I go, whenever I am. There's no escaping it. We must all continue to lead ever faster lives, cramming in ever more stuff, and pursuing all the latest technologies—or become social pariahs. And the reach of the blob known as the federal government isn't far behind the reach of the media.

But, the truth is that the Kingdom of God is also present in our lives. The presence of God's Kingdom doesn't magically make the kingdoms of man vanish from our lives, but it is supposed to transform them. The truth is that my home is in heaven, with God, and so this world will always seem a little strange. It will always seem as if things are not quite right, because in this world they never are. But, I am already in a world, God's world, where things have already been made right.

I may continue to limp along in this world, laboring with ever-greater difficulty as my body continues to wear out. But that labor, if done for the glory of God, is also part of the Kingdom of God. I may lament my own sins and blindness of heart, but I'm someone in whom God has deposited His heavenly treasure, even in this life.

The match seems uneven: the reigning champion of the world—the kingdom of this world and the kingdom of man—seems to be nearly infinite and to occupy the entire universe. But, in reality, there is already a new champion, Jesus Christ the righteous, for He won the battle on Calvary.

So my labor today is not so much to give to Caesar what's Caesar's: I'm pretty sure he'll get what I owe him. The more difficult and beautiful thing is for me to remember to give to God what's His. And, what's His is *me*—someone made in His image; someone redeemed by His Blood; someone inhabited by His Spirit, and someone who is promised a resurrection of his body in my true home in heaven with God.

Prayer:

We praise thee, O God; we acknowledge thee to be the Lord.

All the earth doth worship thee, the Father everlasting.

To thee all Angels cry aloud; the Heavens, and all the Powers therein;

To thee Cherubim and Seraphim continually do cry,

Holy, Holy, Holy, Lord God of Sabaoth;

Heaven and earth are full of the Majesty of thy glory.

The glorious company of the Apostles praise thee.

The goodly fellowship of the Prophets praise thee.

The noble army of Martyrs praise thee.

The holy Church throughout all the world: doth acknowledge thee;

The Father: of an infinite Majesty;

Thine adorable, true and only Son;

Also the Holy Ghost, the Comforter.

Thou art the King of Glory, O Christ.

Thou art the everlasting Son, of the Father.

When thou tookest upon thee to deliver man: thou didst humble thyself to be born of a Virgin.

When thou hadst overcome the sharpness of death, thou didst open the Kingdom of Heaven to all believers.

Thou sittest at the right hand of God, in the glory of the Father.

We believe that thou shalt come to be our Judge.

We therefore pray thee, help thy servants: whom thou hast redeemed with thy precious blood.

Make them to be numbered with thy Saints, in glory everlasting.

O Lord, save thy people: and bless thine heritage.

Govern them, and lift them up for ever.

Day by day, we magnify thee;

And we worship thy Name ever, world without end.

Vouchsafe, O Lord, to keep us this day without sin.

O Lord, have mercy upon us, have mercy upon us.

O Lord, let thy mercy be upon us, as our trust is in thee.

O Lord, in thee have I trusted; let me never be confounded.

Amen.

("Te Deum laudamus" from *The Book of Common Prayer* pp. 10–11)

Points for Meditation:

1. What are some ways in which God allows you to see His kingdom in the midst of the kingdom of man?
2. Meditate on how the discomforts of this world can lead to hope more in the world that is to come.

Resolution:

I resolve to find one way today to give to God what is His: my time, my talents, my treasure, my hopes, my faith, my fears, my worries, my job, my family, and my thanksgiving and praise.

Matthew 22:34–46

When we need advice on important questions in life, we come to wise men.

If I want to know how to do something related to the church, I'm most likely to pick up the phone and call Bishop Grote (of the Reformed Episcopal Church). If you wanted to know how to invest your money more wisely, you'd call a financial planner.

But, what if you had the opportunity to go to the wisest man who ever lived and ask Him the most important question ever asked? Listen closely: the wisest man who ever lived is telling the secret of life. Your all-wise God is telling you what He desires from you more than anything else.

So what is it that God wants from you more than anything else? If we believe the Bible, in this case the very words of Jesus Christ, the most important thing God has commanded us to do is to *love* Him. Love is the fulfillment of the Law, and love is to define our entire relationship with God. This is the *"What?"* question of our lives. "What is the most important thing I can do?" Answer: "Love God." It's pretty simple, isn't it?

Husbands and wives, parents and children—if I were to ask you what is the greatest thing you could do for each other, what would it be? Though we might all give different answers, down deep we all know and agree upon one answer: the greatest thing we can do for another human is to *love* him.

If the greatest thing we can do for one another is to love, then how much more true is it that the greatest thing we can do for God, is to *love* Him? Do you *love* God as you love the dearest, most cherished person in your life? If not, then I say that you have something to learn about loving God.

Now you might say: "I know how to love my wife or I know how to love my kids. They're like me: they're humans, and I can see them. But, *how* do I love God?"

After we have heard and accepted the answer to the *"What?"* question—that

loving God is the greatest commandment—we'd better know as well the answer to the *"How?"* question: *"How* do I love God?" To this question, Jesus has given two answers: Love God for Himself; love God by loving people.

I believe that if we *truly...deliberately...*and *passionately* seek to love God with all our hearts and all our souls and all our minds, and seek to love our neighbors as ourselves, that not only will we have obeyed God's Greatest Commandment to love, but we will also become the Church, the Body of Christ, that God desires for us to be.

Let's look at *how* God would have us to do this.

First, we are to love God by loving Him for Himself. This is what might be called "Mary love." I'm sure you remember the story of Mary and Martha. In Luke 10:41–42 Jesus says, "Martha, Martha, you are worried and troubled about many things. But, one thing is needed, and Mary has chosen that good part, which will not be taken from her."

"Mary love" is the kind of love that loves God for Himself. "Mary love" is the kind of love that worships God for who He is, the kind of love that *catches a vision of God* and is forever transformed by it.

There are many definitions of worship, but one aspect or worship is that it is something done with no ulterior purpose. We don't worship God because then He has to bless us (that is the exact opposite of how things work); we don't worship God because it makes us feel good; and we don't define worship by how good we feel.

We worship God, that is, ascribe "worth-ship" to Him, because He is *worthy* of all glory, honor, and praise, and because we were created to worship. Love of God begins with direct *worship* of God—loving God by loving Him for Who He Is. Love of God begins with acknowledging who God is and then responding in the appropriate ways: with awe...and reverence...and humility.

Mary was content to humbly bow before Jesus Christ, to contemplate who He was, and to respond with adoration and worship. If we really believe, really know who this God is—that He is a consuming fire that makes men fall down like they were dead—then we'd worship Him! This is why churches who worship using the historic liturgies come before God kneeling, confessing our sins with reverence and awe.

Therefore, the first and most important thing we ought to be doing to love God is to *worship* Him. Other people might put other things first, but it seems clear to me that it is *the vision of God, and the worship of God that can't help but come from this,* that is our number one task. It is our vision of God and our worship of Him that will equip and motivate us to love God in all the other ways we should.

But, worshiping God (in the more technical and limited sense of the word) is not our only calling and not the only way God asks us to love Him. If we truly see

God for who He is and worship Him, then we will want to become like Him. This means that *worship* must necessarily lead to *discipleship*.

As we read the Bible, we find that these are the marks of a true disciple:

1. *They are ready to follow God immediately.* "Then He said to them, 'Follow Me, and I will make you fishers of men.' They immediately left their nets, and followed Him" (Matthew 4:19–20, the calling of Peter and Andrew).

2. *They are ready to give up all things to follow Jesus Christ.* "And immediately they left the boat *and their father*, and followed Him" (Matthew 4:22, of James and John).

3. *They are ready to deny themselves in order to follow and exalt God.* Then Jesus said to His *disciples*, "If anyone desires to come after Me, let him deny himself, and take up his cross, and follow me" (Matthew 16:24).

4. *They are ready to obey at all costs.* When God gave the apostles the Great Commission, he told them to make *disciples* of all nations, teaching them to *obey* all things He has commanded (Matthew 28:18–20.)

This kind of discipleship, one that is willing to follow God immediately, to give up all things, and to obey completely, is the appropriate and worthy response to the God we worship. It is the second important way we love God.

Is this the kind of relationship you have with God? Are you willing to drop everything, to give up everything, and follow God? I have a vision that God's people will be a people whose mission is to love God by worshiping Him in such a way that they become disciples of Jesus Christ. For only if someone is first a worshiper, a humble lover and adorer, can he be such a disciple; and only, as we will now see, if we are true disciples, will we love our neighbors as we ought.

Discipleship doesn't happen Sunday mornings but all throughout the week. It happens especially when the Church is intentional about making disciples.

. . .

But, there's a second way of loving God that is just as important as loving God for Himself. The First Great Commandment cannot be divorced from the Second Great Commandment, for both are ways of loving God: *"the second is like unto it,"* and *"on these two laws, hang all the Law and Prophets"* (vv. 39–40).

It's not possible to simply love God in the abstract. Part of the reason we do not feel the presence of God, part of the reason we do not love Him enough, is that sometimes we expect that the only way to experience God is to have a direct experience of Him. We expect to talk with Him as Moses did, or to display a supernatural manifestation of the gifts of the Spirit, or that loving God only entails direct acts of worship such as praying, going to church, etc.

But, God wants all of you—body, mind, and soul—wherever you are, whatever you're doing. The only way to do this is to not only worship God and follow Him as His disciple but also to love the *people* that God has put in your life, and not just on Sunday morning, but 24/7/365.

Though Martha is rebuked by her Lord in Luke 10, the passage I referred to earlier, Martha's kind of love is also important. If Mary caught the vision of God and so became a worshiper and disciple, then Martha caught the vision of man, and so became a servant. This, too, is love, because from our love of God flows our love for our neighbor.

"Martha love" is a servant love. "Martha love" is a practical love of those God puts in our lives. Worshipers and disciples, then, must become servants, evangelists, and disciples. Along with Greatest Commandment comes the Great Commission. Our motivation to go out into the world to serve God is not primarily to make the world a better place (as much as we'd all like to see this). Our motivation is to be true worshipers and disciples of Jesus Christ, and *if* we are worshipers and disciples, we *will* make the world a better place.

This means that because loving our neighbors is connected with loving God we can only fully love God *by becoming servants, evangelists, and disciples. "Inasmuch as you did it to one of the least of these My brethren, you did it to Me"* (Matthew 25:40). Worshipers and disciples must become *servants. "Whoever desires to become great among you, let him be your servant"* (Matthew 20:26). The Son of Man came not to be served but to serve.

We have a call to serve all those around us: God, family, Church, and *neighbors*. If we truly are Christ's disciples, then we will serve as He did. To love your neighbor as yourself means to serve him by serving him as Christ would.

Worshipers and disciples must also become *evangelists*. You may be thinking "Uh oh: evangelists." But, an evangelist is simply one who spreads the Good News of Jesus Christ. There are many ways to do this, but the best way is to simply share your life in Christ with those you already know, and those you meet, as you have occasion. But, we *must* do it: we must love God by spreading His Word. Worshipers and disciples must become evangelists. We must be like the apostles who, when commanded *not* to speak of the name of Jesus Christ said, "We cannot *but* speak the things we have seen and heard" (Acts 4:20).

If you've truly seen God and worshiped Him, this should be a somewhat natural desire on your part.

Worshipers and *disciples* must also become *disciplers*. If we really want to be disciples made like our Lord in all things, then we must disciple others. We are called to edify one another, to use our gifts and talents on behalf of Church, and not just for ourselves.

It's not enough merely to *serve* others around us generally; it's not even enough to *evangelize*, to introduce others to Christ. The ultimate goal is to make them worshipers and disciples as well. The Great Commission is *not* about making a few quick converts but about going and making *disciples*, devoted followers of Jesus Christ who are ready to give up all for His sake.

What greater calling, what more joyful endeavor, than to help the person next to you in the pew, to help the person in your Bible study, to help your friends or family become more like your Lord every day?!

So there they are: the two greatest things that the greatest Person desires for you to do. It's overwhelming, even blinding, to see it all at once. But, that's O.K. You and I have a lifetime to do it, together. The important thing is that we spend today loving God for who He is and loving Him by loving our neighbors.

Prayer:

Ah Lord God, Thou holy lover of my Soul, when Thou comest into my Soul, all that is within me shall rejoice. Thou art my Glory and the exultation of my heart. Thou art my Hope and Refuge in the day of my trouble.

Set me free from all evil passions, and heal my heart of all inordinate affections, that being cured and thoroughly cleansed, may I be made fit to love, courageous to suffer, steady to persevere. Nothing is sweeter than love, nothing more courageous, nothing fuller or better in heaven and earth; because Love is born of God, and cannot rest but in God, above all created things.

Let me love Thee more than myself, let me love others as Thou wouldst have me do, let all I do show that I truly love Thee, as the law of Love commandeth. Amen.

(Thomas à Kempis)

Points for Meditation:

1. Are you more of a Mary or more of a Martha? How might God be calling you to be more like the other person?
2. How is God calling you to worship Him more for who He is?
3. How is God calling you to worship Him more by loving your neighbor?

Resolution:

I resolve to listen today for the one thing that God says is necessary in my life to love Him more, and then to begin to do it.

Matthew 23:1-12

Why does Jesus use such scalding words towards the scribes and Pharisees? His words are so caustic that I feel the sting of them 2000 years later—and they weren't even aimed towards me!

I think it's because Jesus' kingdom is a kingdom of love and humility (which are so closely related it's difficult if not impossible to separate them). But, the scribes and Pharisees, as leaders who lead with pride and not humility, are opposed to His kingdom. I think this may also be the reason Jesus is so harsh towards hypocrites. We're all hypocrites because we don't live up to what we say is right and good. So why such harshness towards hypocrites? It's not all hypocrites that Jesus thrashes but the religious leaders who are hypocrites, those who should be leaders and teachers in love and humility but instead teach pride by their actions.

It's a good thing I like humility. Jesus teaches about humility so much that one is faced with three choices:

1. reject the teaching of Jesus, and therefore Jesus, and do things your way

2. say what Jesus says about humility, but don't do what He does

3. accept the teaching of Jesus and make it your ambition to be humble

Sometimes Jesus teaches with such crystalline clarity and tornadic force that one is reduced to the most elemental things in life. Nothing that Jesus teaches is clearer than His teaching on humility and self-exaltation, and nothing is more fundamental.

In Matthew's Gospel alone, here is what Jesus teaches about humility:

"Then Jesus said to His disciples, 'If anyone desires to come after Me, let him deny himself, and take up his cross, and follow Me'" (16:24).

"Assuredly, I say to you, unless you are converted and become as little children, you will by no means enter the kingdom of heaven. Therefore, whoever humbles himself as this little child is the greatest in the kingdom of heaven" (18:3–4).

"Yet it shall not be so among you; but whoever desires to become great among you, let him be your servant. And whoever desires to be first among you, let him be your

slave—just as the Son of Man did not come to be served, but to serve, and to give His life a ransom for many" (20:26–28).

"But he who is greatest among you shall be your servant. And whoever exalts himself will be humbled, and he who humbles himself will be exalted" (23:11–12).

This is an amazingly consistent and persistent constellation of teachings on humility and how humility is at the center of Jesus' Kingdom. In fact, once you see that Jesus' Kingdom is the Kingdom of Humility, you see exactly what the problem is and has been for thousands of years. For most of humanity, a Kingdom of Humility is an oxymoron, a logical impossibility. It's almost like saying the Pleasure of Pain or the Darkness of Light.

And yet, in spite of what the rest of the world teaches, Jesus insists that His Kingdom is a kingdom of humility. Actually, Jesus' life began, continued, and ended with humility—Jesus is no hypocrite. What He taught was what He lived. Jesus says and Jesus does: we should do both what He says and what He did. And so He was born in a manger in a stable, of two ordinary people. He who was God was born a human baby.

He began His teaching ministry by teaching about humility. Isn't that what the Beatitudes are ultimately about?

"Blessed are the poor in spirit, for theirs is the kingdom of heaven" (Matthew 5:3).

Isn't "poor in spirit" simply another way of saying "humble"? Notice what the blessing of the humble is: the kingdom of heaven, Jesus' kingdom. All of the other blessed conditions that Jesus mentions in the Beatitudes are related in some way to humility.

So Jesus begins His teaching by talking about humility, and then, in chapter 16, when He takes His disciples to a new level of understanding, after Peter's confession, He begins to teach them about the way of the Cross and the need to deny oneself in order to be His disciple.

And there is our definition of humility: to deny oneself. Again, Jesus is no hypocrite but a man of perfect integrity, for what He teaches about crosses is what He chose to do. No sooner does He begin to teach His disciples about their finite crosses than He Himself begins His march to His own infinite Cross.

Jesus taught humility throughout His entire public ministry, but He taught humility most intensely by the events beginning with Maundy Thursday and extending until Easter morning.

"But he who is greatest among you shall be your servant. And whoever exalts himself will be humbled, and he who humbles himself will be exalted."

That's your lesson for today. We all have many competing images of ourselves, and we've become fairly adept at employing them to suit our different tastes and needs. We think of ourselves as our jobs or our roles in families or our roles in social networks. We pick from some of our more salient characteristics and say that this is who we are. I was listening in my car recently to a Confidence Course on tape that I bought at Half Price Records. The author was saying that people who are shy often see their shyness as being who they are and as being a much larger part of who they are than do the people around them.

Who do you see yourself to be? What characteristics define you?

Among the images you have for yourself, Jesus is telling you to take on one special image and role, and that is the role of humble servant: this is the image of Christ Himself. If you see yourself as a teacher, then you might set out as I once did to become a better teacher. You practice teaching and communicating ideas and motivating people. If you see yourself as a mother, then you dedicate yourself to mothering your children and training and shaping and loving and encouraging them. And if you see yourself as a humble servant, then you will set out today to learn how to be more humble and to serve more faithfully.

There are so many ways that our Father and our Teacher teach us to be humble, and often they use different means on different people. You could choose to learn humility today by seeking to love those around you or to serve them. You could choose to learn humility by praying or by praying and fasting, or by doing many other things.

But, I've got another suggestion today, at least partially because it's what I think I need today. What if you practiced humility today by accepting whatever the Lord decides to give you today? Instead of seeing life as being out to get you, instead of becoming angry or upset every time something doesn't go your way, and instead of resenting the difficult things in your life that you can't change, what if you accepted each of them as instruction from the Lord in humility?

What if each disappointment, burden, or undesired event were seen as a means to God and His grace, instead of as a threat to your sovereign desires? I believe that every day is densely packed with opportunities to humble oneself before the Lord.

And therefore, every day is also densely packed with opportunities to be exalted by the Lord—if only you would humble yourself before the one who has taught us how to humble ourselves.

Prayer:

Almighty God, take from me all vainglorious minds, all appetites of mine own praise, all envy, coveting, gluttony, sloth, and lechery, all wrathful affections, all appetite of revenging, all desire or delight of other folks' harm, all pleasure in provoking any person to wrath and anger, all delight of exprobation or insultation against any person in their affliction and calamity.

And give me, good Lord, an humble, lowly, quiet, peaceable, patient, charitable, kind, tender, and pitiful mind, with all my works, and all my words, and all my thoughts, to have a taste of thy holy, blessed Spirit. Amen.

(Sir Thomas More)

Points for Meditation:

1. In what ways are you still proud, exerting your self over God and others?
2. What are some humbling things the Lord has brought your way recently that you might have seen as annoyances or occasions for anger or worry, rather than opportunities to learn humility?

Resolution:

I resolve to accept the things Jesus gives me today as my daily bread, that I might learn humility from Him.

Matthew 23:13–23

It would be easy to hammer the scribes and Pharisees again today. Really, they've made themselves such easy targets! And Jesus Himself spends one of the longest red-letter passages in the Bible wailing on them. So I'd have a good precedent and could claim to be following Jesus.

But, you see, it's too easy. The scribes and Pharisees are long dead, and so it would be too safe to simply beat up on them one more time from the safe distance of two millennia. No, I need a more contemporary target. I could easily pick on the scribes and Pharisees of today, you know, someone like the televangelists who preach about the need to give sacrificially and then ride around in BMWs or Audis.

But, even that would be too easy because I'm not a televangelist. In fact, since this is a devotional commentary, guess who gets stuck playing the role of the scribes and Pharisees today? That's right: you and me. Me, because I'm always the first target of my own slings and arrows. I'm the messenger, and I always get hit first. I'm my own first audience and my own theological guinea pig. And then, of course, if I haven't died from my own prescription, then I generously send it your way!

That's the point of *Give Us This Day*: it's **my** *Give Us This Day*, and it's **your** *Give Us This Day*. We are the ones who must eat our daily bread if it is to do us any good.

And so today I, and then you, must play the role of the scribes and Pharisees. It's not that difficult a role to play, you know. It's not like I, or you, haven't been hypocritical.

There is one major modification that you and I must make when we read such passages, however: being the recipients of the grace and love of Jesus Christ, He does not pronounce a litany of woes against us. It would be wrong to directly apply such passages to a heart that truly loves the Lord. We are not, if we truly love the Lord and are willing to follow Him, the sons of Hell, as Jesus calls the scribes and Pharisees in verse 15. (Such passages easily disprove the notion that Jesus was not judgmental).

So what is there in this passage for you? I find that when I listen to the voice of Jesus in this passage, He is speaking to me. I don't hear him saying, "Woe to you, Charles David, hypocrite!" But, I do hear Him speaking to me nonetheless.

Instead, I see that He has set me down to come and listen to Him. He sits me down patiently and gently today, even though He has come to correct and even rebuke me. He pauses, as if to think of what He should say, but I know that this is just to allow me time to worry about what He might say and to focus my attention all on Him.

In good Jesus fashion, I hear Him asking me a series of thought-provoking questions. This is no lecture: He wants me to be the one actively thinking about my life as His disciple. As He, my Master and Teacher, administers His test to me, He allows me to grade it myself because He wants me to be mature and be honest with myself. He knows that only if I am honest with myself and take responsibility for my life with Him will I ever grow in grace and stature in His kingdom.

"Have you been making a pretense of long prayers, Charles (insert *your name* here)? Have you been doing things in my name so you can receive the glory and attention?"

And then He pauses. He actually expects me to examine myself, and so now I will.

There, I've done it, but it's no fair cheating. I'm not going to let you see my answers because it wouldn't do your soul any good (and it might prove highly embarrassing to me!)

"Have you traveled land and sea to win one proselyte and, when he is won, you make him twice as much a son of hell as you? Have you zealously presented yourself as a Christian, but then when it comes time to live as Christ among other Christians you've acted selfishly?"

Again, He pauses. He wants an honest answer. There's no one but the two of us here, and He already knows the answer. Now that I'm aware of His presence with me, somehow it seems ridiculous that I would ever actually pretend that He isn't here and won't notice. Again, He will wait for you to answer as well. And He doesn't mind if you can't think of anything this time: He just wants you to be honest, not to make up stuff to sound pious.

"Have you rewritten my commandments so that they suit you better and you can feel good about keeping them?"

He pauses a little longer this time. How did He know I needed more time to think about it? Oh yeah, that's right.

"Have you paid the tithe of mint and anise and cumin but neglected justice and mercy and faith? Have you made yourself feel good by keeping outward spiritual things but neglected what I most truly desire? Have you said you were a Christian and even gone to church but not truly had a heart that desires Me?"

He pauses a lot longer this time. I keep looking up at Him to see if He's ready to go on to the next question, but I forget that He's infinitely patient. I keep examining myself and keep finding more ways in which He's calling me to deeper things. It's in this longest silence of His that I see exactly what He's doing. He's not asking me these questions to embarrass me: it's only the two of us, and He already knows my faults. He's not doing it to make me feel like a slug who's just had salt poured all over him (though this may be a by-product of such an examination).

He's asking me these deep questions and pausing so I can discover the variety of ways I've wandered away from Him or settled for images of Him instead of the real deal. He's testing me in so that I may see how much I need Him and miss Him. He's not condemning me: I've already done that to myself! He's showing me the way to forgiveness and His presence. He's showing me, therefore, the way to peace and joy.

But, He has one last word to say to me. He tells me that it's not wise for me to go away sad, storing up all of the ways I have failed Him. What He says He wants is for me to ask forgiveness for all of them, and to ask for His help in being delivered from them. And then He asks me one final question:

"Are you willing to begin today to work on just one of these ways in which I desire for you to come closer to me?"

Am I!

Prayer:

I am perfectly sensible, O my God, that I have in many ways offended Thy divine majesty, and provoked Thy wrath by my sins; and that if I obtain not pardon I shall be cast out of thy sight forever. I desire, therefore, at present to call myself to an account, and look into all the sins whereby I have displeased Thee; but O my God, how miserably shall I deceive myself if Thou assist me not in this work by Thy heavenly light.

Grant me, therefore, at present, Thy grace, whereby I may discover all my imperfections, see all my failings, and duly call to mind all my sins: for I know that nothing is hidden from Thy sight.

But, I confess myself in the dark as to my own failings: my passions blind me, self-love flatters me, presumption deludes me, and though I have many sins which stare me in the face, and cannot be hidden, yet how many, too, are there quite concealed from me! But discover even those to me, O Lord! enlighten my darkness, cure my blindness, and remove every veil that hides my sins from me, that I may be no longer a secret to myself, nor a stranger to my own failings, not ever flatter myself with the thoughts of having repented, and at the same time nourish folly and vice within my breast. Come, Holy Ghost, and by a beam of Thy divine light illumine my understanding, that I may have a perfect view of all my sins and iniquities, and that, sincerely repenting of them, I may know Thee, and be again received into Thy favor; through Jesus Christ, my Mediator and Advocate. Amen.

(Roman Catholic Examination of Conscience)

Point for Meditation:

What is the one way Jesus is showing you today He would like you to come closer to Him?

Resolution:

I resolve to examine myself, listening for the one way Jesus is telling me to come to Him. I further resolve to come to Him in that one way today.

Matthew 23:24–39

Sometimes when I read the lesson for the day I feel like I'm in a biblical supermarket: the Lord offers me so many choices for what to meditate on! Other times, it seems as if there's only one thing to meditate on and for some reason it doesn't compel my heart. I feel like that today.

Here I am, walking down the aisles of the biblical supermarket, la dee da. What have we here? I pick up a can and it says "Condemnation of the Scribes and Pharisees." No, I just ate that yesterday, let's see what the next shelf of cans says. "Stern Judgment against the Scribes and Pharisees." That seems pretty much the same, even though it does come in different flavors. It seems as if that's all God has available for me today, so I guess it's one of those days when I'll just have to be thankful that I'm getting any spiritual food at all today, even if it's not what I wanted.

But, what's this? I come to the end of today's aisle, and what do I see? Still within the walls of Matthew chapter 23, immediately following the lengthy section of woes against the scribes and Pharisees, I find something different. I expect Jesus to continue in the same judgmental tones, but what do I see?

I find one of the most compelling pictures of Jesus in all the New Testament. The one who is stern and judgmental suddenly becomes soft and maternal! I've had cases of theological whiplash before, but this is ridiculous! It doesn't make sense at first.

And then it does. How can Jesus go from perhaps His most withering condemnation to perhaps His most tender compassion in the twinkling of an eye? What unites these two passages is Jesus' concern for those He loves. What He desires is for His people to come to Him, but what He got, especially from those who should most have known to come to Him, was rejection. Jesus is a man of great passions; the Son is a God of great love.

What motivates Jesus throughout Matthew 23 is not a fundamental desire to judge mankind but a deep longing to gather His people to Himself. What the Lord wants is to gather us, His children, to Him, as a hen gathers her chickens under her wings.

This touching picture of the Master's love is sandwiched between two terrible, catastrophic passages. Before is the rest of Matthew 23 and the woes He pronounces upon the scribes and Pharisees. He calls them sons of Hell and pronounces seven woes upon them! They are guilty (verse 32), serpents, and a brood of vipers (verse 33). How can they escape the condemnation of Hell? On them will come all the righteous blood shed on the earth from the blood of righteous Abel to the blood of Zechariah (verse 35)! All of these things will come upon this generation (verse 36).

On the other side of Jesus, as the mother hen, lies Matthew 24 and Jesus' prediction of the destruction of the Temple, the sign of the end of the Old Covenant age, and the coming persecution of Jesus' disciples. All of the things that Jesus warned the scribes and Pharisees about will come soon, to the generation to whom Jesus is speaking!

And yet in the middle of these two chapters of doom is the picture of Jesus the mothering hen. Matthew is a master of dark and light as great as Rembrandt. His use of chiaroscuro reminds me of another painting: Geertgen tot Sint Jans' *Nativity* (which may be seen here: http://www.nationalgallery.org.uk/paintings/ geertgen-tot-sint-jans-the-nativity-at-night).

The dark regions of Matthew's picture, chapter 23 verses 1–36 and chapter 24, make the miniature but bright region of verse 37 of chapter 23 shine with unsurpassed brilliance. Verse 37, however obscured in these chapters, is the harbinger of Matthew 26—the Passion, Crucifixion, and Resurrection. In this one small verse we see the hope of glory, even when things are beginning to look very dark.

Ever since Matthew 16 Jesus has been talking about His own death. Back then things still looked pretty bright, and Jesus' talk of a time of darkness seemed out of place. By Matthew 23, things look very dark indeed and will only grow darker, and this one verse of light is very welcome indeed. It is the Christ child of Geertgen's Nativity.

And yet in a way that only God, the Master Artist, could have arranged and executed, the darkness and the light mingle. In this one verse, in which the Son as Judge is transfigured into the Son as Compassionate Lover, we experience a foretaste of the mystery to come. For the one who is Judge will soon become the one who takes upon Himself the judgment of the world. The one who pronounced woes upon the scribes and Pharisees and condemned them to Hell will soon experience Hell for them. And the ones upon whom doom and damnation ought to come are offered protection under His wing.

It's all right there in verse 37. And it all hangs upon one small phrase. All of this could be avoided. The doom of both chapters 23 and 24 could be reversed, *If.* Jesus would gather us under His wings and protect us *If.*

If *what*? If only we were willing. If only we were willing, Jesus would take upon Him the curse that is rightfully ours. If only we were willing, Jesus would keep us safe.

The strange thing is that as Christians we all know this in an ultimate sense but miss it so often in more proximate senses. We know how willing Jesus was to protect us as a mother hen—He proved it on the Cross. But, what's strange is how often we forget that Jesus wants to gather us under His wing on a daily, momentary basis.

If only I were willing, what blessing might God have in store for me and for others? If only I were willing, what peace of mind I might find in Him. If only I were willing, what delight and rapture I might find in Him!

If only I were willing.

So there it is. I know what Jesus wants from me today. He wants me to live in Matthew, chapter 23, verse 37, right there, under His wing. He wants me to learn from the grave mistake of the scribes and Pharisees and to humbly come to Him once again.

You know what? That's exactly what I'm going to do!

Prayer:

I arise today
Through a mighty strength, the invocation of the Trinity,
Through the belief in the threeness,
Through confession of the oneness
Of the Creator of Creation.

I arise today
Through the strength of Christ's birth with his baptism,
Through the strength of his crucifixion with his burial,
Through the strength of his resurrection with his ascension,
Through the strength of his descent for the judgment of Doom.

I arise today
Through the strength of the love of Cherubim,
In obedience of angels, In the service of archangels,
In hope of resurrection to meet with reward, In prayers of patriarchs,
In predictions of prophets, In preaching of apostles,
In faith of confessors, In innocence of holy virgins,
In deeds of righteous men.

I arise today
Through the strength of heaven:
Light of sun, Radiance of moon,
Splendor of fire, Speed of lightning,
Swiftness of wind, Depth of sea,
Stability of earth, Firmness of rock.

I arise today
Through God's strength to pilot me:
God's might to uphold me, God's wisdom to guide me,
God's eye to look before me, God's ear to hear me,
God's word to speak for me, God's hand to guard me,
God's way to lie before me, God's shield to protect me,
God's host to save me From snares of devils,
From temptations of vices, From everyone who shall wish me ill,
Afar and anear, Alone and in multitude.

I summon today all these powers between me and those evils,
Against every cruel merciless power that may oppose my body and soul,
Against incantations of false prophets,
Against black laws of pagandom
Against false laws of heretics,
Against craft of idolatry,
Against spells of witches and smiths and wizards,
Against every knowledge that corrupts man's body and soul.

Christ to shield me today
Against poison, against burning,
Against drowning, against wounding,
So that there may come to me abundance of reward.
Christ with me, Christ before me, Christ behind me,
Christ in me, Christ beneath me, Christ above me,
Christ on my right, Christ on my left,
Christ when I lie down, Christ when I sit down, Christ when I arise,
Christ in the heart of every man who thinks of me,
Christ in the mouth of everyone who speaks of me,
Christ in every eye that sees me,
Christ in every ear that hears me.

I arise today
Through a mighty strength, the invocation of the Trinity,
Through belief in the threeness,
Through confession of the oneness,
Of the Creator of Creation. Amen.

(St. Patrick's Breastplate. Also see hymn #268 in the 1940 Episcopal hymnal)

Points for Meditation:

1. In what areas of your life do you need to come under Jesus' wing?
2. What image of God's protective love might help you remember to come to God for help?

Resolution:

I resolve to come under Jesus' wing today, consciously choosing to come to Him for safety and peace.

Matthew 24:1–14

Sometimes, a man's got to do what a man's got to do.

In this case, I feel compelled to say a word about Matthew 24 and its relationship to eschatology. It's necessary to do this to understand Matthew 24, as well as to apply this passage to our lives today. In a word, I believe that Jesus is speaking in Matthew 24 about events that would transpire in the 1st century, not His Second Coming.

Let me offer a few points of evidence. First, when Jesus proclaims His woes upon the scribes and Pharisees, saying that they will kill the prophets He sends, He concludes by saying, "*Assuredly, I say to you, all these things will come upon **this generation***" (Matthew 23:36, emphasis mine).

Without getting into arguments about the Greek word for "generation," it's abundantly clear that Jesus is talking to the actual scribes and Pharisees that He's just pronounced the woes upon. *They* will persecute Jesus' messengers, and He says to *them* that all these things will come upon *this* generation.

Second, it's in response to Jesus saying that the Temple will be destroyed that the disciples ask when these things will be and what will be the sign of His coming (24:1–3). They're asking not about the end of all time but about the events leading to the destruction of the Temple. Jesus' answer, therefore, is an answer about the destruction of the Temple.

Third, when the disciples ask Jesus what will be the sign of His coming, they can't mean His Second Coming: they have no idea there will be a Second Coming because Jesus hasn't left yet. They're not even sure at this point that He has to die. The Greek word for Jesus' "coming" here is *parousia*, a word used for a state visit in the Roman Empire or for a dramatic event, such as a miracle, which revealed the power and presence of a god. It's in these senses that Jesus would come to destroy the Temple.

Finally, when Jesus talks about not being deceived and about being killed, He's talking directly to His disciples who are right there with Him.

It might seem as if I'm putting a damper on things and killing the eschatological party. Sorry, there's no Rapture anywhere in this passage. It's true that I am taking our eyes off of *what* will happen *when* right before the Second Coming.

But, that's not a bad thing. The truth is, we know very little about this and any speculation we might enjoy doesn't really have a lot to do with what God's asked us to do in this life.

Far from diminishing life in the Kingdom of Heaven, I hope that by putting this passage in perspective I may magnify it so that we can see it for the exciting adventure and eternal joy that it is. What all of this means to us is that we already live in the New Age because the New Covenant, with its New King, New High Priest, New Temple, New Sacrifice, and New Life, has already come. The destruction of the Old Covenant was an earth-quaking, heaven-shaking event. As we Christians know, the coming of Christ—not only in His birth but in His life, His death, His Resurrection, His Ascension, His coming in A.D. 70, and His presence among us for 2000 years—has absolutely changed the world.

But, since the Kingdom of Heaven is not here in all of its glory, the Kingdom of Man remains. For this reason, we shouldn't be surprised that Jesus' words to His disciples of the 1st century sound fresh to His disciples in the 21st century. Nation still rises against nation, and I suppose they will until the end of time and all is made right. Christians still experience tribulation, and those of us in the U.S. who have been spared thus far should read more about the tribulation of Christians across the world, knowing that one day such things may happen here. Pay attention to the hate crime laws in Europe and Canada, for example, and remember that your children may one day live in a U.S. where persecution of Christians is possible. False prophets are still with us and still deceive many. Lawlessness still abounds, and the love of many has grown cold.

A strange thing happened to me when I was studying for my Ph.D. in Religious Studies. I was studying the identity of contemporary orthodox Anglicanism and broke through something similar to the sound barrier. Previously, though I had been an Anglican since 1988, I had thought of Anglicanism in terms of the various textbooks and introductions to Anglicanism that I'd read. When most of us learn history, we get a very smoothed out, gutless, lifeless history. It's why we think we don't like history, and it's why history looks so different from the textbooks when you look at it up close.

What I discovered is that there really was no golden age of Anglicanism, and that, furthermore, there was no golden age of Christianity. The truth is that if you were to look at the age of the apostles, the age of the Ecumenical Councils, the age of the Reformation, or any age you cared to look at, things in Christianity would be messy and ugly. In every age you would find persecution and heresy, apostasy and wolves in sheep's clothing, lawlessness and love grown cold. But, in every age you would also find saints and martyrs, heroic leaders and courageous teachers, and love reborn and sacrificially given by Christians to their neighbors.

This is what I see in contemporary America. I see a period of almost 50 years of moral decline: the things we tolerate today would have been unimaginable 50 years ago. The things that Christian parents let their children watch and hear and do would have been unimaginable 50 years ago and incomprehensible to most Christians for the past 2000 years. I hear mega-churches that peddle self-help therapy instead of the gospel of Jesus Christ, and I see fuzzy-headed syncretists who think that it's cool to be ambiguous and not have answers and to not be their parents' church. I see mainline churches in decline, and I see a triumphant secularism in every aspect of American public life: education, academia, the media, and politics. I see a nation that might not long endure if present trends continue.

But, I also see a church that transcends America and will outlive the 21st century. I see a Church that struggles to disentangle itself from its hangover from the Roman Empire and its models of the Church. I see a gospel of the kingdom that continues to be preached in the U.S. and throughout the world, and I see Christians heroically and joyfully witnessing to the nations. I see a vast army of Christians who will endure to the end and shall be saved.

Most of all, I see the Son of Man sitting at the right hand of the Father, the King of kings and Lord of lords whose kingdom and throne and scepter cannot be shaken. I see a Christ who has come, has seen, and has conquered. I see my Lord and my God. And that's right where I want to be!

Prayer:

O Lord our governor, we beseech Thee, of Thy mercy,
That we may have the heavenly vision,
And behold things as they seem unto Thee,
That the turmoil of this world may be seen by us
To be bringing forth the sweet peace of the eternal years,
And that in all the troubles and sorrows of our own heart
We may behold good, and so, with quiet mind
An inward peace, careless of outward storm,
We may do the duty of life which brings to us
A quiet heart, ever trusting in Thee.
We give Thee thanks for all Thy mercy.
We beseech Thy forgiveness of all our sins.
We pray Thy guidance in all things,
Thy presence in the hour of death,
Thy glory in the life to come.
Of Thy mercy hear us,
Through Jesus Christ our Lord.
Amen.

(George Dawson)

Points for Meditation:

1. Do current events worry you? How might seeing Christ in heaven help you not to worry?
2. What are some ways in which the glory of God's Kingdom is available to you today?

Resolution:

I resolve to meditate on Christ in heaven and allow my worship of Him to govern how I see the world today.

Matthew 24:15–28

Something of supreme significance happened in the 1st century A.D. It would be easy to read it as we might any other event in history, that is, with a yawn and a reach for the remote control. Julius Caesar was murdered in 44 B.C., we read. At the battle of Thermopylae in 480 B.C. the vastly outnumbered Greeks held back the Persians for three days in one of history's most famous last stands. Interesting. Now let me get on with my real life.

But, I tell you that in the 1st century A.D., something of extraordinary significance happened. Over a 70-year period, a series of most amazing and significant things occurred. At the time, it would have been easy to miss. It was done in a corner of the Roman Empire that didn't seem particularly important at the time. In a small village outside Jerusalem, in the province of Judea, one that some called the King of the Jews was born. Thirty years later, He gathered a small following before he was put to death in another three years by the Romans.

Of course, something much more dramatic happened 40 years later. In A.D. 66 the Jews had revolted against the Romans, who sent the general Vespasian to restore order. In 68, the emperor Nero died, and Vespasian was made emperor. He sent Titus to finish the job. By the year 70, the Romans had breached Jerusalem's outer walls and began a systematic ransacking of the city. The assault culminated in the burning and destruction of the Temple that served as the center of Judaism.

Another century, another collection of random historical facts.

Or is it? This is the way the history books might relate the cataclysm of the first century, but such an account would seriously underestimate the importance of what had just happened. When told from the perspective of God's chosen people, the Jews, and from the perspective of the New Covenant of Jesus Christ, such events would look very different indeed.

From the perspective of the first century Christians (mostly Jews), the events of the 1st century would have seemed like the dramatic death of an entire world and the tumultuous birth of a new one! It would have seemed like the greatest tribulation the world had ever known or ever would. Such an estimation wouldn't be based on a mere counting of the dead. In that case, the Holocaust of the 20th century would have been much worse. Of course, based on mere numbers, the

Holocaust isn't the worst calamity, either: Hitler killed his millions, but Stalin and Mao their tens of millions.

No, in the first century an entire world, the world of the Old Covenant which had existed for 2000 years, died. Nowhere was this more dramatically symbolized than in the destruction of Jerusalem, the city of David, and especially the destruction of the Temple, the center of worship and the religion of the Old Covenant. In fact, with the destruction of the Temple, the Old Covenant could not survive, based as it was on the sacrificial system that had now come to a permanent end.

But, as terrible as this slaughter and destruction were (go read Josephus if you want all the gory details), in keeping with the principles of the Kingdom of Heaven, the old died so that the new could be born. As terrible as the destruction of the Old Covenant was, the birth of the New Covenant was even greater.

And this is one way we may measure how great is the Covenant under which we live, the Kingdom in which we live, and the King we serve: by how terrible the destruction of the Old Covenant was. By this we also know how difficult life in this kingdom will be while still in this life. As you might imagine, there was a lot of resistance to the birth of Christ and His Kingdom—and there still is.

Think of Satan and his minions as a particularly dangerous fire ant mound, and that in the 1st century Jesus stomped all over this mound and destroyed it. However, this aroused the fury of the ants who had been relatively quiet but who now came out in full force. Wherever the Kingdom of Heaven advances, it is met by the Kingdom of Hell, and so we should not be surprised if those things which happened decisively in the first century, prophesied by Christ, are repeated in various guises throughout history.

Whoever reads Matthew 24, let him understand. What happened in the first century forever changed history and mankind. And what happened in the 1st century is still being worked out in our lives in the 21st century. Don't be surprised, therefore, if God's work in your life seems to meet with resistance today. Don't be surprised when life is a mixture of good and evil.

But know this: Jesus Christ has come, and the old world has come and gone. Christ and His Kingdom remain forever, and that makes all the difference in the world today.

Prayer:

Our Father, who art in heaven, hallowed be Thy name. Thy kingdom come. Thy will be done, on earth as it is in heaven. Give us this day our daily bread. And forgive us our trespasses, as we forgive those who trespass against us. And lead us not into temptation, but deliver us from evil. For thine is the kingdom, and the power, and the glory, for ever and ever. Amen.

Points for Meditation:

1. What are some ways you can be reminded that Christ is on His throne and His Kingdom is here?
2. See today's challenges in terms of the spiritual warfare in your life.

Resolution:

I resolve to spend some time thinking of Christ on His throne, preparing for the spiritual warfare I will face today.

Matthew 24:29-41

In 2007 a thought-provoking book titled *The Black Swan* was published. It provides an insightful perspective into seemingly improbable events (i.e., a 'black swan') and our thinking that surrounds them. The author, Nassim Nicholas Taleb, contends that black swans underlie almost everything within our world but that we usually fail to acknowledge the possibility of a black swan event until after it occurs. According to Taleb, most people focus only on things that we already know—or think we know—and that we generally fail to consider what we don't know. The result is that most people are not able to look beyond very narrow confines, and these severely limit their horizon. Most people therefore are blind to the possibility of significantly large events.

And yet, as today's lesson demonstrates, large, unexpected, significant events do happen.

There are three ways we might interpret today's passage and others like it. For reasons I've described (or will describe) in other *Give Us This Day*s, I believe that historically speaking, Jesus is talking to His 1st century disciples about the things that must shortly happen, beginning with His Crucifixion, and continuing with His Resurrection, Ascension, and the destruction of the Temple and the Old Covenant.

Futuristically, this passage could be read in terms of Christ's Second Coming. Even though I don't believe that's what Jesus had in mind, the warnings about Christ appearing and no one knowing the day or hour could be applied to the Second Coming.

But, as happens so often in writings on such passages, I don't necessarily learn much about what such a passage might mean for me today. If I look at what Jesus meant historically, I'm stranded 2000 years ago and reading about events that have already happened a long time ago. On the other hand, if I look at Christ's Second Coming, I'm looking at something that might not come for a very long time. Millennial cults have been around for at least a millennia and, like the poor, will always be with us. Of course, they've all been wrong. And I kind of like the idea that the older Books of Common Prayer have a table that lets you calculate Holy Days until the year 8400! (If you have a 1928 Prayer Book, you'll find it on page lvii, right before Morning Prayer begins.)

But, I am stuck here in the present, and even my discussion about the future in previous paragraphs is now in the past. (Strangely enough, it might be in the present for someone who happens to pick up this *Give Us This Day* and is just coming to that part!)

May I suggest, in keeping with what I've written before, that the cosmic consequences for the work of Jesus Christ 2000 years ago are so powerful that they continue to be felt until the present day and will continue to be felt until the Second Coming? Furthermore, the work of Jesus Christ in creating the New Covenant has a Trinitarian time dimension to it.

What I mean is that the New Covenant, the Kingdom of Jesus Christ, has a past, a present, and a future. The work of God in redeeming the world had an *initial* or *definitive* beginning 2000 years ago. It certainly continues to have a *progressive* aspect as it is worked out in history, even as we live it in the present. And it will, one day, have its *final* consummation in the future. Like any good story, God's story of redemption has a beginning, middle, and end.

And I'm here in the middle, which is organically connected to both the beginning and end. I know what Jesus has done, and I know what He will do in the end. This means that I should have a pretty good suspicion of what He will do in the present with me now.

And so here's where today's lesson applies to you and me. I can't claim to have figured out that Jesus Christ will return in glory and judgment on Tuesday of the 22nd Sunday in Trinity of the year 2008 (the day I first wrote this particular *Give Us This Day*). But, I do know that Matthew 24 sounds a lot like things that are going on in the world today (and as they have for 2000 years). I do know that people are acting as they did in the days of the Flood. They eat and drink and marry. They grow up and get jobs, and they grow old and die. Life is lived as if one day will be pretty much like the next, even as life gradually changes.

We're all uniformitarians when it comes to our lives. We pretty much bank on things being the same and their being safe and predictable. And yet we know that life isn't always like this. We've all made important decisions that forever changed our lives. We grow up and move out and go to college. We begin the grand adventure called marriage and undertake the Herculean labor of being parents. We know people who become desperately sick or die, or we have brushes with death ourselves.

At such moments we realize that life will not always continue the same way, day after day. At such moments, I suspect that even the agnostics and atheists have their consciences pricked that maybe there's more to life, and that this God person just might be real (and worse, might be something like what evangelical Christians say He is!)

Haven't we all had moments where a foolish driver (maybe yourself!) drove in such a way as to jeopardize your life? I can't count the number of times when accidents have been averted while I was in a car, either as driver and passenger, and some of them rather serious ones. In those moments, my heart becomes a rocket and tries to escape my ribcage and flee for his life. I snap to attention, and everything else in life goes away for at least a few moments. Whatever problems I thought I had are instantly put into their proper perspective and are demoted to the category "minor", for just a moment.

But, after we turn out to be O.K., we go back to being uniformitarians and go back to life as usual. We go back to the ultimate game of hot potato, the cosmic round of musical chairs, in which we continue to play the game of life, only dimly aware that at any moment that timer might ring and we might be the one with the hot potato in our hands or no chair to sit on.

And today, since you are here in the present, and Jesus is with you, He's telling you to not go back to the game of life and your uniformitarian ideals. Consider today's *Give Us This Day* as a gentle wakeup call (and don't you dare hit the snooze alarm!)

"Watch, therefore, for you do not know what hour your Lord is coming" (verse 42).

Actually, I think I *do* know what hour the Lord is coming. I think He's coming right now. No—I *know* that He's already here. Just because Jesus isn't coming to finally separate the sheep and the goats and to judge the quick and the dead doesn't mean that He isn't coming and has not, in fact, already come today.

Maybe one of the best ways to read today's passage is not only to fear the Lord because one day He will come in judgment but also to love the Lord who is already here in peace.

Prayer:

We beseech thee, Almighty God, to purify our consciences by thy daily visitation, that when thy Son our Lord cometh he may find in us a mansion prepared for himself; through the same Jesus Christ our Lord, who liveth and reigneth with thee, in the unity of the Holy Spirit, one God, now and for ever. Amen.

(Traditional Collect for Fourth Sunday in Advent from the 1979 *Book of Common Prayer*, p. 160)

Points for Meditation:

1. How strong of a sense do you have of the Lord's presence here and now? What are some things you could do to strengthen this sense?
2. How might today's wake up call change or color your day?

Resolution:

I resolve to allow the presence of the Lord change the way I live today.

Matthew 24:42–51

Most of us adults don't like being watched by our bosses. As children, we know that we're supposed to be watched and that this watching is for our own good. We don't always like it, but as children we know that it's usually a good thing. But as adults, we often rebel at the idea of our boss watching over us.

The question has to be asked "Why?" Why such rebellion against something the boss surely has a right to do? For some people, it might be simply a fear factor or one of intimidation. Another answer is that it offends our adult sensibilities. "I'm an adult and expect to be treated as an adult." And there is a point to that. The implication is that since I *am* an adult, I should be treated as an adult, since I will *act maturely like* an adult."

But, that's the problem for most of us, isn't it? We don't always act like adults, do we? I think that one of the main reasons we don't want our bosses watching over us is precisely because we know that this will put an end to our off-task, frivolous behavior! So our answer, instead of being brought back to maturity, is to get mad at the one who might catch us goofing off!

I hate to break it to you, but God is your boss. Except that all of the normal excuses for not faithfully serving an earthly boss have to be thrown out the window. You can't claim that you don't have to work hard or obey "since the boss is a blooming idiot!" You can't pretend that you know better than the boss or that He's an incompetent punk.

So what is your relationship to God, when seen as that of Master to slave? How faithful have you been in that relationship? Even the boss-employee analogy doesn't go far enough, because the truth is that we're God's slaves. We have fewer rights than we think we do, but also a lot more blessings than we think we do.

The truth is that you have entered into a covenant with the Lord your God, a covenant that was ratified and put into effect in your baptism. When you agreed that God would be your God and you would be His child, you signed away your life: you volunteered to be God's servant, and even His slave.

More than that, you chose to join His Kingdom and to become a minister in it. When you work, whatever work God has given you to do in this life, you are to do it as if serving the Lord. He is your true Master and your real boss, behind any other bosses you have. *The experience of work in this life, then, is not just the daily grind: it's our daily bread that the daily grind helps make.* It's the way that the Lord comes to us each day, for He has incarnated Himself into our daily lives and experiences.

This understanding that God comes to watch over us every day, and even every moment, is part of what the Christian's longing for unity with God is all about. It's what practicing the presence of God is all about. Yes, there is a certain fearful expectation, if we insist on being like the wicked and unfaithful servant.

But, how blessed it is to have God as your boss! When working for him, we don't work for earthly pay and aren't time-servers who will do the minimum amount of work to still keep our job. When working for God, it's more like being a father or mother. It's a job you don't get paid for doing: in fact, it's a job that costs you a great deal, in time, energy, money, and every imaginable resource. As fathers and mothers, we're recompensed, all right, but the rewards are intrinsic to the experience itself. There's no cold, objective, symbolic exchange of money: instead, there is the ultimate reward of God's blessing for doing His will.

God delights in catching His children doing what they're supposed to be doing. As a teacher and a parent, sometimes I feel as if I've too often looked for the worst in my kids. It's not that I wanted to find it: it's just that it's been one of my jobs to keep order and make sure people were doing what they were supposed to be doing. It's kind of like the way teachers take out the red pen only when an answer is wrong. The truth is that my watchful eye has often been necessary and has allowed for true learning and peaceful lives. It's prevented the world of my classroom or my home from descending into a re-enactment of *The Lord of the Flies.*

But, how blessed I have always felt when I would return to the classroom and find peace and order and my kids busily working!

How blessed as a father, when I go to inspect a kid who's been assigned a house job, go to check up on him, and find that he's still at work! How happy when I go to check on the ruckus in the boys' room only to find that it was a happy noise, and not injury and crying. How overjoyed, when I happen to wander past some of my children and find them at peace with one another and enjoying one another's company!

One of the things I've found useful in my life is to keep before me this simple phrase: "Am I doing what I'm supposed to be doing?" It's a phrase I developed for use by a classroom of kids with learning disabilities I had one year. I asked them to think of this question throughout the day as a way of focusing. Throughout the day or week, I'd occasionally remind them of this important question.

It's amazing how that simple question can immediately raise my awareness of where I am in my life at any given moment. I don't usually have to think too hard for an answer. It's usually clear. Maybe I'm goofing off, and so once I've raised the issue with this question, my conscience quickly seizes the control knobs and steers me back to God. Maybe I'm in a sinful attitude, and God is calling me to change it. Maybe I'm working, but there's something more important I've been called to do instead. And maybe, the question finds me in that most blessed of states: doing exactly what God desires for me to do.

Today, rather than thinking about what will happen if God catches me being the wicked and unfaithful servant, I'm going to think about what will happen if He catches me doing what I'm supposed to be doing. It's not just about the state I'll be in when it comes time for me to die: it's about what state I'm perpetually in, moment by moment. And, after all, it's this moment-by-moment state that will determine my final state.

Today, I'm going to think of God not as a meddlesome boss who I'd rather not see, but as a loving Father coming to visit one of His children. Today, I'm going to think in terms of pleasing my Father whom I love, hoping that when He does come by and look He'll find me doing His will. And then, like any good father, He'll give me a great big hug, which we adults call union with God.

Prayer:

I desire, O God, this day most earnestly to please Thee; to do Thy will in each several thing which Thou shalt give me to do; to bear each thing which Thou shalt allow to befall me contrary to my will, meekly, humbly, patiently, as a gift from Thee to subdue self-will in me; and to make Thy will wholly mine. What I do, make me do, simply as Thy child; let me be, throughout the day, as a child in his loving father's presence, ever looking up to Thee. May I love Thee for all Thy love. May I thank Thee, if not in words, yet in my heart, for each gift of Thy love, for each comfort which Thou allowest me day by day. Amen.

(Edward Bouverie Pusey)

Points for Meditation:

1. If God were to evaluate you on your typical day, how much of the time would He find you "doing what you're supposed to be doing?"
2. Meditate on the joys of pleasing your heavenly Father.

Resolution:

I resolve to work today so as to please my Lord.

Matthew 25:1-13

One of my favorite shows growing up was *Batman*. My favorite arch villain was King Tut played by Victor Bruno. (Julie Newmar's Catwoman was a close second). King Tut was in real life a mild-mannered Harvard professor of Egyptology, but when he got hit on the head with, for example, a flower pot, he turned into King Tut. In one episode, he actually figures out that Bruce Wayne is Batman. He mumbles to himself, mulls over what he's seen and heard, calculates and says out loud to himself, "carry the 3...ergo, Bruce Wayne...is *Batman*!"

At the end of the episode, however, he gets hit on the head again and turns back into the mild-mannered Harvard professor of Egyptology. When he sees Commissioner Gordon and Police Chief O'Hara and others looking at him, he looks up at them and says, "Oh dear! Have I done it again?"

Well, that's the way I feel today.

Do you remember what yesterday's lesson was about? I know. I, too, have to scramble to think what it was about. Oh yeah, I remember. It was about no one knowing the day or hour when Christ will return, and I applied it to mean that God is our boss and we should work like He is working, so that whenever He comes He'll find us doing what's pleasing to Him.

And then we come across today's lesson—and it's exactly the same thing! I mean, the characters in the parable are changed and so on. But, it's really still all about the master/ bridegroom being gone and what we'll do in His absence. Why can't Jesus move onto something else?

But, the reason I feel like King Tut—"Oh dear, have I done it again?"—is because *I'm* the one who's done it again. It's hard to believe that 24 hours have expired and transpired (and perspired). But in that time, in spite of my spending so much time having written yesterday about watching for Jesus throughout my day—guess what? I haven't done a very good job. My whole day was about *things* I'm sure He wanted me to be doing, and yet so little of the time was spent thinking about *Him*.

The truth is that I need to hear this message about always being prepared for Christ in my life again. A second reminder, after I bungled the first one, isn't such a bad thing after all.

In retrospect, I feel like a kid who's a picky eater. I turn my nose up at leftovers, and I don't like what I get served, even if it's good for me! God never fails to feed His children with His daily bread, but that doesn't mean we always like it. This is one of the things I like about using a lectionary system for reading the Bible or preaching: I don't get to keep going back to my favorite verses but instead have to find what is good about what God has just served me.

Left to myself, I'd probably go back to my old favorites time and time again: Psalm 19, Psalm 27:4, Matthew 16:24, 1 Corinthians 13, Philippians 2, Revelation 1, and so on. Left to myself, I could eat pizza almost every day. In fact, during one summer I worked at Pizza Hut, I did! But, a strictly pizza Biblical diet would not be such a good thing!

So today, I'm supposed to be one of the wise virgins. What was the difference between the wise and foolish virgins? One cared enough to prepare, and one didn't.

Don't you know that one day, when He returns, you'll be re-united with Jesus, the Bride with the Bridegroom? This life is to prepare for the next, eternal, life. But, if you've been a foolish virgin who has not prepared and has not cared enough to bring extra oil, you just might be surprised when He does return!

You sometimes hear stories of soldiers being reunited with their wives after a long period of separation, sometimes years. I'm blessed, in that I've never been away from Jackie more than a week at a time. So I can only imagine how joyful and exuberant such a reunion must be for us. Imagine the joy we'll all have when we're completely reunited to our Lord in heaven!

The way we prepare for the Second Coming of Jesus Christ is to prepare for His coming to us today.

Thanks, I needed to hear that again. And I won't complain, Lord, if you serve it to me again sometime soon in the future.

Prayer:

My spirit longs for thee,
within my troubled breast,
though I unworthy be
of so divine a Guest.

Of so divine a Guest
unworthy though I be,
yet has my heart no rest
unless it come from thee.

No rest is to be found
but in thy blessed love;
O let my wish be crowned
and send it from above.

(John Byrom)

Points for Meditation:

1. Are there ways in which you've been complaining about the daily bread that God gives you each day?
2. What are some ways in which Jesus is likely to show up in your life today?

Resolution:

I resolve to spend today looking and longing for the presence of my Lord.

Matthew 25:14–30

Having paid close attention to the last three chapters of Matthew's Gospel, this parable strikes me in a different way today. Jesus is still talking in that long red-letter passage about when "these things shall be," of which the disciples inquired. He's still talking about what He is about to do: His Crucifixion, Resurrection, and Ascension, which entail the coming of the New Covenant and the destruction of the Temple.

Historically speaking, then, to whom is He speaking? It's probably a good thing to know this first, rather than jumping in and applying it to ourselves out of context. In the first century, at the end of His earthly life, what might constitute the talents that the master had given, and who might be the good and faithful, and the wicked and lazy servants?

The wicked and lazy servants seem to be Jesus' favorite whipping boys: the scribes and Pharisees. They had been given the Law, the very oracles of God, and they had been given the Temple. They were given the keys to the kingdom. They were the ones to whom God had entrusted His little lamb. And what had they done with these great talents? They had hidden their true nature from the people, where they could not be profitable to them.

The good and faithful servants, then, are all of those, including the tax collectors and prostitutes, who had turned to Jesus in faith and had received the Word from Him.

When we apply this parable to ourselves, the most important thing to consider is which kind of servant are we? What have we done with the talents or treasure which God has entrusted to us? We should understand from the beginning that the greatest talent and greatest treasure that God has given to us is Himself in the person of His Son, Jesus Christ.

Before I hear about how well you've used the intelligence, charm, communication skills, and wisdom God has given you, I want to know what you've done with that greatest of treasures: Jesus Christ.

Have you realized His worth? Have you sold all to seek Him? Or have you buried Him somewhere in the crevices of your life? Do you know right where He is when you need Him, and yet most of your life He's invisible to you?

I think there's an interesting relationship between what we do with the treasure of Christ and what we do with the gifts and talents God has given us. This is seen most interestingly in a man BC and a man AC (Before Christ and After Christ in his life). Most of us have known people who have turned from a life without Christ to a life with Christ. Is he the same man AC?

Spiritually speaking, we know He is not. And yet when God has made Him a new creature, does God rearrange his face? Does He make the man any smarter or dumber (I'm not talking about wisdom here but about raw IQ points), or give him increased physical strength? We know that these things remain the same. In the same way, I believe that when God changes a person's life by his being united to Christ that He doesn't give that person an entirely new personality with entirely new gifts and talents.

And yet that's the way we think of spiritual gifts most of the time. We often miss how God uses spiritual gifts in our lives today because we're used to thinking in terms of speaking in tongues, a gift which was not there at one time in a person's life and then was. And we therefore undervalue the gifts that don't seem extraordinary.

St. Gregory of Nazianzus rightly said of Christ's Incarnation, "*What is not assumed is not redeemed.*" By this He meant that Christ had to be human in every way in order to redeem every part of man. One implication is that Jesus came as God and man to become the perfect man, one whose natural gifts and talents were completely redeemed and made perfect.

When, through, the Holy Spirit, we are given spiritual gifts, therefore, I don't think that we usually receive new talents or powers but that instead we have been freed and empowered by God's grace to use our "natural" talents in the way in which they were intended. Take, for example, the intellect. A man with a powerful intellect could use that intellect for hateful, despicable purposes towards someone else, or he could use it for selfish, prodigal purposes, becoming a connoisseur of knowledge but not putting it to any good use.

Or, redeemed by Christ, he might become the next C.S. Lewis who used his natural gift of intellect to defend the honor and glory of God and show Him to a generation (and more than a generation). C.S. Lewis didn't suddenly become smart when He became a Christian. But, C.S. Lewis didn't use his intellect for the spiritual gift of edification, teaching, or wisdom until the Holy Spirit had made that "natural" gift a "spiritual" gift.

I've been watching the X-Men movies lately. They (super)naturally appeal to me. I used to draw all sorts of pictures of freakish monsters of all different sizes and abilities, and I've always been fascinated by a comparison of various powers. Some of the powers that the X-Men mutants have seem to be pretty dull and wimpy, while others blaze in glory and are godlike. At one point in one of the movies, Magneto (who has one of the better gifts: the ability to manipulate anything made of metal) turns to a teenage mutant who has the ability to manipulate fire and says to him: "You're a god among insects."

St. Paul and others may be a god among insects compared to some of us. But, you have been given the greatest talent and gift of all: Jesus Christ. And by him all of the natural abilities you were born with and all of the experiences you've had since then have been redeemed.

How you treat this greatest of gifts, Christ Himself, will govern how you treat all of the other gifts and talents He's given you. Giving these gifts and talents back to the Lord won't necessarily magnify them in the eyes of the world. A man with little natural intelligence who becomes a Christian will not suddenly become Albert Einstein. But, he might become the most loving father, the most faithful gardener, or the most fervent worshiper of God.

It may seem as if God has given you only a few small things. But, use those few small things through the Spirit, and you will inherit the greatest thing of all: everlasting life in Christ.

Prayer:
Receive, O Lord, all my liberty. Take my memory, my understanding, and my entire will. Whatsoever I have or hold, You have given me; I give it all back to You and surrender it wholly to be governed by your will. Give me only your love and your grace, and I am rich enough and ask for nothing more. Amen.

(Ignatius of Loyola, from *The Spiritual Exercises*)

Points for Meditation:
1. What natural talents has God given you? How might they be used in a more spiritual way, as God intends?
2. Meditate on what it means to be made a steward of the mysteries of Christ.

Resolution:
I resolve to choose one gift or talent that God has given to me and find one way to direct it to God's purposes today.

Matthew 25:31–46

We Americans are the richest people who have ever lived. I'm using statistics that are now almost a decade old (and I think these numbers are even higher now), but 34% of our families own two TVs, and 40% own three or more. Our average family has two cars, while 18.7% of us have three or more, not to mention computers, DVRs, stereos, houses, etc. We live longer, with better medical treatment than ever before, we have unlimited access to things to entertain us, and our choices in food are so great that they're bewildering.

We live like kings, and yet the perception of many of us is that we are just getting by, perhaps because we are comparing ourselves to the wrong thing: the celebrities and the super-rich of the world.

In the same way, we Christians are the richest people on the face of the earth. Every Christian is inheriting the greatest kingdom ever known. And yet as we live in this sinful world, we sometimes complain about what is not yet here—heaven in all its glorious perfection—instead of being thankful for the good things we already have in the kingdom of God.

But, there's something you should know today—the Kingdom of Heaven that Jesus has been talking about for three chapters has come! The King is on His throne, and His kingdom is here, although not in all of its power and glory. You might also want to know that you have been privileged to rule with the King, starting today.

The Kingdom of Heaven, as I've said before, has three temporal aspects: *initial, progressive,* and *final.* This is true both corporately, for the kingdom as a whole, and for the lives of individuals. Christ's Kingdom was initiated at His first coming, in our lives at baptism and in our justification. His Kingdom is progressively revealed throughout history and through the process of sanctification. Finally, His Kingdom is consummated at the final judgment, and in our glorification.

There's a dangerous tendency sometimes to think more of the first and the last than about the middle. We read the Old Testament or the Gospels and see God acting in power, and we think about God's final defeat of His enemies at the end of all time. But, do we pay enough attention to His establishment of His kingdom here and now?

John the Baptist proclaimed the coming of Christ before Christ's public ministry.

And what did he say? What he *didn't* say is "Look! the Kingdom of Heaven is 2000 years or more away, and God is far from you!"

What he did say, in Matthew 3:2, was "Repent, for the kingdom of heaven is *at hand*!"

When Jesus sent out the 12 disciples in Matthew 10 and gave them power to do the things He did, He told them to say as they healed the sick and spread the gospel: "The kingdom of heaven is at hand."

That same kingdom is here today! The King is here. He came to earth, and the genealogies of Matthew and Luke demonstrate that He was born of the kingly line: it was because He was a king that Herod wanted him killed, and even at His death Pilate unwittingly testified to His kingship.

He sits at the right hand of the Father now, from where He rules both heaven and earth. He is *here*. Jesus Christ is present on planet earth, wherever you are at this moment, and He is still the King of Kings. Is He somehow here *less* completely than before the Crucifixion, Resurrection, and Ascension?

God is *now*. He inhabits all time, and His rule is established forever. The same King who proved His mastery over the natural forces of land and sea, over the supernatural forces of darkness, and over sickness and death is here now. He witnessed your conception and birth, and He will be present, watching over you on the day you die.

He's here, in space. God has become man and has tabernacled with men. And yet sometimes we feel that God is far off.

I believe that many of us carry around in our heads a mistaken mental picture of God. I believe that many of us see God sitting around in the vast void of space and that we imagine heaven is somewhere infinitely away among the stars. Such a view of God makes prayer very difficult, and the presence of God is so remote that He cannot be in every square inch of our lives.

But, what if God inhabits the space all around you, as a spirit lives with a body, so intimately connected that you can't easily separate them? When God the Father spoke to the Son from heaven on a few occasions in the Gospels, that voice was very near to Christ, and those around heard it. We live in a God-drenched world.

God is accessible. In *The Divine Conspiracy* Dallas Willard uses the illustration of electricity. Most people today have had electricity so long that it has ceased being a miracle to them. But, even in the 20th century there were homes that had no electricity. Through programs of rural electrification, such as the TVA, suddenly electricity became instantly accessible. All one had to do was to know how to gain access and a world of radio and central heat and air conditioning, of electric lights and appliances, opened up. It was as if someone had said to those people: "The kingdom of electricity is here!" We can imagine their surprise and joy when they discovered this newfound access![8]

In the same way, the kingdom of God is here and now, accessible to all who are part of the Kingdom. But all too often, like the TV or radio waves that are bouncing around the walls this very minute, we forget about God or believe His power to be too remote.

The King, whose kingdom you live in, comes to you every day. The same King who gave blind Bartimaeus back his sight, the same Lord who gave Lazarus back His life, and the same Lord who wept and whose bowels were filled with compassion while here on earth is here in your presence today. He's present in the Sacraments and in His Word. He's present in prayer and in the Body of Christ around you.

But, *if the Kingdom of God is Here, then we should begin ruling with Christ Now!* You and I, in Christ, are seated in the heavenlies (Ephesians 2:6). We have started to rule with Him. Rule what? A king's rule is the range of his effective will. You already have rule over several countries that God has given you. The question you need to ask yourself is not, "Do I have the authority to rule?" but *"How* should I rule?"

You're to rule yourself first and foremost, meaning body, mind, and soul. This is the point of Christian maturity. You have material resources that God has given you rule over, and you have been given daily labor by Him that you are to govern. You have God-given relationships that you are to govern wisely, especially those of us who are parents and spouses.

We pray for this effective rule every day: "Thy kingdom come, thy will be done on earth as it is in heaven (i.e., that all would progressively come under His rule and will).

The amazing thing is that we get to cooperate in establishing His Kingdom by doing His will. "My bread is to do the will of my Father," He said, and He might just as easily have said, "My *daily* bread is to do the will of my Father."

Because Christ rules, and we in a lesser way, we can even say that Christ rules *through* us. He isn't here physically on the earth, but through His Church He is. He rules through the Church, who is His Body, as He dwells in us through His Spirit.

---

8   Dallas Willard, *The Divine Conspiracy* (New York: HarperCollins, 1998), 30–31.

As with His earlier disciples, He commissioned us to do the same things He did while on earth. In John 14:12 He said, "He who believes in me, the works that I do shall he also do; and greater works than these shall he do; because I go to the Father." Later, He also says, "As the Father has sent me, so send I you."

And so we rule in God's kingdom the same way Jesus Christ did: we serve, for "He who wants to be great in the Kingdom of Heaven, let him be the servant of all." You must *serve* those whom God has put under your rule. The life of a parent, for example, is a never-ending work of feeding, cleaning, diapering, praying, educating, training, playing, disciplining, and sacrificing.

As Jesus teaches us today, in Matthew 25, we rule by loving. When the Son of Man comes in all His glory with the angels to judge the nations, on what basis will he separate the sheep from the goats? On whether or not in His name they fed the hungry and gave drink to the thirsty. On whether or not they saw a stranger and invited him in or visited those who were sick or in prison.

By doing good works, by loving, and by serving (that is, Christ in us), we rule in the kingdom of heaven. If you do these things—if you rule by serving—great will be your reward in the Kingdom of Heaven!

Prayer:
Our Father, who art in heaven, hallowed be Thy name. Thy kingdom come. Thy will be done, on earth as it is in heaven. Give us this day our daily bread. And forgive us our trespasses, as we forgive those who trespass against us. And lead us not into temptation, but deliver us from evil. For thine is the kingdom, and the power, and the glory, for ever and ever. Amen.

Points for Meditation:
1. Look for opportunities today to care for someone who has a need. Look for opportunities to console those who are lonely or discouraged.
2. How might it change the way you look at your life to think of it as a rule that God has given you to exercise?

Resolution:
I resolve to ask the Lord for one way He wants me to rule in His kingdom today and, having heard His will, to go out and do His will, as it is in heaven.

Matthew 26:1-16

In Matthew, we have been climbing God's holy hill. The going has been rough lately, actually ever since Peter made his profession and Jesus began to teach about His coming death. But, Jesus' words on the coming destruction of the Old Covenant and Temple have been even tougher to get through. Obviously, something big is about to happen!

And then, here in Matthew 26, after struggling to have come this far in our journey, the rest of the mountain opens up for us. We can see that what we've been through so far is child's play compared to the last three chapters of Matthew. Suddenly, everything gets more intense. It reminds me of Einstein's theory of relativity, which theorizes that when an object with mass accelerates and gets close to the speed of light it comes closer and closer to weighing an infinite amount.

The closer we start getting now to Calvary, the heavier we get. And so after Jesus had finished His sayings in chapters 24–26, He tells His disciples the Passover is soon approaching and the Son of Man will be delivered up to be crucified. There, He's said it plainly, not only that He must die but also how He will die. Immediately after this, the antagonists of the story, the chief priests, scribes, and elders of the people, take counsel together against the Lord and against His Anointed, saying, "Let us plot a way to kill this Jesus by trickery." By verse 14, Judas Iscariot goes to the chief priests and makes his demonic deal with the chief priests.

But, sandwiched in between the forces of darkness and some notorious villains is a light that shines in that darkness. She is the woman who anointed Jesus for His burial. She is the woman who extravagantly took an alabaster flask of very costly fragrant oil and poured it over the head of Jesus. She is the woman whose deed will shine in the world wherever the Gospel is preached.

And we're supposed to be like her.

It might help to know that the fragrant oil she used was probably worth about a year's wages and was therefore very costly to her. So costly was it that the disciples (especially Judas) are indignant at the waste. Why, after all, the money could have gone to the poor!

But, what this woman did (John tells us it was Mary of Bethany), extravagant as it was, she did for the most valuable thing in the world: her Lord. What an honor to anoint the Anointed One! In Matthew and Mark, she anoints Jesus' head, as the priests and kings and prophets were anointed in the Old Testament, for He is *the* Prophet, *the* Priest, and *the* King. But, in John's account, she anoints His feet, wiping His feet with her hair. She does this a full chapter before the Lord washed His disciples' feet on Maundy Thursday. Apparently, she had an idea of not only how important Jesus was but also of how we should serve Him.

This Mary is the same Mary who chose the one thing necessary, to sit at the feet of the Lord and worship Him. The feet that she anointed were the same feet at which she sat, adoring.

And we are to be like her. But there's just one thing—the physical body of Jesus Christ is up in heaven, and so we can't anoint His feet. Besides, I'm all out of spikenard and don't have the money to go buy some more.

There is one thing you could do. When Jesus' physical body ascended into heaven, the Holy Spirit was sent to breathe life into the mystical Body of Christ on earth, the Church. We *do* have the Body of Christ with us, and we are to anoint it. Mary took her glory, her hair, and wiped the feet of Jesus, besmirched with the dirt of the earth, with it. She took something very important to her and sacrificed it to the Lord.

As Mary anointed the body of Christ, so must we. Do you remember the parable of the talents (it was just last chapter)? How do you think the Master would want you to invest the gifts and talents He's given you? He's given you your spiritual gifts so that you might edify, anoint, and adorn the Body of Christ (Ephesians 4:12).

Do you believe that the Church is truly the Body of Christ? St. Paul certainly thought so, and so has the majority of Christians throughout history. This is no mere figure of speech. Something about God taking on human nature, something about Christ's sacrifice, and something about our union with Christ through baptism and faith leads to the blessed belief that through the power of the Holy Spirit we *are* the Body of Christ on earth. We are how He works in the world today.

The question for today, then, is, "How might I go about edifying, anointing, or adorning the Body of Christ today?" What you do to and for your brothers and sisters in Christ (for they are the Church) is what you do to Jesus Himself. It might be the case that one of your brothers or sisters in Christ is among the poor, who are still with us, and that God is asking you to serve him in some way. It might be that you have the gift of teaching, and yet have buried that talent. Maybe your local church is looking for volunteers for an important ministry and God is asking you to anoint His Body in this way. Some of you may be called to anoint Christ's body with your tears, in the difficult work of prayer.

There are more spiritual gifts than the 20 listed in Scripture, and there are many ways to use each of these gifts to anoint the Body of Christ. Ask God today to show you how He would like you to care for His Body, remembering that He has called you to this sacred task.

When you do, something beautiful will happen: as with Mary's spikenard, the house, God's house, will be filled with the fragrance of your ointment. And that fragrance is the fragrance of Jesus Christ, the Anointed One, whom you have just anointed.

Prayer:
O Almighty God, who hast built thy Church upon the foundation of the Apostles and Prophets, Jesus Christ himself being the head cornerstone: Grant us so to be joined together in unity of spirit by their doctrine, that we may be made an holy temple acceptable unto thee; through Jesus Christ our Lord. Amen.

(Collect for Saint Simon and Saint Jude from *The Book of Common Prayer*, p. 254)

Points for Meditation:
1. Where have you smelled the fragrance of the saints anointing the Body of Christ in your life?
2. Consider what spiritual gifts God has given to you and how they might be used to edify the Body of Christ.

Resolution:
I resolve to listen for the one way the Lord is asking me to anoint His Body today, and then to do what He wills.

Matthew 26:17-30

One of my favorite painters is the surrealist Salvador Dali. In 1976 Dali painted a painting titled "Gala Contemplating the Mediterranean Sea which at Twenty Metres Becomes the Portrait of Abraham Lincoln," (commonly called "Lincoln in Dalivision). In this painting, Dali used 252 tiles that, when seen up close, look like his wife, Gala, looking out a window. But, as you move back from the painting, a picture of Abraham Lincoln emerges. Not long after this, the world of photo mosaics was born.

And that's what the Gospel of Matthew is like. The entire meaning of the Gospel, the Good News, is about to be revealed in a startling way so that all of those wonderful individual pictures Matthew's been showing us now reveal themselves to be part of a much larger picture.

For several chapters, now, Jesus has been teaching about the coming of the New Covenant and the cataclysmic events that would usher it in. He actually began teaching about it in the very first words of His public ministry: *"Repent, for the kingdom of heaven is at hand"* (Matthew 4:17). He then proceeds to talk about the Kingdom and the blessings it will bring upon those who are poor in spirit and who hunger and thirst for righteousness, after which He teaches about the new Law in the New Covenant. He demonstrates that there is a new power in this New Covenant by the many miracles He performed.

In choosing the 12, He prepares for the continuation of this New Covenant after He must die, be raised up, and then ascend into heaven. He tells parables about what life in the kingdom will be like, and He miraculously feeds both the 5000 and 4000 as a way of teaching about how He will feed those who hunger after righteousness in the New Covenant.

Beginning in Chapter 16, He begins to teach about a terrible price that must be paid in order for this New Covenant to be put into place. That price is His own life, which He will give for the life of the world, and it will involve a sacrifice on the part of His disciples as well. He teaches some more about the coming of the New Covenant, teaching in many different ways that Israel of the Old Covenant has rejected her Savior, killing the prophets and soon the Son Himself. His harshest words are for the leaders of Israel, who should have prepared the people and led them to the Messiah and the New Covenant but who instead are determined to keep the people in great darkness. And then He teaches about how terrible the events will be that mark the fullness of the coming of this New Covenant.

Here in Chapter 26, when we come to the Last Supper and the institution of the Lord's Supper, suddenly the entire book of Matthew comes into focus. Each of the stories and teachings we have heard are all part of the larger picture of the coming of the New Covenant and the coming of the Kingdom of Heaven. But, it's not until we come to Matthew 26 that things start to make more sense. The Lord's Supper bridges the gap between Jesus' teaching about the New Covenant and that Covenant being put into effect. It's amazing how short the account of it is. It would look rather unobtrusive, if we weren't already alerted to its immense significance. In Matthew's account, he spends nine verses talking about the preparations for the Passover and the coming betrayal of Him. The description of the actual supper lasts only four short verses, and then Jesus and the disciples leave for the Mount of Olives.

It all happens so quickly, that it would be easy to miss. O.K., so Jesus is at the Passover with His disciples. We would expect that, since this was a required feast, and we've heard about Jesus going to Passovers before. We've been hearing about Jesus being betrayed and going to die and then being raised up on the third day for some time, and it seems time to get the inevitable over with. We all know that Jesus has to go into Gethsemane to pray and be betrayed and then experience the terrible events of the Passion and Crucifixion.

So why this interlude with the disciples at the Passover? It's just a religious obligation, and one that was part of the Old Covenant, isn't it?

But, these four verses are not only what connects the parts of Matthew's Gospel: they're also what connects us to Matthew's Gospel and the narrative of the coming of Christ and the New Covenant. Just as Jesus had gathered up His chosen 12 apostles to be His Body and continue the work of the Incarnation, now He also provides the means by which they will continually be fed and strengthened to be His Body and do His will on earth. In the Lord's Supper He gives Himself to them for heavenly food, the bread which comes down from heaven. In this supper, He gives Himself to them, His Body and His Blood, that they might become His Body and be one with Him.

Having established His Church and given Himself to her by His supper, Christ also made it possible for that Body to continue to live and be one with Him, even after the 12 were dead. In this humble supper, He seals the New Covenant for all time, even as all of the Old Covenant is consumed and fulfilled within the New Covenant. All of the sacrifices of the Old Testament and all of the feasts and festivals are contained in this humble meal. All of the Gospel, from the Incarnation, in which the Father gives His Son and His Body and Blood for us, to the Crucifixion to the Resurrection and the Ascension are served to us, here in this humble fellowship meal.

Here is the Passover Lamb, the Lamb of God that takes away the sins of the world. Here is the meaning of all that God had told Israel 1500 years before, and here is the meaning of our lives 2000 years later.

Here is the betrayal of mankind, Adam's sin being repeated by Judas, and Adam and Judas' sins being repeated by us. But, here also is the sacrifice that takes away the sins of the world, for all who eat with faith. Here is the Crucifixion of our Lord for our sins, and here is our own death. But, here also is His Resurrection and our new life with Him.

This humble supper is the fulfillment of the Passover and the prediction of the Crucifixion. It is the fulfillment of the Incarnation, and the prediction of the Resurrection. For us, it is the fulfillment of all, because in it we find Christ. In it, we remember God's promises and mighty deeds, and we anticipate the future hope of glory. And in it, we come to understand the meaning of the narrative of our lives and all of the smaller images that sometimes don't make sense by themselves.

It would be easy to read these four small verses and pass by as if nothing particularly significant had just happened. It would be easy to read them quickly and without due attention because we've seen it all before.

But, here is the meaning of our lives. Here is the New Covenant. Here is Jesus Christ, His life, His Body and His Blood, offered to us anew, each and every time we come to this humble supper.

So now is the time to prepare for the next time you come to this supper. Do not treat it lightly. Do not pass over it, as if it were nothing. For in it, is Life itself, for in it, is Jesus Christ, who is the New Covenant and all its blessings.

Prayer:

Almighty God, whose blessed Son Jesus Christ has ordained in the Holy Sacrament the perpetual memorial of His death and the communion of His risen life, grant that we may keep the feast spread out before us and approach the sacred mystery of Your love with humility and awe. May we, by Your grace, feed by faith upon the Body and Blood of Your Son and be made partakers of Your heavenly grace; through the same Jesus Christ our Lord. Amen.

Points for Meditation:

1. If you are in anguish because of sin or difficult circumstances, remember the heavenly food Jesus offers to you at this time.
2. How might you more adequately prepare to eat the Lord's Supper the next time it's offered to you?

Resolution:

I resolve to prepare adequately for the next time I come to the Lord's Supper.

Matthew 26:31-46

We know that Jesus was constantly in prayer, but we don't have many of His prayers written down for us. He's left us *the* prayer, of course, in the Lord's Prayer. And we have what is called the high priestly prayer of John 17. But today, I'm especially glad for His prayer in the garden of Gethsemane.

This prayer of Jesus seems a lot like my prayers, and I think that just as Jesus taught by His words and His miracles, His example of prayer in tribulation has much to teach me today.

There are a lot of interesting things about Jesus' prayer in the garden, but there's one fact that stands out to me like a Neanderthal at a cocktail party. Do you see it?

It could be that Gethsemane is a garden. That's interesting. The life of the first Adam began in a garden, and here is the life of the Second Adam, ending in a garden. And, of course, when Jesus is resurrected He is mistaken for the gardener, so He rises in a garden. What an intriguing irony: the garden which was Paradise but which was also the place where man fell is now a battlefield for Man.

It's interesting as well that Jesus has to remind His disciples to watch and pray, lest they fall into temptation. There's that word temptation again, and in a garden. And maybe Jesus tells them this because He knows He Himself is being tempted. This would make sense: that the serpent would return to the Garden to tempt the Second Adam, just as he tempted the first Adam. So maybe Jesus, the Second Adam, undoes what the first Adam did by resisting the temptation in the Garden.

It could be. But maybe, the one startling fact that I see is something else. Maybe it's the fact that Jesus even has to pray at all. Why would one who is God have to pray to God? Because the one who is God is also man, and as a man, He had to pray. It's a mistake, a mistake well on the way to heresy, to think that just because Jesus was God that He wasn't fully man in His human nature, with all of man's needs and limitations—except for the notable exception of sin.

So it's fascinating that Jesus has to pray at all. His prayer in the garden points to another aspect of His humanity: His soul was exceedingly sorrowful, even to death. Jesus knew what was coming. He had known for some time that He was to be crucified in Jerusalem, and He knew what pain and agony were in store for Him. He knew as well that He would be raised the third day—He'd already begun teaching His disciples that.

So why is He so sorrowful and deeply distressed? Didn't He know that it would pass and that He'd be resurrected? Yes, He did. But, would that completely anaesthetize the pain of the Cross? I'm not sure that any of us can comprehend what the Cross would have felt like to Jesus, not only the pain of the crucifixion that any criminal of the first century might have experienced, but the tailor-made Cross just for Him, weighted down with the sins of the world.

There is another remarkable thing. Being human, Jesus asks the Father to take the Cross, the cup, from Him. Knowing that it was the will of the Father, as a man He still wants to find a way out, if at all possible. Here He is, just a short time after He has offered the cup of life and salvation to His disciples, and He's left holding the cup of the wrath of the Father for the sins of the world. It could hardly have seemed fair. And so He asks, out of sorrow and distress, for the cup to be taken from Him. In fact, He pesters the Father and asks three times.

But, none of these are the one fact that stares out at me today like headlights in a cat's eyes. No, the thing that strikes me most about Jesus' prayer in Gethsemane is that the Father says, "No, my Son." Here is Jesus, the only perfect man who ever lived, the very Son of the Father, the most pleasing person in the eyes of the Father, and the person who most faithfully prayed to the Father, asking the Father for something out of His sorrow and distress. And His loving Father tells Him, "No."

There's an important lesson here for us this morning. Have you ever wondered why some of your most fervent, persistent, righteous prayers are answered "No" by the Father? It doesn't seem to make sense. But here, in the Garden with Jesus, such things make sense. Here in the Garden we're confronted with the righteousness of the Son and His anguished prayers, and we're confronted with the sleeping disciples. That's us: sleeping through life while the Son does all the hard work! We know that we're the ones who should feel such anguish. We know that we're the ones who deserved the suffering of the Cross—and much more.

And when we see our Lord praying so fervently and righteously, our lives come back in focus. We suddenly see what we really deserve and what God has given us instead. We see our righteous Lord in anguish for us, when He has done nothing to deserve it. And, everything in our lives seems small in comparison. It has a way of shutting one's mouth.

As I watch and hear my Lord suffer for me, another thought occurs to me. What if my suffering, and yours, is *necessary* for the redemption of the world? What if we are to fill up what is lacking in the sufferings of Christ? What if God can't save the world without suffering being involved? What if it's hardwired into the plan of redemption?

I know that I am united to Jesus Christ and that for the most part that is nothing but bliss. But, I also know that I am united to Him in His suffering, as He is to me, and so is it so strange that I also should suffer? Actually, the fact that I suffer shouldn't be strange at all. I deserve far worse, and one day it shall all be ended and all that will remain will be Christ within me and the perfection of heaven.

And if God the Father can say "No" to even the Son, then I understand a whole lot more why He so often seems to say "No" to me, when I ask for my suffering and distress to be taken away.

This is why I love Jesus' prayer in the Garden of Gethsemane. This is why it seems so human to me: it feels like my life many times, and now I understand it much better. I know as well that the prayer in the Garden and also the Crucifixion were limited in time. They passed, and so shall all of the difficult and painful things in my life. And if I have to endure them with my Lord, *for* my Lord, for several more decades, then I can do it.

Through Jesus' prayer in the Garden, I come to the point where I want what He wants, which is nothing but the will of the Father. And if that means some suffering, then I'm O.K. with that because the Father whose will I desire to do is my good and loving Father. And He's the One who raised His Son from the dead and has promised to raise me up as well.

So thank you God, for now I'm ready to pray in my own little garden today. Now I know who You are and who I am, through the prayer of Your beloved Son, who continues to pray for me in heaven.

Prayer:

Our Father, who art in heaven, hallowed be Thy name. Thy kingdom come. Thy will be done, on earth as it is in heaven. Give us this day our daily bread. And forgive us our trespasses, as we forgive those who trespass against us. And lead us not into temptation, but deliver us from evil. For thine is the kingdom, and the power, and the glory, for ever and ever. Amen.

Points for Meditation:

1. Meditate on Jesus' prayer in the Garden of Gethsemane. How can it help to put your life and its suffering into perspective?
2. How might you make your prayers more like Jesus' prayer?

Resolution:

I resolve to accept the Lord's will in my life today when I pray faithfully and don't receive what I ask for.

Matthew 26:47–56

Today we come to the Word of God.

When we say "the Word of God," we often use it in two different senses of the Word. We say, on the one hand, that the Bible is the Word of God. In its strongest sense, we see this when the prophets say things like, "Thus says the Lord."

We also use "the Word of God" to mean the Son of God, Jesus Christ, the Word made flesh. In both cases we have the revelation of God to man, and the two are joined more intimately than we can imagine.

But today, I see before me a strange dance. I see, on the one hand, the Word of God, those ancient prophecies of the Israelites, spoken by the prophets of old. Matthew, especially, pays attention to the fulfillment of Scripture, especially at both the beginning and the end of His Gospel. "So all this was done that it might be fulfilled which was spoken by the Lord through the prophet, saying, 'Behold, the virgin shall be with child, and bear a son, and they shall call his name Immanuel,' which is translated, 'God with us'" (Matthew 1:23, quoting Isaiah 7:14). Matthew also draws attention to the fulfillment of Micah 5:2, about the shepherd who would come from Bethlehem; to the fulfillment of Jeremiah 31:15 and lamentation of Rachel weeping for her children at the slaughter of the innocents; and to John, the voice of one crying in the wilderness spoken of in Isaiah 40:3.

Something interesting happens in Matthew 26: we see Jesus, the Word of God, choosing to lead a life that will fulfill the perfect will of the Father, as spoken through those ancient prophecies. Here, in Matthew 26, we see the ancient, immovable, written Word of God spread out before us. And here, in Matthew 26, we see the living, incarnated Word of God choosing the steps of His life to be in perfect harmony with the Word, the will of the Father, spoken by the prophets.

This conforming of His will to the will of the Father is no easy thing for Jesus. We're mistaken if we think it is. Have we, like the disciples, fallen asleep so soon? Don't you remember the agony of the Lord in the Garden of Gethsemane, immediately after which the betrayer and armed multitude came for Him? He's just asked for the Father to take this terrible cup from Him.

Leave it to Peter to offer a way for Jesus to avoid the will of the Father. Good old Peter. The one who would not have his feet washed by his Master and the one who denied that the Son of Man should ever go to Jerusalem to suffer and die is now the one who would stop this prophecy one way or the other. Poor Peter! One little sword among so many swords and clubs and men. It's a good thing Jesus intervened. Little did Peter know that Jesus could have defended Himself very easily. He could have called twelve legions of angels to protect Himself.

But, there's that little matter of the Word of God, which Jesus knew must be obeyed. How could the Scriptures be fulfilled, if Jesus had delivered Himself? How could the will of the Father be kept if He chose His own will?

Jesus seems almost amused by what is happening. Was it really necessary, He asks them, to bring so many men, with swords and clubs? He was theirs for the taking any time earlier. "Aren't these rather bizarre circumstances under which you're arresting Me?" He seems to ask. It's as if Jesus is, even at the last, teaching. He's teaching them that the secret betrayal and seizure at night, the Mickey Mouse trials He'll undergo, and the Crucifixion all suggest that something very strange and momentous is taking place.

Even the end of verse 56, "*Then all the disciples forsook Him and fled*," is a fulfillment of the Word of the Lord, even if it's only me and not St. Matthew that's pointing it out—"*Strike the shepherd, and the sheep will scatter*" (Zechariah 13:7).

It's tempting to admire Matthew's cleverness in write a story that manages to cobble together so many different Old Testament prophecies. What an insightful writer he is! Of course, it was Matthew who learned to correctly understand the Old Testament from Jesus, and not the other way around.

What strikes me today about how Jesus the Word of God submits to the will of the Father through the written Word of God is this: that because He knew the Scriptures, He knew what He had to do. And then, knowing and loving the Father, He did it.

The same is true for you today. If you know the Word of God, and intend to do the will of the Father, then you'll know what you need to do. I'm not saying that if you randomly open your Bible you'll suddenly be enlightened as to what to wear this morning or whether you should get the grande or the venti at Starbucks. But, if you know the Word of God, you'll know the will of the Father in all the important things.

In fact, (since I'm assuming many of you know your Bibles well), if you just sit still for a few moments, God's will for your life will come streaming into it. Probably more than you want it to! It's not magic, but if you put together the written Word of God and an honest heart that truly desires the will of the Father, there's a good chance you'll end up with wisdom and the blessing of having done the will of the Father.

This provides an enormous incentive to know the Word of God better. It's no use cutting corners, and a lazy hermeneutic that reads verses out of their larger context has often gotten men into trouble. But, as you learn to read the Word of God richly and deeply so that it gets into the fibers of your muscles and the fissures of your brain and the blood of your heart, then learning and following the will of the Father becomes possible. For when you read the Word of God in this way you are united to the Word of God, the incarnate One who not only perfectly understood but also perfectly obeyed the written Word.

When you submit yourself to the Word of God, seeking the will of the Father, then you, too, will be enabled to endure the Gethsemanes the Father has willed for your life.

Prayer:

Our Father, who art in heaven, hallowed be Thy name. Thy kingdom come. Thy will be done, on earth as it is in heaven. Give us this day our daily bread. And forgive us our trespasses, as we forgive those who trespass against us. And lead us not into temptation, but deliver us from evil. For thine is the kingdom, and the power, and the glory, for ever and ever. Amen.

Points for Meditation:

1. Meditate on your life in reading the Word of God. Is there some aspect of reading, studying, or meditating on God's Word that He is calling you to work on?
2. What aspects of His perfect will does the Father seem to be impressing on you today through the Holy Spirit?

Resolution:

I resolve to read the Word of God tomorrow (you've just done it for today!), looking for His will for my life.

Matthew 26:57-75

"What do you think of this Jesus?"

Careful how you answer!

They answered and said, "He is deserving of death." Then they spat in His face and beat Him, and others struck Him with the palms of their hands, saying, "Prophesy to us, Christ! Who is the one who struck you?"

Really? What could a good moral teacher and healer of sicknesses possibly have done to merit death? Maybe the religious leaders of the day were just jealous, and, yes, that's part of the answer. There was some truth in their answer that Jesus was deserving of death, from their perspective. It's all summed up in a nice, neat syllogism they all carried around in their hearts and heads. It went like this:

> *Major Premise*: Under God's Law, anyone who commits blasphemy deserves to die.
> *Minor Premise*: Jesus has committed blasphemy.
> *Conclusion*: This Jesus must die.

It's all there in black and white. There's no escaping it: once you accept the premises of a syllogism then the conclusion is inevitable.

The problem is that we humans often begin with wrong premises, ones that are sometimes terribly, tragically wrong. And such is the case today. Looking at the syllogism, it's easy to see what went wrong: it's the minor premise. Jesus did not, in fact, commit blasphemy.

But, the Jews certainly thought He did. Why would they think that? Isn't blasphemy about taking the Lord's name in vain and using it as a curse word? But blasphemy has a much broader meaning as well. According to Webster's (1913 edition), blasphemy is "An indignity offered to God in words, writing, or signs; impiously irreverent words or signs addressed to, or used in reference to, God; speaking evil of God; also, *the act of claiming the attributes or prerogatives of deity*."

And there it is: "the act of claiming the attributes or prerogatives of deity." That was why the high priest, scribes, and elders said that Jesus deserved death: He had blasphemed. He had claimed not only to be the Messiah but dared to say even more. Caiaphas the high priest asks Jesus: "*I put you under oath by the living God. Tell us if you are the Christ, the Son of God*" (v. 63).

Silent before, now Jesus answers. "*It is as you said*" (v. 64a). In other words, "Yes, I am the Christ, the Son of God."

More than this, He claimed to be the Son of Man of Daniel 7 sitting on the right hand of power of Psalm 110 and coming on the clouds of heaven. Whatever the real motives of the Jewish leaders, they had enough justification for them to condemn Him. Here was one who not only claimed to be the Messiah but also claimed to be divine. What further need did they have of witnesses?

What do we make of such a claim? When looked at from the point of view of Caiaphas, the scribes, and the elders, such a claim to be both the Messiah and God seem preposterous. If you're the Christ, prophesy about whom is the one who struck you. You can't be the high priest, because I, Caiaphas, have inherited the high priesthood from my father-in-law, Annas. If you're the king, then why do you come in such low estate? And if you're God, then why don't you call down twelve legions of angels to save you?

It must have seemed as if the powers of this world had everything covered. Rome was still king of the hill, and Israel a lackey of Rome. Yes, there'd been a little trouble recently but the ringleader is about to be dealt with. Even after we come to the end of Matthew 28, it seems as if the world went on as normal and as if nothing had changed.

And today, looking outside my window to the houses and street below, it looks pretty much like any other day. This story about Jesus is tucked away neatly in my Bible and is safely contained within its pages.

But there, we've done it again! We've swallowed a fallacious premise, and so our whole conclusion about the ordinariness of our lives and the power of God is in error. We've gladly gobbled up the religion of materialism and scientism and live according to the following syllogism (though unconsciously):

> *Major premise*: The visible world is all that exists.
> *Minor premise*: God is not visible.
> *Conclusion*: God does not exist.

Now I'm not saying that this is what any of us would ever actually say or believe, but it's how we act so much of the time. All around us are the Caiaphases and scribes and elders and armed multitude, and they seem to govern the world. It sure seems like they're in charge and that it is the kingdom of man that, in the end, will prevail.

But, look again at verse 64, Jesus' answer. To those in charge of the world at that time He said that He was the Christ, the Son of God, and that they would see the Son of Man sitting at the right hand of the Power and coming on the clouds of heaven. No one except Jesus, not even the apostles yet, could see what Jesus saw. The One who had fulfilled all prophesy now makes a prophecy of His own, and it was sure to come to pass.

That generation saw the Son of Man, sitting at the right hand of the Power and coming on the clouds. In Daniel 7, the Son of Man comes with the clouds of heaven *to the Ancient of Days*, where He was given dominion and glory and a kingdom. The coming of the Son of Man on the clouds is the Son of Man *ascending* on the clouds into heaven and to the right hand of the Father. "Now when He had spoken these things, while they watched, He was taken up, and a cloud received Him out of their sight" (Acts 1:9).

It is in the Resurrection and the Ascension that we see Jesus' words fulfilled. It is only after the Resurrection and Ascension that He fully receives the kingdom promised to Him.

But, all of these things have happened for us: the prophecy of Jesus has been fulfilled. And yet sometimes we're tempted to play by the old rules, to act as if nothing special happened 2000 years ago. On Good Friday, it must have seemed as if God's side and His people were losing. The bad guys were in control and were about to squash the last hope of salvation. But, that's not how the story ended. We know how it ended: with a complete victory for God!

And we know how our story will end as well. No matter how dark things may seem today, no matter how much evil men still seem to triumph in this world, Christ has won the victory! It might well be, as it was with Jesus, that we will need to lose or appear to be losing for a season, so that the will of the Father might be fulfilled.

But in the end, those who stand with Jesus and proclaim Him as Messiah and God will rule with Him, and all of those who appeared to have been winning will have their kingdoms crumble into the sea.

Prayer:

O Lord God, our Governor, we beseech Thee, of Thy mercy, that we may have the heavenly vision, and behold things as they seem unto Thee, that the turmoil of this world may be seen by us to be bringing forth the sweet peace of the eternal years, and that in all the troubles and sorrows of our own hearts we may behold good, and so, with quiet mind and inward peace, careless of outward storm, we may do the duty of life which brings to us a quiet heart, ever trusting in Thee. We give Thee thanks for Thy mercy. We beseech Thy forgiveness of our sins. We pray Thy guidance in all things, Thy presence in the hour of death, Thy glory in the life to come. Of Thy mercy hear us, through Jesus Christ our Lord. Amen.

(George Dawson)

Points for Meditation:

1. How consciously throughout the day do you direct your thoughts toward God? How many of your decisions are governed by an appeal to Him?
2. Are there times when you feel you should stand up and proclaim that you are a Christian?
3. If you are facing a trial in your life and evil seems to be triumphing, remember the end of your life's story!

Resolution:

I resolve to hope today in Christ and His Kingdom, even when things look dark.

Matthew 27:1-10

He had been plotting it for weeks now, the evil thing that had to be done. For some time he had grown frustrated and disappointed at the sharp difference between what was promised and what was. It wasn't at all what he had bargained for, he told himself, and so he had the right to take matters into his own hands.

It wasn't just that things were not as they were promised to be: he didn't feel valued. He alone knew the true value of things: that's why they had all agreed to entrust the common purse to him. He alone had seen how wasteful they all could be. What embarrassing extravagance: to pour a year's worth of ointment on *his* feet!

So what if he skimmed a little off the top every once in a while? He was owed. He'd given up a lot to become part of this company, and he'd staked his reputation on this Jesus. And where had it gotten him? Nowhere. It was time to act on the plans he had only dreamed about previously. It was time to put the escape plan into effect.

And so he had great plans when he went to the chief priests and asked what he could receive for delivering Jesus to them. 30 pieces of silver, eh? The price of a slave. It wasn't as much as he was hoping for, but there wasn't exactly a large market for betraying would-be Messiahs. 30 pieces of silver was something to build on, and it would get Jesus out of the way so that he could begin a new life without him or his failed mission.

It had seemed delicious in his mind, as he anticipated the plans he was making. He had thought about it for so long and waited so patiently. Finally, he would be in charge of his own life again, and things would be made right. The actual transaction was not as delicious as he had anticipated, but it was kind of thrilling, this deal made in the dark, this being important to important men. It felt good to be the one making things happen again, and he told himself that the real pay off would come once he had made his new beginning.

He wasn't exactly sure what he had expected they would do with Jesus. The truth is, he hadn't really thought much about it. It was just a dirty job that had to be done, and what was that to him?

But, somehow it seemed different to actually see Jesus condemned, and a new feeling came over him. Suddenly, it became more personal. Yes, he wasn't happy with his life, and things hadn't turned out the way he had planned. But, that wasn't really Jesus' fault. And he didn't really want them to *kill* Jesus.

He tried to shake off the feeling, but it wouldn't go away. It didn't seem like such a glamorous and glorious thing now, what he had done. In fact, it didn't feel good at all. Worse yet, it would not go away, and the pressure it was exerting on him was growing. Far from the peace he had sought to buy, he had instead inherited a war within himself.

"I know what I'll do. I'll make things right. I'll just go and undo what I've done. I'll tell them it was all a mistake and that I was wrong to approach them. They'll have to listen to my confession. They're priests: they'll know how I can make things right."

But, when he came to them, bringing back the 30 pieces of silver, saying, "I have sinned by betraying innocent blood," all they said was, "What is that to us? You see to it!"

He looked wildly around him. He rushed towards where the Court of Israel adjoined the Priest's Court, where sacrifices for the penitent were being offered. There he threw down the 30 pieces of silver, and fled. They could have it—they could have it all! All he wanted now was for things to go back to the way they were. But, that was now impossible. He knew he had betrayed innocent blood—he'd known it all along. He had felt the truth in his mind when he first started thinking about it. Hadn't he met with resistance even in his own heart? But, over time he was able to master his conscience and pretend it wasn't still speaking to him.

How stupid! Look what he'd done! And he couldn't undo it, and no one could help him. He had sinned and betrayed his master, and there's nothing anyone could do about it.

Everywhere he went, everyone—the people, the houses, the earth and the sky— accused him, and he had no defense. He found himself in the desolate valley of Hinnom. Scrambling among the clay soil, he found his way to the jagged rocks that rose perpendicularly there. Before he knew it, he was at the top of a large rock.

He could see more now, on top of the rock. He could clearly see what had to be done. Slowly, he unwound the long girdle that held his garment, the same girdle that had carried the 30 pieces of silver. He secured it around a branch of a nearby tree and made everything ready. Here was a final solution that would go according to plan.

. . .

This is what came of Judas' plans and his attempts to do things his way instead of Jesus' way. It's a tragic and sad story, for it's the story of fallen mankind. Judas is truly a son of Adam, carrying out the wage of sin to its logical, inevitable end.

Judas could have stopped this terrible trajectory any step along the way. He could have repented of stealing from the treasury. He could have submitted himself to Jesus, waiting for the Kingdom of Christ instead of relying on the kingdom of men. Even after he had betrayed his Lord, he could have allowed his remorse to become repentance. Jesus would have forgiven even this worst of betrayals.

But, Judas chose to do none of these things but instead chose to continue to try to find his own solutions and answers.

The wages of sin are death, and if we allow the sin in our lives to grow, at some point it takes on a life of its own, choking out the true life we've been offered. A sin is not just an isolated minor fault or failing but is the seed of a life that is lived apart from God. And the fruit of a life lived apart from God is Judas' end. Judas is a picture of the inevitable end of sin.

But Jesus, whom Judas, you, and I have all betrayed, stands ready to forgive. No matter how small or great your sins, or how numerous, Jesus stands ready to forgive you. Today, therefore, is a day to examine your conscience and your life, and to make your confession to God.

Prayer:

Almighty God, Father of our Lord Jesus Christ, maker of all things, judge of all men: I acknowledge and bewail my manifold sins and wickedness, which I from time to time most grievously have committed, by thought, word, and deed, against thy divine Majesty, provoking most justly thy wrath and indignation against me. I do earnestly repent, and am heartily sorry for these my misdoings; the remembrance of them is grievous unto me, the burden of them is intolerable. Have mercy upon me, have mercy upon me, most merciful Father; for thy Son my Lord Jesus Christ's sake, forgive me all that is past; and grant that I may ever hereafter serve and please thee in newness of life.

Almighty God, my heavenly Father, who of his great mercy hath promised forgiveness of sins to all those who with hearty repentance and true faith turn unto him, have mercy upon me, pardon and deliver me from all my sins, confirm and strengthen me in all goodness, and bring me to everlasting life; through Jesus Christ my Lord. Amen.

(Taken from The General Confession of Sin & the Absolution of Sin from *The Book of Common Prayer*)

Point for Meditation:

Consider your sins before God today. Take note of even seemingly minor ones so that they do not grow.

Resolution:

I resolve truly to be sorry for my sins today, to confess them all, to receive the forgiveness of God, and to turn from them.

Matthew 27:11-26

If you have a pen or pencil, I'd like you to take it out. I have a little exercise I think will help you to understand the Word of God to you this morning. Have you got a piece of paper and pen ready? Actually, you can write it right here on this *Give Us This Day* printed copy.

Here's what I want you to write. First, write down "The King has come." Underneath this, I want you to take the word "has" and move it to the beginning of the sentence, but leave everything else in the same place.

What have you now written? *"Has the King come?"*

Look closely at these two sentences. They both contain the same four words and in almost the identical order. All that's happened is that you've slightly rearranged the words. And yet in slightly changing the statement of truth, "The King has come," to the question of doubt, "Has the King Come?" you have completely reversed the meaning.

Hath God said? Hath God said that you shall not eat of every tree?"

This is how Satan thinks and works. You see, he doesn't have words of his own: all he can do is take God's work and words and corrupt them. He asks questions that make us doubt God and His Word. God said to Adam and Eve: *"If you eat of the Tree...you shall surely die"* (Gen. 2:18). And Satan came along and said, "You shall *not* die."

And so this morning, God says to you that the King of kings has come. But, the Satanic question, asked by many, is: "Has the King Come?"

In Matthew 27 we see three kinds of people: Pilate, Judas, and the chief priest and elders, who don't have a lot in common. But, the one thing that unites them is that they are all people who didn't receive Jesus as the King who had come. Oh yes, there is a *fourth* kind of person who is not willing to accept the King the way He comes as king—and that is the group composed, to some extent, of you and me and all humanity.

The first questioner of Jesus Christ the King is Pontius Pilate. For him, and those like him, Jesus Christ was an inconvenient King.

Pontius Pilate was the governor of Jerusalem and Judea. During his ten years as a governor, from the years A.D. 26–36, Judea had thirty-two riots. The Jews hated the Romans and were constantly on the verge of rioting, and Pilate himself was often the cause for rioting.

In the year A.D. 26, shortly after Pilate become governor, Pontius Pilate came riding into the city of Jerusalem with his troops bearing their standards, carrying medallions of Caesar on them. This infuriated the Jews, and the rioting Jews first came by hundreds and then by thousands to the home of Pontius Pilate in Jerusalem and staged a demonstration for five days. Pilate was incensed with the protestors and killed some of them. Pilate was finally removed from office in A.D. 36 because of his brutal handling of the Jewish riots of that year.

For Pontius Pilate, to admit Jesus Christ was a king would have been highly inconvenient: it might have even meant he'd lose his job. When Jesus arrived in Jerusalem, Pilate had already arrived in Jerusalem with 600 troops, ready for another riot. He didn't want a king who would create a royal mess for him. So, for the sake of keeping the peace, Pilate refused to acknowledge Jesus as King, even though he had some idea that He was. Though it meant war with God, Pilate wanted to keep his human peace.

Sometimes we're like Pilate. Sometimes, it's inconvenient for us to acknowledge Jesus as King. Maybe, in the midst of friends or relatives who are not Christians, we're willing to act as if Jesus Christ were not King. Or maybe, we know that if we truly allow Jesus to rule as King in our entire lives we will have a riot on our hands—a riot of our old man, the sinful nature.

Nothing will stir up your natural propensity to sin and exalt yourself faster than truly proclaiming that Jesus is King. And that means rearranging your life to please and obey Him. It might be inconvenient to get up on Sunday morning to worship the King. Because it might inconvenience him, Pontius Pilate denied the King. Instead of proclaiming that the King had come, Pilate in essence said, "Has the King come?"

Are you willing to follow Pilate?

. . .

There is a second questioner of the King in Matthew 27, and that's Judas Iscariot, whom we read about yesterday and who was probably looking for a political king. Disappointed, he represents those for whom Jesus Christ is a weak or wimpy king.

The apostasy of Judas Iscariot was probably not just a sudden moment in which he betrayed His King. His betrayal of His Lord was likely to have been a gradually growing disillusionment with Jesus as King. It's likely that Judas accepted Jesus as King, as Messiah, and yet rejected Him as the same. Although this sounds contradictory, the truth is that Judas likely accepted Jesus as King, but only on Judas' terms. Judas wanted Him to come and rule in the way Judas expected, as a political king who overthrew the hated Roman Empire.

But, then Jesus began to say some disenchanting things, such as "My kingdom is not of this world." And what about John the Baptist dying and apparently coming to naught? What would have been Judas' reaction to Jesus as King when he refused to allow the people to make Him king by force on their terms, and not His? After the feeding of the 5000, the people came to make Jesus king by force, and what did this King, this Messiah do? He retreated to go off and pray by Himself. Some king! "Wimp!" we can almost hear Judas thinking.

You see, Judas' mastering passion was ambition and greed. He wanted a king with whom he could rule here on earth and parade himself around as someone. He wanted a king whose earthly treasure would be divided with him.

But, this King Jesus talked about being a servant and dying. When this King came riding in on a donkey, humbly and lowly, Judas had had enough. By the time that Jesus had washed the disciples' feet, as a mere servant, it was only a small step to complete betrayal for Judas. Jesus was not the king who ruled in an earthly and immediate way like Judas wanted, and so Judas rejected Him.

But, aren't we too often like Judas, accepting Jesus only as a king in our image, and not truly as the King of kings and complete Master of every aspect of our lives?

We all love the hypothetical Jesus, the one who stands for whatever we want Him to be. Too often, we say we want this hypothetical, figurehead Jesus of a King, but we don't really want Him as the King of kings. We don't really want Him to rule in our lives as the dread, sovereign ruler over our entire life, the one who has the power of life and death over us. We will not let Him rule in *His* way, according to the rules of *His* kingdom. He can rule in our lives, alright, but only when He rules as we'd like Him to.

What if the King comes to you in unexpected ways—ways that you didn't desire and plan for? What if He comes to you in the lowly things of life? What if He comes to you in suffering? What if He comes to suffer, and what if He as your king asks you to suffer for and with Him? Would you still receive Him and hail Him as King?

What if there were no mountain top experiences and no ecstatic visions, but instead, He offered a life to be lived by faith, one humble day after another? What if the path to glory is through humility and the way to rule in His kingdom is to serve? And what if He asks you to love, to give up yourself and your own ambitions, and to accept what He is trying to tell you and has been trying to tell you for some time? What if He didn't instantly answer all of your prayers or help you out of every mess you were in the way you expected to be helped?

What if He comes lowly, riding on a donkey into your life? Will you still receive Him as your king and vow to obey Him? Or will you follow Him in the way Judas Iscariot followed Him?

. . .

There is a third kind of person who rejects Jesus Christ as King in Matthew 27, and that is the chief priest and elders. They rejected Jesus as King, Matthew tells us in verse 18, out of *envy*. Jesus was very popular with the people because He demonstrated the power of God with His miracles and the truth of God with His words. But, the truth He spoke was different from what many of the Jewish leaders were teaching, and so they saw Him as a competitor to be eliminated.

They were kings like Herod: they didn't want another king, because *they* wanted to be kings. This isn't surprising, because they acted as if they were God. So Jesus the King was a threat to their own rule, and so they rejected Him, murdered Him in their hearts, and then put Him to death.

It's not just the chief priests or elders who have a problem with pride and envy: too often we too want to be God instead of God. We've coronated ourselves, and we sit on our man-made thrones, ruling by our own selfish desires. This is the essence of sin. We want Him to do our will and don't want to do His will. Sure, we'll submit to Him, but only when it fits in with our plans and our will. We want to be God, or at least the king, and that will lead to a rejection of the true King every time.

We say with our lips that Jesus is our Lord. We say that we our His disciples, *Christ*ians, and that we will faithfully obey Him. As Christians, most of us, if Jesus Christ were here in the flesh and told us to do something, would say "Yes, Lord, right away, Lord." And we'd be glad to do it.

But, the King comes to you in this life through those who have His authority and are to act as His representatives. If the King sent an angel, you'd probably also obey. But what if He asks you to submit to the people in your life that He has put in authority over you? Will you do it? What if the King asked you who are children to obey your parents? Do you obey as you would the King? What if the King asked you to submit to the dictates of your boss? Your pastor preaches and exhorts you to apply the Word of God in your life—do you listen and obey as to the Lord?

Even the circumstances of your life are things allowed by the King. Do you kick against them and curse the King? Or do you see the circumstances of your life as the lowly donkey on which your King comes to you each day?

You see how it's not just Pilate or Judas or the Pharisees who had a problem with the authority of Jesus in their lives.

. . .

There is one final group of people in Matthew 27, although they're hiding in the shadows...It's the disciples themselves. Though they're scattered and though they hide...the King came for weak human beings just like them. He came *as* one of them. Though they failed Him time and time again, He loved them. Though we have failed Him time and time again, He loves us to the end, and He died on the Cross for us. The King came in a lowly form, as a human, as a helpless baby. He came riding on a donkey to die and to die the most horrific and lowest form of death by crucifixion.

But, this is the same King who has the power to rise again from the dead and to destroy sin and death. This is the same king who restored Peter and breathed out His Spirit on those weak men on the day of Pentecost.

It is this King who has come and who rules over you every day of your life. Brothers and sisters in Christ: behold your King has come. May He rule without measure in your lives!

Prayer:

To Jesus Christ our Sovereign King
who is the world's salvation,
All praise and homage do we bring
and thanks and adoration.

Your reign extend O King benign,
to every land and nation;
For in your kingdom Lord divine
Alone do we find salvation.

To you and to your Church, great King
We pledge our heart's oblation;
Until before your throne we sing
In endless jubilation.

Christ Jesus, Victor!
Christ Jesus, Ruler!
Christ Jesus, Lord and Redeemer. Amen.

(Words by Martin B. Hellrigel)

Points for Meditation:

1. What are some of the areas in your life where the King rules? How have you been responding to the King's presence and commands?
2. What are some ways in which the King seems to disappoint you? How might you see Him and His rule in a different light today?

Resolution:

I resolve to consider one area of my life today where I may more faithfully acknowledge my King and His rule in my life.

Matthew 27:27-44

Whenever I used to see someone getting beat up or pushed around by a gang of people in the movies, like some of the many biker movies of the 60s I've seen, I have a visceral reaction.

I get mad or become sorrowful. Something about the injustice of it all gets to me. I have the same reaction when I see or hear about bullying in schools, a common occurrence.

But, how does it feel when the Son of God Himself is the one being picked on? What makes the bullying of Christ all the more startling is the knowledge that He could have chosen to do something about it if He wanted to.

For all of those who have ever been bullied or ganged up on, for all of those who have been unfairly persecuted, and for all of those who have borne the injustices of this world to any degree, we have Jesus Christ today.

It's really remarkable how God could enter into human history, as one of us, and allow Himself to be so abused by us. Knowing what we know of Jesus, it's repulsive in the extreme and almost incomprehensible. And yet here it is again, as we read about the Passion and Crucifixion of Christ one more time.

Everyone in the world seems to be joining in on this gang pummeling, torture, and execution. And, in fact, we ourselves have joined in. This, what we are witnessing today in Matthew 27, is the consequence of your sins and my sins and the sins of the world. It started with the betrayal by Judas, one of the 12 whom Jesus had hand-picked and who had lived and traveled with Him for three years. The hastily assembled Sanhedrin, the leaders of Israel—the high priest, chief priest, scribes, and elders—are next. They falsely condemn Him, spit in His face and beat Him, mocking His prophetic nature.

The spitting part is personal to me. I always looked up to my oldest brother Paul growing up. He was 2½ years older than me (strange—he still is!), and he helped open up new worlds of knowledge, music, and movie-making to me. But he was, like a lot of us Erlandsons, not at the top of the social heap in high school and might have fit into the nerd category.

One day when I (and I think my other brother was there as well) was up at the local elementary school with Paul, a group of high school students showed up.

They began giving Paul a hard time—I'm not sure why. Bullies don't really need a reason, except to make themselves feel superior. They began taunting him. One of them punched him in the chest and another spat in his face. I remember wondering why he didn't do anything about it but also knew that he couldn't. I felt sorry for him and humiliated as well.

And that's how I feel today, reading about my Lord. As if this weren't enough, Peter, the Rock, denies Jesus three times and goes to lick his wounds. Pontius Pilate passes Jesus around like a hot potato, doesn't defend Him, and decides to send Him to be crucified.

But first, Pilate's soldiers gather a whole garrison around Him and begin to mock Him. They strip Him, put on a scarlet robe, and crown His head with a crown of thorns. They mock Him as the King of the Jews, spit upon Him, and strike Him in the head with the reed that had served as His scepter.

Then the crucifixion itself begins, and He is treated as a criminal and crucified with criminals. The people who pass by show no pity but blaspheme Him, asking Him to come down from the cross if He is the Son of God.

Where are we in this picture? The disciples have all fled, and we were once among those who bullied Him. We were among those who rejected Him and reviled Him. We, by our sins, have had our part to play in the sad story we read today. We were the ones who made His suffering and death necessary.

But, no Christian can ever believe the story ends there: we know what this suffering and death are all about. Knowing this, we still cannot help but be sobered by what had to happen.

I see us in another character in today's story, and that is Simon of Cyrene. Like Simon, we must take upon us the Cross of Jesus. We, who were the ones He came to be with and the ones He came to die for, must be united with Him. We must unite ourselves to Him in His death, that we might unite ourselves with Him in His Resurrection.

And so, like Simon, we must take up His cross today. Life isn't always fair to us Christians, either. Just as our Lord was reviled, we too will find that sometimes we are reviled. As Christendom loses its hold on the U.S. and the Western world, we will see more and more that the world is a bully to Christians. It's remarkable that there was ever a time when this wasn't clear and didn't seem to be the norm.

There are some who will call us ignorant and intolerant and accuse us of hypocrisy and many other things. And even if we don't face immediate hostility or persecution, there are any number of ways in which this fallen world can seem to bully us. Life itself seems to be the greatest mocker, sometimes whispering and sometimes shouting that if Jesus Christ really is God then why doesn't He come down and make everything right? If He truly is God then why doesn't He deliver us out of all our difficulties?

I myself wish that all were immediately right with the world and that the bullyings and injustices of the world would cease this moment. It didn't stop for Jesus, not before He had been bullied, tortured, and killed, and it won't stop for us, either, not during this life.

Why do we expect that Jesus had to suffer for us but never suspect that we might have to suffer for Him? In this life, we will have to carry a cross. It can either be the one that justly crucifies us as criminals or the one that we carry with Jesus that crucifies the Old Man so that the New Man may live in us.

Take heart today, therefore, in the bullying and mocking of the world and in the cross that has been assigned to you today. As a Christian, that bullying and mocking and that cross are no longer means of torture and punishment. Instead, they have become the means of being united to your Lord.

Use the pain and suffering, the bullying and mockery, in your life today as a means of remembering and being united to the pain and suffering, the bullying and mockery, that ultimately redeemed the whole world.

Prayer:

Almighty God, whose beloved Son willingly endured the agony and shame of the cross for our redemption: Give us courage to take up our cross and follow him; who lives and reigns for ever and ever.

(Prayer of the Holy Cross from the 1979 *Book of Common Prayer*)

Almighty God, whose most dear Son went not up to joy but first he suffered pain, and entered not into glory before he was crucified: Mercifully grant that we, walking in the way of the cross, may find it none other than the way of life and peace; through Jesus Christ your Son our Lord. Amen.

(Contemporary Collect from Monday in Holy Week from the 1979 *Book of Common Prayer*)

Points for Meditation:

1. In what ways does the world seem to bully or mock you? How might you understand such things in a new light today?
2. Spend some time today thanking Jesus for His sacrifice for you.

Resolution:

I resolve to carry my cross for Jesus today, whatever that cross may be.

Matthew 27:45–56

So this is what it has all come to.

Three years of teaching about and living in the Kingdom of Heaven, and this is what it has all come to. He wasn't kidding about going up to Jerusalem to be delivered to death, a death on the cross. Not just three years but 2000 and three years. All of the promises made to Abraham, everything revealed to Moses, and all of the promises made to David. They all converge here, and it seems as if they have come to nothing.

Out goes the Light of the World, and darkness envelops the world for good. He who was divine seems to be abandoned by God, and He cries out, helpless after all.

> *This is the way the world ends*
> *This is the way the world ends*
> *This is the way the world ends*
> *Not with a bang but a whimper.*[9]

In the rematch of the ages, God vs. Satan, it looks like Satan has finally won.

And often our lives look and feel like Good Friday or Holy Saturday. Jesus has died, and that's that. Yes, we know all about the promised Resurrection, but today all I see is the death of the Lamb of God. And I think: "Is this all there is?" It seems to me like much of life, where death still seems triumphant and where things seem to have gone tragically wrong. Some of us may feel this way especially on a day like today, when the fate of the nation seems to hang in the balance, and the balance seems weighted the wrong way.

How powerful sin and death must be, that they were powerful enough to kill the King of Glory! How powerful, that they seem to separate even Father from Son, Son from Himself, and body from soul. So powerful are they that they must have their Day, and it is a long and dark one to me.

But even here, even on Good Friday (an ironic name indeed!), there are hints of victory. Even in death and dying, there are hints of the resurrection to come. Nature seems to be God's harbinger. Did you notice how it was dark for three

---

9   T.S. Eliot, "The Wasteland".

hours before Jesus died? It's as if Nature were telling us what would happen. But, did you also notice how the earth quaked and the rocks split? It's as if they were dying with Jesus and showing how great that death was. But, it's also as if they are showing us that the old world was about to be torn in two so that a new world could come. Did you notice that?

Did you notice what else happened when He died, when the darkness was at its greatest? The veil of the temple was torn in two from top to bottom. This veil was the enormous, thick veil that separated the Holy Place from the Holy of Holies. How embarrassing it must have been. It's almost as if the Temple itself had ripped its pants at the most embarrassing part of its anatomy!

In fact, the ripping of the veil was a symbol and harbinger of what would happen in 40 years, just as Jesus had prophesied, when not only the veil but also the entire Temple would be destroyed. It's as if immediately, when Jesus died, the Old Covenant began to die as well. Like a bad Hollywood actor of old, it took the Old Covenant a long time to die on stage, but it began to die at the moment Christ died. For at that very moment, the old was being torn down to make way for the new, even if few could see what was really happening.

And did you notice how when the rocks were split, so did the graves, those markers of death? It's as if, unbeknownst to just about everyone, Death itself had begun to die and as if from this time Death was a marked man. At the moment Christ died, the saints of God were about to be resurrected. Coming out of their graves after the resurrection, they went into the holy city and appeared to many. St. Matthew can't keep the Resurrection out of the Crucifixion, for they hang together!

And something else amazing happens in the midst of all this death: a pagan comes to know the Son of God. As a result of the earthquake and other things that happened, the death of Christ brings a Roman centurion to exclaim, "Truly this was the Son of God!"

Often to me, this life seems like a Good Friday. There is still so much suffering and dying and death. How powerful sin and death must be that they still have the power over all of us in this life, 2000 years after the Crucifixion. It still appears as if Jesus is locked in mortal combat with sin and Death and Satan.

But, that's not true. How powerful the death and resurrection of Jesus must be, that 2000 years later the graves of the saints of God cannot contain them and that one day there shall be a resurrection of body and soul. And pagans are still coming to Christ, 130 million in China alone, according to the latest reports. The earthquake that is Christ, who destroyed the Old Covenant and Temple so that He might create the New and better one, is still rippling through the universe. And a strange earthquake it is, whose vibrations and power do not abate but only seem to grow stronger.

And so in this life of death and suffering, we cry out with a loud voice to God, and, yielding up our spirits to Him, He receives us. He receives us because there is One who was born that He might die and who died that we might live.

The 2000 some odd years were not a waste after all—it's just that we've been blind.

> "On the tenth of this month every man shall take for himself a lamb. Your lamb shall be without blemish, a male of the first year. Then the whole assembly of the congregation of Israel shall kill it at twilight. And they shall take some of the blood and put it on the two doorposts and on the lintel of the houses where they eat it. Then they shall eat the flesh on that night, roasted in fire, with unleavened bread and with bitter herbs they shall eat it. For I will pass through the land of Egypt on that night, and will strike all the firstborn in the land of Egypt, both man and beast. Now the blood shall be a sign for you on the houses where you are. And when I shall see the blood, I will pass over you; and the plague shall not be on you to destroy you when I strike the land of Egypt. So this day shall be to you a memorial; and you shall keep it as a feast to the Lord throughout your generations. You shall keep it as an everlasting ordinance" (a compression of Exodus 12).

This Passover is an everlasting ordinance, as He promised. It's one that we still celebrate today: "Christ our Passover is sacrificed for us: Therefore let us keep the feast, not with old leaven, neither with the leaven of malice and wickedness; but with the unleavened bread of sincerity and truth" (1 Corinthians 5:7–8).

In that death which seemed so dark, He gave us His Body and Blood. Having made all things ready the night before, at the Last Supper, He prepared Himself to be a perpetual Passover for us. What else could He have done? In spite of His impassioned pleas in Gethsemane, what else could He have done? He who for His entire life made Himself a living sacrifice could only make Himself a living sacrifice in His death as well.

That sacrifice, that offering, that death, still lives in us today.

Therefore, let us keep the feast by offering ourselves up to Him, by crucifying our flesh, and by offering ourselves as living sacrifices; joined in death with Him that we may be joined in His life!

Prayer:

I earnestly desire thy fatherly goodness, mercifully to accept my sacrifice of praise and thanksgiving; most humbly beseeching thee to grant that, by the merits and death of thy Son Jesus Christ, and through faith in his blood, I, and all thy whole Church, may obtain remission of our sins, and all other benefits of his passion. And I offer and present unto thee, O Lord, my self, my soul and body, to be a reasonable, holy, and living sacrifice unto thee. And although I am unworthy, through my manifold sins, to offer unto thee any sacrifice; yet I beseech thee to accept this my bounden duty and service; not weighing my merits, but pardoning my offences, through Jesus Christ my Lord; by whom, and with whom, in the unity of the Holy Ghost, all honor and glory be unto thee, O Father Almighty, world without end. Amen.

(Adapted from the Prayer of Consecration from the Holy Communion Service of *The Book of Common Prayer*)

Points for Meditation:

1. What signs and symbols of the resurrection do you see, even in this life of suffering and death?
2. Take time to meditate today on Christ's death on the Cross for you.
3. In what ways do you still need to die to self?

Resolution:

I resolve to find one way to die to my self today, that I might be better united to the death of my Lord.

Matthew 27:57–66

Today's passage is just a little bit eerie. But, Holy Saturday is always that way to me. It's like the unearthly eye of the storm, in which you feel calm but can't feel peace because you just know something big is about to happen.

For today, we must allow Jesus to be dead. Not dying, as on Good Friday, which we know how to think about and meditate on. And not alive and resurrected, as on Easter Sunday, which we also know how to meditate on.

But, actually dead. It reminds me of the last eternal piano chord that plays on into silence at the end of the Beatles' "A Day in the Life." It's actually rather numbing.

There's no doubt about it: Jesus is dead. He who said He was the Resurrection and the Life to Martha when Lazarus had died has now died Himself. He who said He had come to give Himself for the life of the world has now had his life snuffed out.

Even the disciples see that it's all over now. Joseph of Arimathea asks for the body because now it will obviously have to be buried, since it's a corpse. He wrapped it in a clean linen cloth and laid it in his new tomb, because that's what you do with dead bodies. And then he rolled a large stone against the door of the tomb and departed because death is for keeps. There would be no escaping the cold hard clutches of death, not even for Jesus.

The enemies of God want to make absolutely sure He's good and dead and stays that way. So Pilate allows the Jews to make the tomb as secure as they could, sealing the stone and setting a guard over it: as if stone could move by itself or as if the mortified disciples would dare to steal the body and make up a lie about it.

And so today, Jesus is dead and in the tomb. And yet, His soul did not die: the early church did not believe in soul sleep but that the spirits of the dead went to Hades. There is a wide range of opinions about exactly where the soul of Jesus went and what He was doing during this time.

And I'm not going to attempt to argue for any of them.

But know this—that on Holy Saturday, it seemed as if all were lost. It seemed as if death had swallowed up life itself. It was as if the death of Jesus turned everyone instantly into zombies, continuing to live for a while but marked for a certain and irreversible death.

All was eerily quiet and still, more so than when all five kids in my house are quiet and still at the same time! That pregnant pause surely seemed like the end of the world as they knew it. All that remained was to live out the remainder of this mortal life.

But, something was happening, even during this eerie time. Those who were so certain about the triumph of death over Jesus and the ultimacy of death in our lives were wrong.

That silence you hear isn't the fade out music that escorts us out of life: it's the death of the old life and the birth of the new. It's the transition between death and life.

Some of you may have heard it in this life from time to time. I know I have. You may have experienced it when you were between jobs or between stages in your life, perhaps during a period of engagement. Or, more soberly, you may have experienced it during the times of life when you lose sight of the meaning of life for a time. What you thought was going to happen didn't and what might happen hasn't yet, and you walk the earth as a zombie.

But, this transition will not last. Even when I appear to be equipoised between death and life, this is a temporary phenomenon, although one that may last an earthly lifetime. I know how the story ends. (I've peeked at the next page, Matthew 28, but I won't spoil the ending for you!) This eerie, confusing silence will soon pass, and in its wake something startling this way comes!

Prayer:

Grant, O Lord, that as we are baptized into the death of Thy blessed Son our Savior Jesus Christ, so by continual mortifying our corrupt affections, we may be buried with Him; and that through the grave, and gate of death, we may pass to our joyful resurrection; for His merits, who died, and was buried, and rose again for us, Thy Son Jesus Christ our Lord. Amen.

(Collect for Easter Even from *The Book of Common Prayer*)

Points for Meditation:

1. Meditate on the death of Christ as payment for your sins and how serious they must be.
2. Meditate on the love of Christ who died for you.

Resolution:

I resolve to spend some time today anticipating the joys of the resurrection!

Matthew 28:1–10

For some reason, something totally unexpected dazzles me about the resurrection passage this morning. It's not the great earthquake. It's not the countenance like lightning and the clothing white as snow of the angel. And it's not the resurrected Jesus.

What I find deafening is the relative quiet of the passage, and what I find dazzling are the subdued tones with which St. Matthew paints his picture. This is why God didn't choose me to write one of the four Gospels. I would have written purple prose. I would have extolled the virtues of the Mighty Hero who triumphed over the Devil and Death. I would have made the passage explode!

But, St. Matthew plods along with his normal prose, describing things not as a composer of a hymn or fable but as someone who just wanted to write down exactly what people had witnessed. He doesn't add his opinion or try to fill in the delicious gaps in the account which exist. It doesn't sound like he's trying very hard to glorify what happened. Look—he doesn't even use a single exclamation point! !

Which is exactly why I love the Gospel narratives of the resurrection. I find that this is the way that God comes to me—not with a bunch of the heavenly boys whooping it up, but with a quiet narrative of what really happened. My knowledge of the resurrection comes not from a Stephen Spielberg or George Lucas movie but from a brief historical narrative.

It's this mismatch between the extreme glory of the Resurrection of Jesus Christ and the quietness with which it has been related to me that gets my attention today. And now that I think about it, it requires a lot of faith.

I mean, think about how improbable the story is. A man dies and is placed in a tomb Houdini couldn't possibly escape from, carefully secured by an armed Roman (or perhaps Jewish) guard. And then he not only rises from the dead but also escapes the tomb. All of this has happened 2000 years ago. Now I'm a pretty educated guy and somewhat skeptical of things sometimes. I've bought this story, hook, line, and sinker.

Why? A sociologist could explain it by the influence of my parents and the American culture I was born into. A psychologist might explain it by whatever needs and neuroses and complexes he figured I had.

The answer lies in the power of the Resurrected Jesus. What else could explain why this improbable story has such a hold over someone like me and 2 billion other someone's in the world and has found its way into every culture in a way that other religions have not?

It's not just the resurrection that's so improbable: the teachings of Jesus are so counterintuitive. I mean, what's all this about if you want to be great, learn to be the servant of all? The #2 religion in the world (numerically), Islam, is mostly about power and domination, and has been from the beginning. Only in Christianity do you have an all-powerful God who improbably, impossibly, becomes a man and stays one. Some other religions have had gods who are incarnated as humans for a while but not permanently. And the other two religions with one all-powerful God, Islam and Judaism, will have nothing to do with a God who actually stoops to become a man.

But, there's something about this all-powerful God showing His strength in weakness that compels me to believe and live by my beliefs. The God who is powerful and loving enough to hide Himself in the form of a man and be born as a baby is the same God who hides in humble narratives and ordinary lives. He's the same God who creates in unimaginably beautiful world and leaves undeniable and certain hints of Himself, and then frustratingly refuses to demand attention beyond all doubt.

This is like my life. If I pretended for a moment that I didn't believe in the God who became man and in the God-man who rose from the dead, I could imagine that my life is just an ordinary, materialistic, secular life. I've had no night visions and no angelic visitations. I've seen no miracles, not in the deepest sense of the word. And yet my belief in God is so powerfully and inextricably a part of me that it defies explanation, aside from the power of God.

The resurrection of Jesus Christ happens offstage. Have you ever noticed that? Nobody was there at Ground Zero at H Hour. But, what we see are the results of an explosion that makes the atom bombs of Hiroshima and Nagasaki look like the effect of a single bacterium falling to the ground. From that moment, the Kingdom of Heaven has been exploding. It knocks over the strong Roman guards, and it rolls away the massive stone. It transforms the lives of the disciples so that this tiny frightened band of brothers turns the world upside down in a matter of years. 40 years later it decimates the Old Covenant and its Temple and sacrifices.

50 years ago it swept into my life, causing me to be born to believing parents, and it's been exploding, slowly, quietly, in my life ever since.

It is the shock and awe of the empty tomb, and it is the Day of Pentecost without the miracles. It's the small still voice that was strong enough to create the world and yet gentle enough to perform spiritual heart surgery on me.

It is the Sacrament of Life, the invisible grace of God made visible in every imaginable way in my humble and small life.

It is the Resurrection of the Lord Jesus Christ, *my* Lord Jesus Christ, and it's the meaning and end of my life. For I am a Christian.

Let me go out quickly from the empty tomb today with fear and great joy and run to bring word to His disciples and those who have not yet heard!

Prayer:

O God, who for our redemption didst give thine only-begotten Son to the death of the Cross, and by his glorious resurrection hast delivered us from the power of our enemy; Grant us so to die daily from sin, that we may evermore live with him in the joy of his resurrection; through the same thy Son Christ our Lord. Amen.

(Easter Collect from *The Book of Common Prayer*)

Points for Meditation:

1. Now that you've meditated on the Resurrection of Jesus, how does it color the situation of your life today?
2. Spend some time today meditating on your own resurrection.
3. Spend time today praising God for the Resurrection of the Son.
4. Sing some Easter hymns today!

Resolution:

I resolve to rejoice today, for Jesus Christ has risen from the dead, and if possible to share that joy!

Matthew 28:11-20

Matthew 28:18–20 has rightly been called the Great Commission, for great it is.

"Go, therefore, and make disciples of all the nations, baptizing them in the name of the Father, and of the Son, and of the Holy Spirit, teaching them to observe all things that I have commanded you; and lo I am with you always even to the end of the age."

Why is the Great Commission so great? Because in the Great Commission we see how great the salvation and kingdom of our God truly is. In the Great Commission we witness—indeed, are *made participants in*—God's redemption of the cosmos. In the Great Commission we see that the New Covenant which came by the life, death, resurrection, and ascension of Jesus Christ is now perpetuated *through us*, as God with man labors to redeem man.

Here is the greatness of the Great Commission: that God, who created man out of the dust of the earth, now takes fallen man, who deserved nothing but to be returned to dust, and makes His home with him.

Here is the greatness of the Great Commission: that God, who created men out of the dust of the earth by breathing His Spirit into them and making them living beings, now takes lifeless, cowardly, doubting, and betraying bodies, breathes His Spirit into them, and makes them a living being called the Body of Jesus Christ. And it is this mystical Body of Jesus Christ that He will use to disciple the nations, to bring in His Kingdom, and to redeem the cosmos. Surely, He could have chosen to do it without us: but He chose to use us, His betrayers and those who nailed Him to the Cross.

. . .

But, as great as the Great Commission is, I find that we often minimize it, finding ways, as we do, to escape the greatness of the commission of our Lord. We minimize the Great Commission by reducing it to "evangelism."

Well, I've got news for you: I don't believe in evangelism.

There, I've said it. Bring on the ecclesiastical tribunals and stop reading *Give Us This Day* in protest: but I don't believe in evangelism.

I don't believe in evangelism because I believe in *discipleship* instead. Of course I believe in what we call "evangelism," but not in the way it is often portrayed. I'm not even sure that "evangelize" is ever used as a verb in the Bible. Yes, there are evangelists, and there is a sacred and essential task of introducing people to Jesus Christ. But, I've heard many well intentioned Christians and churches proclaim that "evangelism is the number one priority of the Church" or "evangelism is the most important task of the Church."

Where do we get such an idea from? Where in the Bible are the proof texts for such theology? Often Matthew 28, the Great Commission, is cited, but as we know, the Great Commission is all about *discipleship*. One of the primary ways in which we minimize the Great Commission, therefore, is by shrinking its scope to the task of "evangelism." But, what Jesus didn't say in the Great Commission was: "Make a few quick converts and then move on to the next victim." What He said was: *"Go therefore and make disciples of all the nations, baptizing them in the name of the Father, and of the Son, and of the Holy Spirit, teaching them to observe all things that I have commanded you"* (v. 20).

I view evangelism as being an essential and important component of discipleship, which is the larger task to which we are called. We are called to be disciples and to make disciples: that is the primary task of the Church. If I never "lead" someone to Christ but lead a faithful life of being a disciple of Jesus Christ for decades, have I somehow failed in life? Maybe I've planted countless seeds or watered or fertilized but have never been lucky enough to be the one who comes just at the right time to observe the first push of the new life through the soil. And maybe I've spent my life doing the backbreaking work of discipling those who others have first "led" to Christ.

I find the whole notion of evangelizing and "leading" people to conversion to Christ very vague and unhelpful at times. At what moment does the task of evangelism end? When someone says the Sinner's Prayer? When they have an emotional experience of God for the first time? At what point do we abandon one who has just been "evangelized" and then go on to evangelize someone else because it's the most important task, leaving the work of discipleship undone?

As I've said, I think it's more useful to think of evangelism as being only the first phase of the biblical process of discipleship, which is a lifelong endeavor and which is not a solo flight into spirituality.

Another reason the Great Commission is so great is because it is the fulfillment of the first commandment God gave man. What was that first commandment? Even before the commandment *not* to eat of the Tree of the Knowledge of Good and Evil (it would be hard to build a life around *not* doing something!), God commanded Adam to be fruitful and multiply. So important is this sacred task that when God saved mankind through the ark of salvation, He repeated it to Noah twice.

But, simply having children isn't enough any longer. Now that our children are all born in sin, it is not enough to populate the earth with Adolf Hitlers and Saddam Husseins, or even Mother Teresas without the grace of discipleship in her life. To be fruitful and multiply now requires that we have children and disciple them. This is why the task of bearing children and keeping them in the covenant is so crucial and always has been. It's why every threat to the family as God ordained it, such as abortion or homosexuality or divorce or unwed mothers, is so destructive to human life and well-being.

I've come across some eye-opening research that suggests the importance of bearing children and keeping them in the faith. There are six billion people in the world, about two billion of whom are Christian. How many new Christians do you think are made each year? Go ahead—guess.

The truth is that there are about 23 million new Christians every year (based on an average of the years 1990–2000.) Now, how many of those 23 million new Christians made each year came from conversion from some other religion or no religion? The answer is about 1.8 million, which means 21.3 million are born into Christian families. In other words, 12 times as many Christians are made each year by Christians having children as are made by all of the churches' and Christians' efforts to "evangelize."

Now the really interesting part of discipleship is that sociologists of religion have shown that the primary way that people become Christians is based on the density of the social networks they have. In other words, if someone is an atheist at a university, and all of his friends and colleagues are committed atheists, we should pity the poor Christian student who thought it was his duty to "convert" the professor. I'm not at all saying that we shouldn't do such bold things: God performs miracles. But, I am saying that it *would* be a *miracle* because it is not the normal way that God works.

Now where is it that we have the greatest density of social networks? It would have to be a social situation where you had the most time possible for the disciple of Jesus Christ to disciple someone. It would have to be the social situation where the discipler is as highly motivated as possible to persevere in the laborious, often dull, exhausting work of making a disciple of Jesus Christ. And it would have to be the social situation where the person to be discipled is at the most impressionable time in his life.

Now let me see...where in the world could we ever find a social situation that meets all these criteria? In the Christian family! It's no surprise, then, that God's primary means of fulfilling the Great Commission has always been through the covenant He establishes with families. If you don't believe me, then go back and read the whole Old Testament.

I'm working even now on an idea for a book based on this concept, which I call *The Great Commission Family*. If you want to find a way to enter fully into the glory of the New Covenant; if you want to be an active part of the Great Commission: then I submit that you should look no further than doing everything you can to have children and disciple them. If your circumstances do not permit this for whatever reason, then find any of the multiple ways you can assist and support Christian families in this sacred, most-important task of discipleship. There are many Christian families failing at this task, and they need your help.

But, lest we're tempted to think it's all about the family, Jesus puts the task of discipleship squarely in the context of the Church. It is the Church as a whole to whom Christ promised His presence and Spirit. The task of discipleship is given to the entire Church, and only a Church has all of the gifts and talents necessary to equip us for this work.

Hillary Clinton was wrong. It doesn't take a village: it takes the *Church*.

Prayer:
Oh my Lord, I know that you are always with me. Help me to obey your commandments, and lead me to share my faith with others, so that they may know you and love you as well. Amen.

Points for Meditation:
1. What opportunities do you have every day to share Jesus Christ with people? This sharing of Christ may take many forms.
2. If you spend time with children, meditate on how your interaction with them may more profitably be seen as a means of fulfilling the Great Commission.

Resolution:
I resolve to meditate further on the meaning of the Great Commission and take some time today to see if I have been considering it wrongly.